TOWARD AN
ARCHITECTURE OF
ENJOYMENT

Also by Henri Lefebvre
Published by the University of Minnesota Press

The Urban Revolution
Translated by Robert Bononno
Foreword by Neil Smith

Dialectical Materialism
Translated by John Sturrock
Foreword by Stefan Kipfer

State, Space, World: Selected Essays
Edited by Neil Brenner and Stuart Elden
Translated by Gerald Moore, Neil Brenner, and Stuart Elden

Also on Henri Lefebvre
Published by the University of Minnesota Press

*Henri Lefebvre on Space: Architecture, Urban Research,
and the Production of Theory*
Łukasz Stanek

TOWARD AN ARCHITECTURE OF ENJOYMENT

Henri Lefebvre

Edited by Łukasz Stanek

Translated by Robert Bononno

University of Minnesota Press
Minneapolis • London

This book was supported by a grant from the Graham Foundation for Advanced Studies in the Fine Arts.

English translation copyright 2014 by Robert Bononno

Introduction copyright 2014 by the Regents of the University of Minnesota

All rights reserved. No part of this publication may be reproduced, stored in a retrieval system, or transmitted, in any form or by any means, electronic, mechanical, photocopying, recording, or otherwise, without the prior written permission of the publisher.

Published by the University of Minnesota Press
111 Third Avenue South, Suite 290
Minneapolis, MN 55401–2520
http://www.upress.umn.edu

Library of Congress Cataloging-in-Publication Data

Lefebvre, Henri, 1901–1991, author.
 [Vers une architecture de la jouissance. English]
 Toward an architecture of enjoyment / Henri Lefebvre; edited by
   Lukasz Stanek; translated by Robert Bononno.
 Includes bibliographical references and index.
 ISBN 978-0-8166-7719-1 (hc)
 ISBN 978-0-8166-7720-7 (pb)
 1. Architecture—Philosophy. 2. Architecture—Psychological aspects. I. Stanek, Lukasz, editor. II. Bononno, Robert, translator. III. Lefebvre, Henri, 1901–1991. Vers une architecture de la jouissance, Translation of. IV. Title.
 JNA2500.L4513 2014
 720.1—dc23

2014001742

Printed in the United States of America on acid-free paper

The University of Minnesota is an equal-opportunity educator and employer.

20 19 18 17 16 15 14   10 9 8 7 6 5 4 3 2 1

CONTENTS

Translator's Note   vii

Introduction. A Manuscript Found in Saragossa:
Toward an Architecture   xi
Łukasz Stanek

Toward an Architecture of Enjoyment

1. The Question   3
2. The Scope of the Inquiry   24
3. The Quest   32
4. Objections   50
5. Philosophy   60
6. Anthropology   80
7. History   87
8. Psychology and Psychoanalysis   102
9. Semantics and Semiology   117
10. Economics   128
11. Architecture   136
12. Conclusion (Injunctions)   146

Notes   155
Index   177

TRANSLATOR'S NOTE

The title *Toward an Architecture of Enjoyment* is taken directly from Henri Lefebvre's French working title, *Vers une architecture de la jouissance*, and, in that sense, is unproblematic. The proverbial elephant in the room makes its appearance in the form of *jouissance*, a word ripe (some might say rife) with connotations that has repeatedly proven problematic to translators of contemporary French prose. Its range of associations and ambiguity is legendary, and justifications of its *translation*, rather than its wholesale adoption, have now become commonplace. The usual fallback position, and one I obviously do not follow here, is to leave it untranslated. One would have to examine this tactic on a case-by-case basis to explicate the underlying rationale, but the primary reason can be traced to its use in psychoanalytic texts, particularly the work of Jacques Lacan, for whom it was a core concept.

The most recent and most accurate translation of Lacan's *Écrits*, by Bruce Fink, "translates" it as such; it is assumed, as Fink notes in a short glossary at the end of the book, that readers of Lacan are sufficiently familiar with the term and its meanings to preclude the need for English translation. But even for Fink, in the context of Lacanian psychoanalysis, *jouissance* is a form of "enjoyment": "I have assumed that the kind of enjoyment beyond the pleasure principle (including orgasm) denoted by the French *jouissance* is well enough known by now to the English-reading public to require no translation."[1] Of course, such familiarity is open to question, particularly outside the narrow circle of Lacanian psychoanalysts and those scholars who engage regularly with his ideas. There appears to be a tacit assumption on the part of many that its appearance in French must inevitably refer back to Lacan, thereby foreclosing any further attempt at interpretation. Lacanian discourse may have poisoned the well of *jouissance* for generations, but translators must be open to the possibility of other readings. Unfortunately, given Lacan's significance as a thinker and the widespread distribution of his ideas, directly or indirectly, in twentieth-century scholarly writing, the term has become accepted as a common element of academic discourse, in need of no further explanation—and no translation. As a result, its use (and abuse) is widespread. It is worth considering, however, that the word predates its use by Lacan and has been employed, even by his contemporaries, in ways that are less troubled with multiple and often confused interpretations. In French, the word has a lengthy pedigree; its earliest use has been traced to the fifteenth century, where it is intended primarily as a form of usufruct.[2] In the sixteenth century it began its association with what we may call "pleasure," initially the pleasure of the senses generally and then, around 1589, sexual pleasure. Littré in his majestic, though now somewhat superannuated, dictionary of the French language traces the verb from which it is derived, *jouir*, to Latin *gaudere*. Other than its nontranslation in psychoanalytic contexts, it has been variously rendered as "pleasure," "enjoyment," "contentment," "satisfaction," "bliss." The emphasis so often found on sexual pleasure and on orgasmic relief is misplaced; while *jouissance* can certainly have this meaning, its semantic range is much broader, and sexual release is not its primary meaning, as a glance at any large French monolingual dictionary will reveal. In fact, it is the sense of overall "well-being" that the verb *jouir* designates: "to experience joy, pleasure, a state of physical or moral well-being procured by something."[3] The release should be seen as one that is organic rather than purely orgasmic, one that covers a panoply of sensual and psychic satisfactions. (Moreover, since when has it been decided that "sexual pleasure" must be limited to the moment of orgasm, to the exclusion of all that precedes and follows, or that sexuality must be so instrumental, resolutely directed toward the achievement of a goal?) There are pros and cons to each of these potential translations, and each would have to be examined in the context in which it was made. But the question remains: how does Henri Lefebvre employ the term here, in this book, in the context of architectural space?

Every translation is an act of interpretation.[4] This inevitably entails the elucidation of meaning—the evaluation of a word's connotational and denotational elements within a microcontext of some sort (the sentence or paragraph, generally). In fiction what a word connotes may hold more weight for the translator than the various senses found in a dictionary entry. But with certain text types, nonfiction especially, we are most concerned with a word's denotation, the class of objects that theoretically fall within its scope of reference. The characteristic that indicates that a word is a technical term (as *jouissance* would be for Lacanian psychoanalysis) is its restricted scope of reference. That scope can be relatively large or relatively small, but it is not unlimited, does not extend to the limits of general language as a whole. The language of the sciences, law, or finance are prime examples of such restricted scope. To leave a word untranslated is to imply that it is so uniquely bound up with a culture that it is untranslatable (*croissant* or *baguette*, for example) or to signify that it is a term of art employed as intended by specialists in a given field, usually for historical reasons (*voir dire* in the field of law, for example). *Jouissance*, of course, has escaped the cage of Lacanian psychoanalysis and been used with an equally complex range of associations, primarily psychoanalytical, by other scholars, but its appearance in an English context is intended to isolate and identify its pedigree in Lacanian psychoanalysis. To have left the word untranslated would have been to have made such an assumption, whereas it is used, as Lefebvre's text demonstrates, "to lay out a broad field of investigation ... often ... within and against a whole family of concepts such as *bonheur, plaisir, volupté*, and *joie*" (see the Introduction).

There are a number of overriding factors in the use of "enjoyment" as a translation for *jouissance*: its inclusion in the title of the book and the weight that must be assigned to this, and its recurrence throughout the text in various and wide-ranging contexts. While Lefebvre was familiar with Lacan's work, nothing in *Toward an Architecture of Enjoyment* indicates his employment of the word in the sense(s) used by Lacan—in other words, as a psychoanalytic "term of art." "Pleasure" as a translation of *jouissance* is a possibility, but the French language has a perfectly adequate word to express that concept, *le plaisir*, and its translation is relatively unproblematic. More important, as Łukasz Stanek notes in his Introduction, Lefebvre changed the title from *Vers une architecture du plaisir*, which had been suggested by Mario Gaviria, to *Vers une architecture de la jouissance*. There was, therefore, no justification for its use here as a translation of Lefebvre's *jouissance*. Additionally, given the nature of Lefebvre's text and his theorization of space, a more active word was needed. "Pleasure" and "bliss," and their synonyms, refer to states of being rather than to a mode that would involve the active engagement of the subject over time, a way of being. "Enjoyment," in spite of its humble workaday simplicity and lack of academic standing, has the virtue of reflecting such activity, one that is commonplace, easily accessible, and liable, even likely, to be associated with the experience of architecture or an architectural site or a (lived) space generally. Both concrete and capable of duration, it accords with Lefebvre's vision of space as something not merely conceived or perceived, something abstracted or purely representational, but something lived and, yes, *enjoyed* in the process of organic unfolding. Lefebvre's notion of space and, by extension, architectural space is that of an actualized, embodied space and would strongly call into question any attempt to interpret his use of *jouissance* as something abstract, much less purely psychoanalytical. Lefebvre was notoriously antipathetic toward academicism and its jargon and what he referred to as the "violence of scholarly abstraction."[5] In his discussion of psychology and psychoanalysis and their relation to architecture, he writes, "Knowledge struggles to reduce: uncertainty to certainty, ambiguity to the determinate, silence to speech, spontaneity to deliberation, the concrete to the abstract, pleasure to thought, and pain to the absence of thought" (chapter 8). Such a view would support a more general reading of *jouissance*, one that affords room for the living, breathing subject to engage with the world fully and completely.

INTRODUCTION

A MANUSCRIPT FOUND IN SARAGOSSA

TOWARD AN ARCHITECTURE

Łukasz Stanek

The *Manuscript Found in Saragossa* is a gothic novel by Jan Potocki (1761–1815), a Polish aristocrat touring Napoleonic Europe, that recounts the story of a mysterious manuscript found in the Spanish city of Saragossa and features the adventures of Walloon soldier Alphonse van Worden who, on his way through the mountains of Sierra Morena to Madrid, meets thieves, inquisitors, cabbalists, princesses, coquettes, and many other colorful characters.[1] With Potocki's book in mind, I arrived in Saragossa on a warm evening of September 2008 to be received by Mario Gaviria, the renowned Spanish urban sociologist, planner, and ecological activist. In the early 1960s Gaviria was a student of Henri Lefebvre (1901–91) at Strasbourg University and became a friend and collaborator in the period when Lefebvre was formulating his theory of production of space, published between 1968 ("The Right to the City") and 1974 (*The Production of Space*) and developed further in *De l'État* (On the State, 1976–78).[2] Belonging to Lefebvre's inner circle, Gaviria would visit him many times in his maternal house in Navarrenx, and they would make trips to the nearby new town of Mourenx and then to the Ossau Valley and further south: Pamplona for the San Fermin festival, Tudela to celebrate the fiesta in Gaviria's *peña*; they would rest for several days in his house in Cortes on the border between Aragon and Navarra, and then Lefebvre and his partner, Nicole Beaurain, would take off to his summer house in Altea in the province of Alicante. During our conversation in Saragossa Gaviria recalled their collaborations and in particular the 1973 study on tourist new towns in Spain, for which he commissioned Lefebvre to write about "the architecture of pleasure." Yet the manuscript that Lefebvre delivered hardly met the expectations of Gaviria, who considered it too abstract and decided not to include it in the results of the study submitted to the commissioner.[3] He should still have this manuscript, Gaviria mentioned, and offered that we look for it together. The next day, we drove to Cortes, and it was in the library of the seventeenth-century house that, after several hours of searching, he found *Vers une architecture de la jouissance*, a typescript with Lefebvre's handwritten corrections.[4]

Among Lefebvre's writings, a book about architecture is unique. However, a look at the table of contents of *Vers une architecture de la jouissance* shows that architecture is listed among philosophy, anthropology, history, psychology and psychoanalysis, semantics and semiology, and economy; and this marginal position seems to be confirmed by Lefebvre's broadening of the investigation from "architecture" to "spaces of jouissance," as

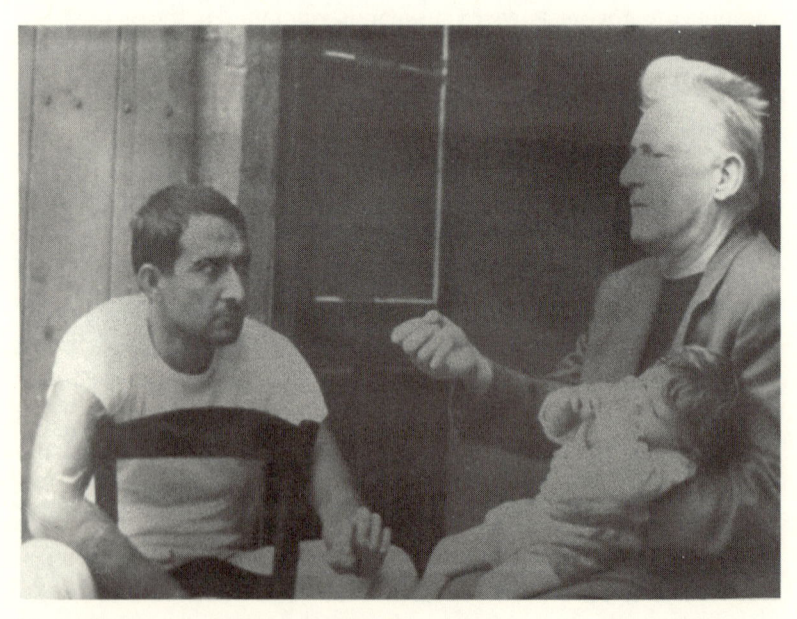

Mario Gaviria, Henri Lefebvre, and Lefebvre's daughter Armelle at Gaviria's family house in Cortes (Navarra, Spain), early 1970s. Archive of Mario Gaviria, Saragossa, Spain. Courtesy of Mario Gaviria.

he summarizes the book in its "Conclusions."[5] Straddling a range of disciplines, the book needs to be understood as resulting from an encounter between Lefebvre's philosophical readings of Hegel, Marx, and Nietzsche; the impulses provided by his contacts with architects and planners; and multiple studies in rural and urban sociology he carried out or supervised beginning in the 1940s—which is how I read his theory of the production of space in my *Henri Lefebvre on Space* (2011).

From within this encounter, Lefebvre formulated such transdisciplinary concepts as "space," "the everyday," "difference," and "habitation." These concepts facilitated exchanges between multiple discourses: political-economic analyses by David Harvey since the 1970s; followed by "postmodern geographies" by Edward Soja within the "spatial turn," or the reassertion of space in critical social theory; and philosophical readings of Lefebvre's work by Rémi Hess, Stuart Elden, Christian Schmid, and others.[6] Since the late 1990s, architectural and urban historians, critics, and theorists such as Iain Borden, Margaret Crawford, Mary McLeod, and Jane Rendell demonstrated the potential of Lefebvre's concepts for architectural practice and research.[7] Facilitated by the transhistorical character of Lefebvre's definition of space, whose production in capitalist modernities allows for a retrospective recognition of space as always-already produced, historians examined architecture's instrumentality within social processes of space production.[8] This was complemented by discussions in postcolonial and feminist theories focused on the everyday practices of submission and normalization, transgression and resistance; Lefebvre's work has been a key reference here, despite his moments of "infuriating sexism" and "disturbingly essentialist rhetoric."[9] In this perspective, minoritarian practices of the production of space were recognized as sites where the agency of architecture in the reproduction of social relationships can be addressed and, potentially, challenged, toward a rethinking of architecture's manifold possibilities.[10]

The transdisciplinary understanding of architecture, which inspired these studies and which was implicit in *The Production of Space*, is spelled out and advanced in *Toward an Architecture of Enjoyment*. If architecture understood as a professional practice or a collection of monuments has a marginal presence in the book, it is because Lefebvre addresses architecture beyond its restriction to a disciplinary division of labor and redefines it as a mode of imagination.[11] The starting point for this redefinition was the concept of habitation, understood as the half-real, half-imaginary

Table of Contents of the manuscript *Vers une architecture de la jouissance* by Henri Lefebvre. The book was handwritten by Lefebvre and typed by Nicole Beaurain. Archive of Mario Gaviria, Saragossa, Spain. Courtesy of Mario Gaviria.

distribution of times and places of everyday life. Prepared in the first two volumes of *The Critique of Everyday Life* (1947, 1961), this concept of habitation was advanced by the studies on the everyday practices of inhabitants in mass housing estates and individual suburban houses, carried out by the Institut de sociologie urbaine (ISU), cofounded by Lefebvre in 1962 and presided over by him until 1973.[12] Specific and yet shared by everybody, habitation became for Lefebvre a form of leverage to rethink the possibilities of architecture and to reconsider its sites, operations, and stakes.

This rethinking of architecture in *Toward an Architecture of Enjoyment* was embedded in the vibrant architectural culture in the period between the death of Le Corbusier in 1965 and the mid-1970s, when various paths within, beyond, and against the legacy of modern architecture were tested. Lefebvre's theory of the production of space, drawing on his research at the Centre d'études sociologiques (1948–61) and the universities of Strasbourg (1961–65) and Nanterre (1965–73), was a major reference in these debates, which he occasionally addressed, including architectural and urban semiology by Roland Barthes and Françoise Choay, the emerging postmodernist discourse by Robert Venturi and Charles Jencks, the phenomenological writings of Christian Norberg-Schulz, and texts by readers of Martin Heidegger in France. In particular, he would oppose the restriction of Marxism in architectural debates to the critique of architectural ideologies by Manfredo Tafuri and his followers, with which *Toward an Architecture of Enjoyment* takes issue. After 1968 Lefebvre would comment on students' designs at the *unités pédagogiques* and the Institut d'urbanisme de Paris, determine with Anatole Kopp the editorial policies of the journal *Espace et sociétés*, give advice on the reform of architectural education within governmental commissions, and participate in juries of architectural competitions. Direct contacts with architects were also a part of this continuing exchange: with Constant Nieuwenhuys in Amsterdam and Ricardo Bofill in Barcelona; with Georges-Henri Pingusson, Ricardo Porro, and Bernard Huet, all of whom he invited to his research seminars in Nanterre; and with Pierre Riboulet, Jean Renaudie, and Paul Chemetov during the visits to the buildings recently designed by them. Comparing his work to that of an architect as an intellectual speaking on behalf of urban space, Lefebvre gave multiple interviews on radio and television, where he would insert comments on architecture, urbanism, and space production into his broad assessment of social, political, and cultural topics.[13]

Lefebvre's interventions into these discussions were highly polemical, and this was also the case with *Toward an Architecture of Enjoyment*, where many concepts were introduced in contrast to others, rather than by a self-sustained definition. It is not the aim of this introduction to give a comprehensive account of these polemics in French politics, urban sociology, philosophy, and architectural culture around 1968—which was done in *Henri Lefebvre on Space*. Rather, my aim is more singular and more speculative: to read Lefebvre's book as a study on the architectural imagination, which participates in the social process of space production but is endowed, in his words, with a "relative autonomy."[14] In what follows I will take clues from *Toward an Architecture of Enjoyment* in order to explore architectural imagination as negative, political, and materialist. Negative, that is to say aiming at a "concrete utopia" that strategically contradicts the premises of everyday life in postwar capitalism—which is how Lefebvre assessed the potential of the practice of habitation. Political, because habitation becomes the stake of political struggle, as Lefebvre's studies in rural and urban sociology and his specific interventions into political debates after 1968 show. Materialist, both in the general philosophical sense of Marxist historical materialism and as starting with the materiality of the body and its rhythms. Taking the liberty to read *Toward an Architecture of Enjoyment* in the manner Lefebvre was reading his favorite authors—as fields of possibilities, beginning with their historical context and moving beyond it—I will start with a discussion of the research project on spaces of tourism in Spain, as an opportunity and pretext for Lefebvre's speculation on architecture.

Modernity at Its Worst and Its Best

There is a real chance that, after its publication, Lefebvre's *Toward an Architecture of Enjoyment* will in some bookshops sit next to Alain de Botton's *Architecture of Happiness*, just as Nietzsche's *Gay Science* occasionally ends up in the LGBT section.[15] While such an encounter would be enchanting and not fully accidental given the sharing of some quotes by both authors, in contrast to de Botton's escapism *Toward an Architecture of Enjoyment* needs to be read as part and parcel of Lefebvre's formulation of the theory of the production of space.

Landscapes of leisure on the Spanish Mediterranean coast were strategic sites for this task. "A remarkable instance of the production of space on the basis of a difference internal to the dominant mode of production is supplied by the current transformation of the perimeter of the Mediterranean into a leisure oriented space for industrialized Europe," wrote Lefebvre in *The Production of Space*.[16] In this book, spaces of leisure exemplify the reproduction of capitalism through the production of space: they result from the "second circuit of capital" in real-estate investment that compensates for the tendential fall of the average rate of profit in the primary circuit of capital, related to manufacturing.[17] They are sites of the reproduction of labor power and of the bourgeois cultural hegemony over everyday life. Yet at the same time, Lefebvre argued that in spaces of leisure "the body regains a certain right to use": they are indispensable parts of space production by postwar capitalism and yet reveal its "breaking points."[18]

This fundamental ambiguity of spaces of leisure was the focus of the research project in Spain, and to investigate this ambiguity was the main motivation of Gaviria:

> Around 1968 [he recalled], there was a lot of criticism about the consumer society, and leisure and tourism were seen by critical Marxist thinkers as

Henri Lefebvre, Nicole Beaurain, and their daughter Armelle in Sitgès (Catalonia, Spain) in the early 1970s. Photograph by Mario Gaviria. Archive of Nicole Beaurain, Paris, France. Courtesy of Nicole Beaurain.

consumption of space, as alienation of the working class. Yet my point was that the space of pleasure was something else: if you go to the Alhambra you realize that its experience cannot be reduced to consumption; it is something else, or *also* something else. This is what we talked about with my collaborators and colleagues in Benidorm, also with Henri, and this is what I asked him to write about.[19]

One cannot think of a more provocative case study for a Marxist philosopher than Benidorm, a tourist new town described recently by the sociologist José Miguel Iribas—himself a former member of Gaviria's team—as "stand[ing] out as the purest example of concentration at the service of mass-market tourism."[20] Yet to focus on Benidorm was more than a provocation, and Gaviria's opposition to mainstream Marxism reveals the broad theoretical and political aim of Lefebvre's book: the critique of asceticism in Western intellectual and political traditions. *Toward an Architecture of Enjoyment* targets asceticism under its many forms—as bourgeois morality, capitalist accumulation, modernist aesthetics, structuralist epistemology, biopolitical statecraft—but this critique culminates in Lefebvre's rejection of the asceticism of the communist Left. The suspicion of sensual enjoyment and consumption was deeply entrenched in left political discourse ever since the early nineteenth century, tracing any hint of betrayal of the proletariat changing sides toward the petit-bourgeoisie and condemning the "individualism" of those who disturb collective solidarity and do not comply with the norms and larger aims set by the organization.[21] This asceticism was upheld by Western Marxism during the postwar period: even if Herbert Marcuse in his essay "On Hedonism" (1938) recognized in the drive for sensual enjoyment a "materialist protest" against the relegation of happiness beyond the present, he was quick to add that hedonism only shows that the unfolding of "objective and subjective" human capacities is impossible in bourgeois society.[22] With alternative arguments entering wider circulation with decades of delay, like Walter Benjamin's "promise of commodities," Aleksandr Rodchenko's call on the socialist thing to become a "comrade" of the proletarian, or Werner Sombart's argument about the progressive historical potential of waste and expenditure in eighteenth-century Europe,[23] Western Marxism, and the Frankfurt School in particular, defined postwar left discourse about the emerging consumer society as normalized amusement and regenerative recreation, strictly functionalized within the reproduction of capitalist relationships. This critique extended toward state socialism in Central and Eastern Europe, marked by new types of social hierarchies defined by access to consumer goods. Just as socialist realism in architecture and its "palaces for the people" was, more often than not, ridiculed in the West, so was later discourse on consumption in "real existing modernism" invisible to postwar Western Marxists, with tobacco seen in Bulgaria as one of the main achievements of the socialist state; fashion explained in the Soviet Union and the German Democratic Republic in terms of cultural, economic, and social progress; or perfumes considered a "democratic luxury" and a "gift" from the industry to Soviet women.[24] Having all but disdain for "goulash socialism" in Hungary, "small stabilization" in Poland, and "normalization" in Czechoslovakia, many Marxists in the West found they were in unlikely agreement with the dissidents behind the Iron Curtain, who saw post-Stalinist socialism as being founded on "the historical encounter between dictatorship and consumer society," in Vaclav Havel's description of Czechoslovakia in 1978.[25]

Lefebvre's opposition to this tradition was inscribed into his rethinking of Marxism against its productivist discourse, in line with Paul Lafargue's *Right to Be Lazy* (1880) and more recent references to Pierre Naville's argument (1967) that the historical movement "from alienation to jouissance" implies a shift from work to "nonwork," the latter understood as an activity that cannot be commodified.[26] Strategically linking his reading of Marx's revolutionary project with Nietzsche's subversive one, Lefebvre's theorizing of the relationship between work and nonwork resonated with numerous French activist groups throughout the 1960s. This included the Internationale situationniste and its condemnation of the "poverty" of the students' everyday life "considered in its economic, political, sexual, and especially intellectual aspects" as the title of their influential pamphlet (1967) went.[27] The opposition to communist asceticism was also conveyed by French counterculture around the journal *Actuel* that featured ephemeral groups such as the Dutch Provos and Kabouters, the U.S. yippies and Weathermen, and the members of the movement "Vive la révolution" from the Parisian suburb of La Courneuve who proclaimed that "doing a revolution in Europe is to find out if one can be happy in La Courneuve."[28]

In the interviews given by Lefebvre in *Actuel* in the early 1970s, he endorsed Nietzsche's "amendment" of the mechanistic and ascetic character

Cover of the tourist guide *Benidorm en color* by Vicente Ramos (1975). This tourist town developed from a small village was a focus of Gaviria's research.

of materialism, including Marxist materialism, and agreed with Octavio Paz's accusation of Marxism for its tendency to see the body as "a fragment of dead matter." Instead, Lefebvre suggested an understanding of the body as an ensemble of rhythms and called for a rhythmanalytical pedagogy of the body—a project advanced in *Toward an Architecture of Enjoyment*.[29] At the same time, the images published in *Actuel* became sources of Lefebvre's references to architectural experiments of the period. They subscribed to a search for alternative ways of life, including the stacked structures of Habitat 67, funnel cities by Walter Jonas, the "center for sexual relaxation" by Nicolas Schöffer, but also landscape interventions by Haus-Rucker-Co and Hans Hollein, geodesic domes by Buckminster Fuller and Drop City, walking cities by Archigram, inflatable structures by Ant Farm, proposals for an appropriation of space by People's Architecture of Berkeley, and the bubble of Marcel Lachat attached to a facade of a housing estate in Geneva. Many of these ideas found their way to the "correction" of a contemporary mass housing project in the Quartier d'Italie in Paris, published by *Actuel* in 1971.[30]

It was against such architectural production as the new estates in the Quartier d'Italie that Gaviria suggested studying spaces of leisure. The starting point was his own studies of housing estates in Madrid: Concepción (1965), Gran San Blas (1966–67), and Fuencarral (1968). These studies were carried out by Gaviria in the framework of the "seminar in rural and urban sociology" and belonged to the first attempts outside France to test Lefebvre's theory of the production of space in urban research.[31] The studied estates shared many of the drawbacks of the collective housing estates constructed at this time in France, being not sufficiently connected to city centers by public transportation and inadequately equipped with facilities. However, Gaviria stressed the intensity of urban life in these estates, which was based on a "spontaneous urbanism" differing from that foreseen by the planners and yet "well understood by some street vendors who change positions according to times of the day and days of the week." In order to reveal it, the team mapped shops, services, clubs, and cafes as well as the routes of the vendors of candy, flowers, and shoe cleaning in the Concepción estate, and this was complemented by charting the paths of the pedestrians in Gran San Blas.[32] Besides participatory observation, the Concepción study was carried out by means of the analysis of design documentation, questionnaires, and nondirected interviews, as in the ISU studies.

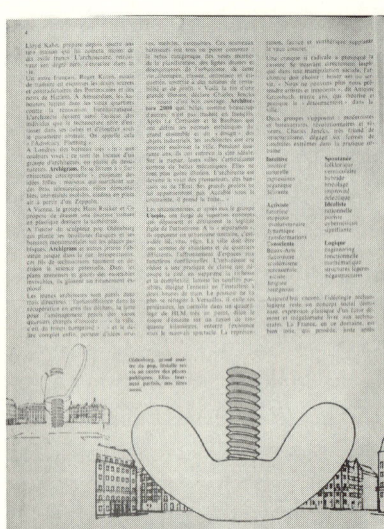

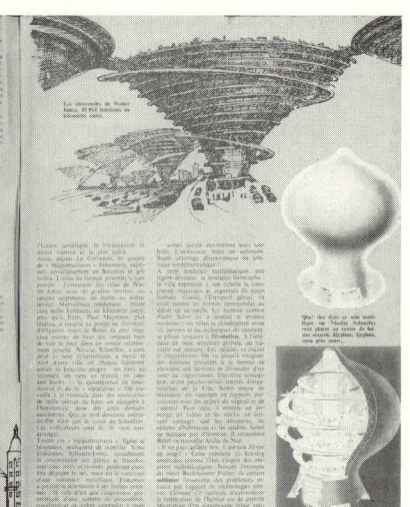

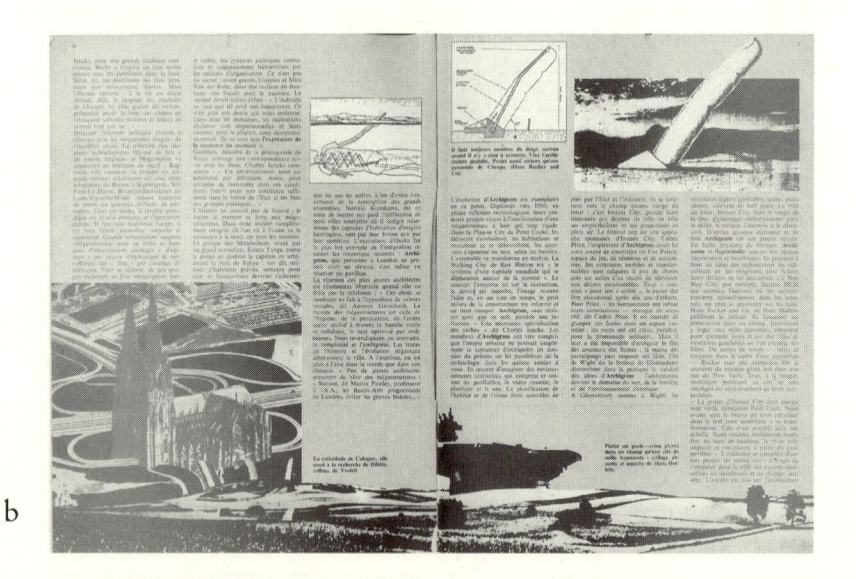

a

b

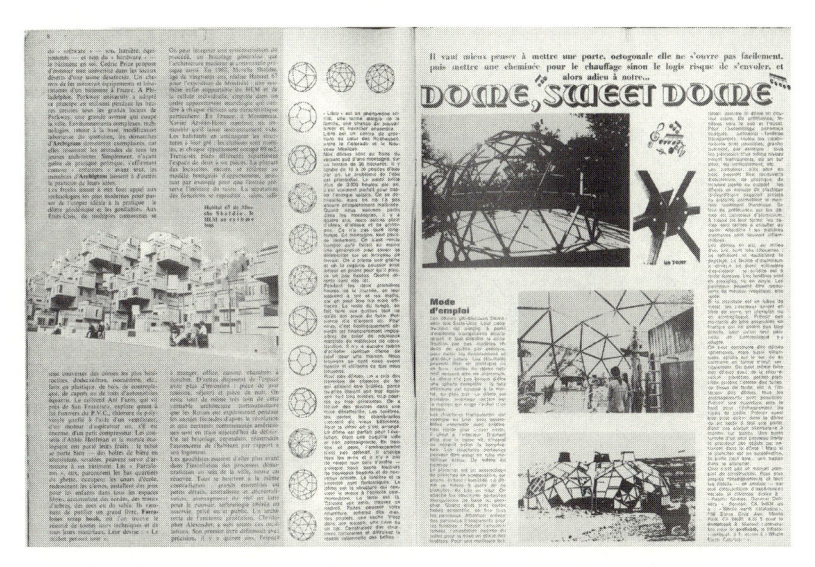

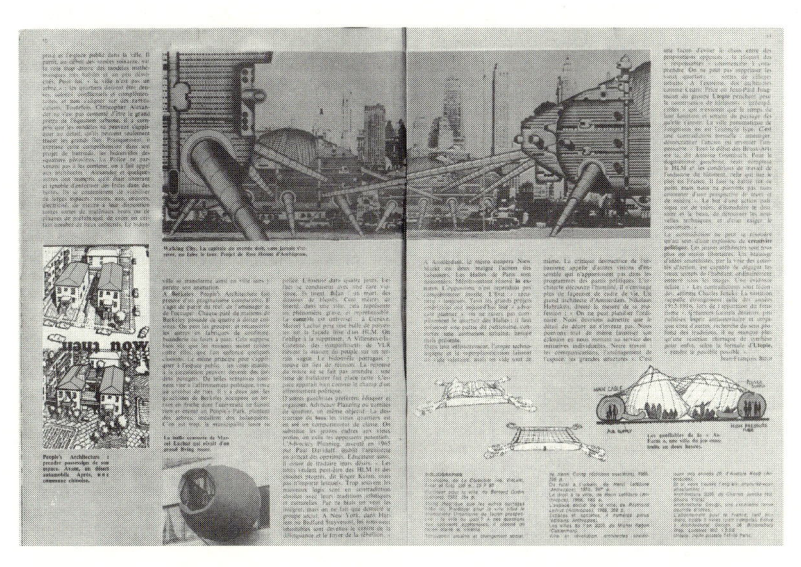

Projects by (a) Claes Oldenburg, Walter Jonas, Nicolas Schöffer; this project of a "center for sexual relaxation" by Schöffer was criticized by Lefebvre in *Toward an Architecture of Enjoyment*; (b) Haus-Rucker-Co; (c) Moishe Safdie, Drop City; (d) People's Architecture, Marcel Lachat, Archigram, Ant Farm. Published in *Actuel* 18 (March 1972): 4–11. Lefebvre must have seen these illustrations, because *Actuel* published an interview with him in the same issue.

MAIS, QUE VOIS-JE? JE NE VOIS PAS TRISSE !
BONCH
BLANG
BLANK
RAS LE BOL DE CETTE TURNE!
JE VAIS CHERCHER LE NIRVANA À DENFERT !

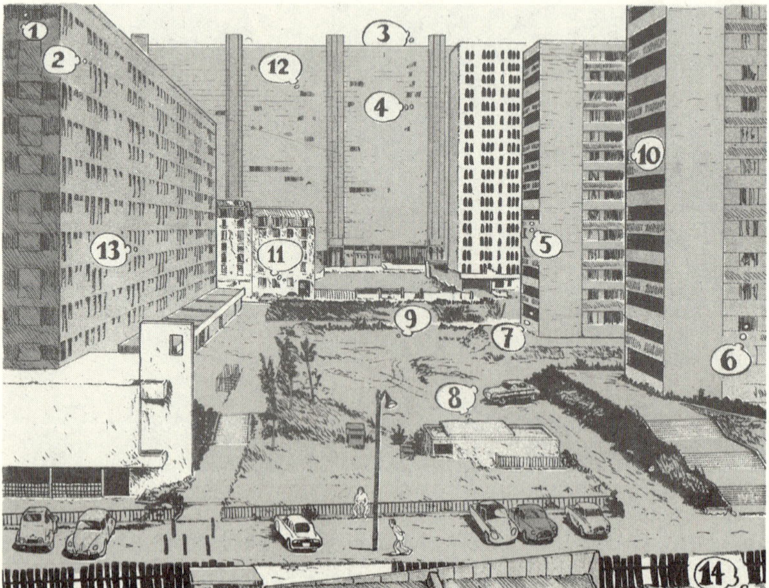
1
2
3
12
4
10
5
13
11
9
7
6
8
14

Left: The "revised and corrected" Quartier d'Italie, as depicted in *Actuel* 12 (September 1971): 40–41. These unsigned drawings show the rue du Château-des-Rentiers and the "Deux Moulins," part of the 1957–72 redevelopment project in the thirteenth arrondissement of Paris. The caption describes the proposed interventions, assessing their feasibility and cost: (1) a metal or plastic bubble attached to the facade; (2) a flexible tube; (3) a Swiss chalet; (4) a mural ("all tenants agreed"); (5) a raised platform linking the buildings; (6) a polyester toboggan; (7, 8) inflatable domes; (9) plastic tents; (10) a facade chosen by the inhabitants; (11) old house "belonging to die-hards who resist developers"; (12) hanging garden; (13) two emptied stories; (14) a pit with construction materials to be recycled, "like in Drop City, Colorado."

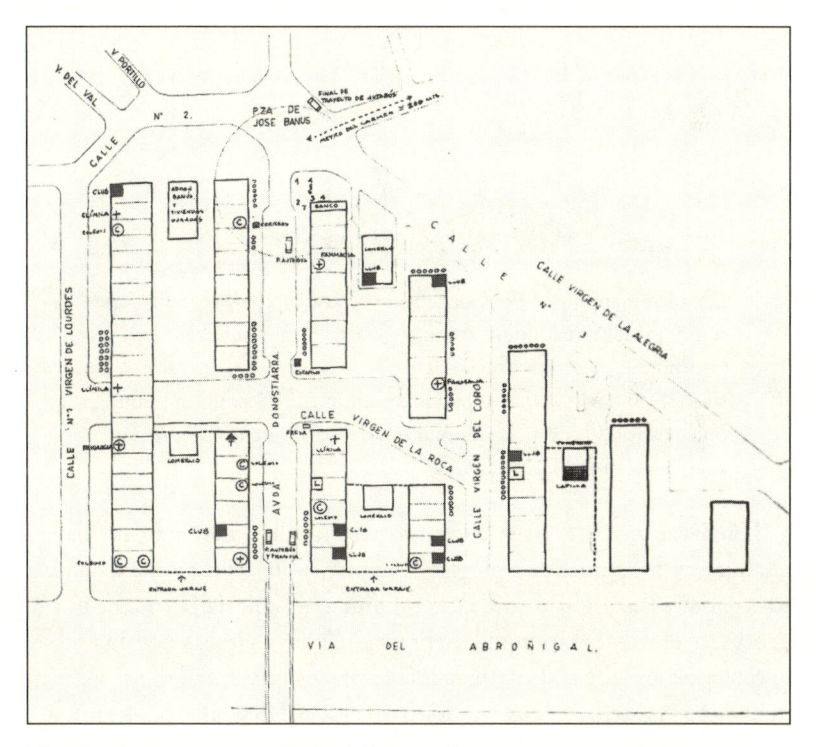

The Concepción estate in Madrid, designed by Lorenzo Romero Requejo, Francisco Robles Jiménez, Jacobo Romero Hernández, and Federico Turell Moragas, 1953–58. The mapping of the estate by Mario Gaviria and his team shows functions that contributed to its urban character: clubs, small shops, services, and gardens. From Mario Gaviria, "La ampliación del barrio de la Concepción," *Arquitectura* 92 (1966): 30. Courtesy of Mario Gaviria.

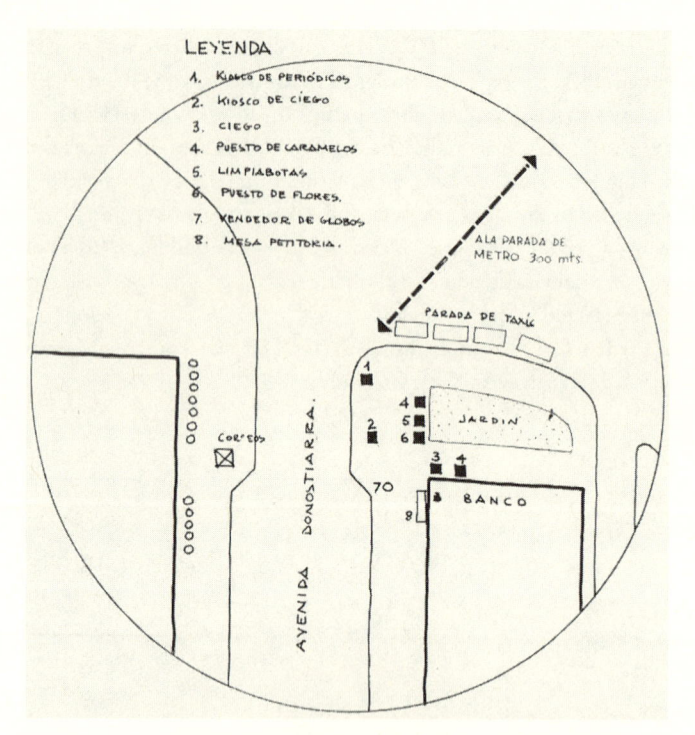

Detailed mapping of the Concepción estate, showing (1) newspaper stand; (2) national lottery stand (operated by a blind person, a tradition in Spain); (3) blind person; (4) candy stand; (5) shoe shiner; (6) florist stand; (7) balloon salesman; (8) petition point. From Mario Gaviria, "La ampliación del barrio de la Concepción," 30. Courtesy of Mario Gaviria.

Lefebvre's visits to Gaviria's seminar in Madrid were part of his exchanges with Spanish sociologists and architects, at the time when his ideas about the "right to the city" became particularly pertinent in the processes of urbanization in late Franco's Spain as it was dominated by speculation and the real-estate market, housing crises, and the absence of democratic procedures that would channel social demands on the municipal level.[33] "Based on the research by Henri Lefebvre concerning the street as structured and structuring element, we have developed a detailed study of the relationships between empty spaces and built structures in new peripheral quarters," wrote Gaviria in reference to Lefebvre's lectures in Strasbourg.[34] In view of the urbanization processes in Spain, Gaviria saw the critique of the Charter of Athens (1933, published in

1943) and its principle of division of urban functions into work, housing, leisure, and transportation as the fundamental contribution of Lefebvre.[35] Instead of reducing urban design to the factors of circulation, insolation, and formal composition, Gaviria embraced the complexity and ambiguity of urban life.[36] As he wrote in his introduction to the Spanish translation of *The Right to the City*, "it is easier to build cities than urban life."[37] He contrasted the sharply defined, contained, continuous, and visually linked spaces of traditional urbanism with the discontinuity of spaces of functionalist urbanism subscribing to the Charter of Athens and collaborated with architects on recommendations for urban designers.[38]

In view of these studies, new tourist towns appeared as strategic approximations of the "other" of postwar housing estates. As Lefebvre argued already in his 1960 study on Mourenx, functionalist ensembles

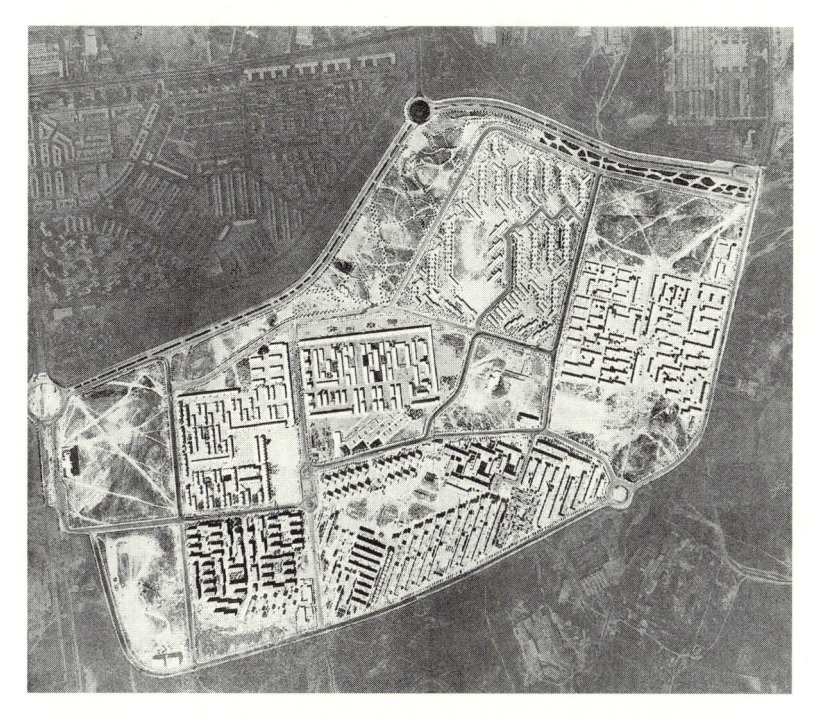

Aerial photograph of the Gran San Blas estate in Madrid, designed by Luis Gutiérrez Soto, Julio Cano Lasso, José Antonio Corrales Gutiérrez, and Ramón Vázquez Molezún, 1958–62. From Mario Gaviria, *Gran San Blas: Análisis socio-urbanístico de un barrio nuevo español* (Madrid: Revista Arquitectura, 1968), 7. Courtesy of Mario Gaviria.

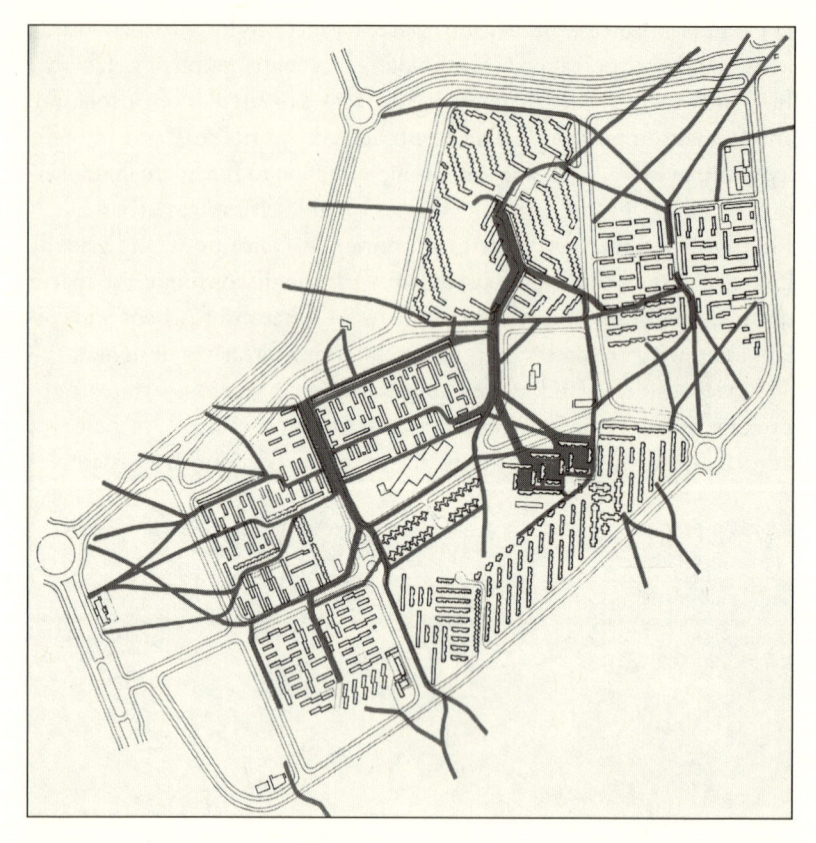

Spontaneous pedestrian paths in the Gran San Blas estate. From Mario Gaviria, *Gran San Blas*, 83. Courtesy of Mario Gaviria.

were expressing the paternalism of the state and they were anachronistic, since they did not account for the society moving beyond Fordism, in which the urban space was about to replace the factory as the place of socialization, exploitation, and struggle.[39] Similarly, in his critique of housing estates at the peripheries of Madrid, Gaviria argued that they failed to adapt to the specificity of the Spanish cultural, social, economic, and even climatic context and were lacking architectural innovation—which, rather, can be found in tourist new towns.

For Gaviria, Benidorm was a case in point: developed according to a 1956 master plan drafted by the urban planner Pedro Bidagor, the basic unit of the city was an open block without height restriction but with a system of setbacks that accommodated shops, services, gardens, pools, and parking spaces and contributed to the compact character of the city. Learning from Benidorm, Gaviria stressed density as an essential feature of urbanity at the same time rejecting the monofunctional character of this city—a critique raised by Lefebvre in his seminars held for Gaviria's team in Benidorm in 1972 and 1973.[40] Gaviria wrote that the architecture and urbanism of leisure are "differentiated forms of the occupation of space and everyday life," prefiguring "certain aspects of the society of leisure" that can be generalized beyond the Spanish context.[41] If in the late 1950s Lefebvre saw Mourenx as an "urban laboratory"—the site of emergence of new collective subjectivities—for Gaviria it was the tourist towns such as Torremolinos, Benidorm, Salou, and Platja d'Aro that became laboratories for the employment of free time.

The argument that the future of society will be defined by leisure was widely discussed in 1960s France, in particular by Joffre Dumazedier and his influential hypothesis about the "civilization of leisure."[42] At a time when the expenses for food of a workers' family dropped to less than half of disposable income, Dumazedier argued for the increasing importance of leisure, defined either functionally (as recreation, entertainment, distraction, and personal development) or negatively (in opposition to professional and domestic work, taking care of the body and mind, religious service, and education).[43] In this condition, leisure facilities became part of French urbanism and planning on every scale of the territory: neighborhood, city, agglomeration, and region. New spaces were created, such as national parks and large-scale tourist facilities in Landes and Languedoc-Roussillon, as well as new holiday villages (*villages de vacances*) in southern France and Corsica, and new skiing resorts.[44] The tourist town La Grande Motte in Languedoc-Roussillon created a man-made landscape populated by ziggurats, while Port Grimaud at the Côte d'Azur experimented with traditional urban morphologies. Leisure was at the center of international debates among architects across the Iron Curtain, with reviews of the journal *L'architecture d'aujourd'hui* covering the facilities on the shores of the Mediterranean as well as those on the Black Sea coast.[45] The debate about spaces of tourism culminated in the congress on "architecture and leisure" organized by the Union internationale des architectes (UIA, International Union of Architects) in 1972 in the Bulgarian city of Varna.[46] Dumazedier, a participant of several UIA congresses, argued that models of holiday accommodation will influence the preference for housing, a clear tendency in French architectural culture since the 1950s, when holiday villages had become an occasion for experimenting with new housing typologies by architects such as Paul Chemetov, Pierre Riboulet, and the partnership Candilis-Josic-Woods.[47] With tourist developments seen as fields of experimentation for future society, Dumazedier extrapolated his findings twenty years ahead and speculated about "housing and leisure in 1985": the kitchen becoming a poetic oeuvre (rather than a functional, laboratory unit); the replacement of the dining and living rooms by a multimedia "room of festivals and spectacles," where inhabitants watch self-produced movies; and the transformation of bedrooms into multifunctional, personalized spaces.[48]

Leisure spaces thus seemed to be the field where new tendencies of the production of space were surfacing, and this is why they were the focus of several research studies by the ISU as well as several dissertations supervised by Lefebvre.[49] These spaces, he argued, revealed a new division of labor emerging in Europe: that between the industrialized North and the perimeter of the Mediterranean, which became the space of nonwork, including holidays, convalescence, rest, and retirement.[50] This argument was largely based on Gaviria's research, and in particular his "Ecologic study of urban concentrations created in Spain during the last years as centers for tourism" (1973), commissioned by the March Foundation of the March Bank of Mallorca,[51] for which *Vers une architecture de la jouissance* was written. Gaviria argued that the Mediterranean coast of Spain and the Canary Islands had become, since the early 1960s, a target of "neocolonial" urbanization by real-estate agents and tourist operators, mainly from industrialized countries in Europe. This urbanization was supported by the Francoist government seeking economic gains and state-guided modernization, but also by the consolidation of Spanish territory around the ideas of modern tourism.[52] These processes were facilitated by new means of transportation, the development of infrastructure, improved financial instruments, computer-aided data processing, and the tendency toward complete urbanization—as Lefebvre wrote in an introduction to one of Gaviria's books.[53]

If spaces of leisure are part of the simultaneously homogeneous and fragmented "abstract space"—the product, instrument, means, and milieu of postwar capitalism—they also require a range of new conditions: besides being accessible by private and public transportation and offering inexpensive land and labor power, fiscal incentives, and flexibility of regulations, they also need, in Gaviria's mocking description, "few people on the beach, fishermen fulfilling their decorative mission in the old harbor, and indigenous folk who are kind and forthcoming to tourists."[54] While Lefebvre discussed the production of abstract space as predicated upon the creative destruction of the peculiarity of places, the experience in Spain pointed at "quality space" characterized by ecological, aesthetic, cultural, and historical values, which are necessary for the expansion of the leisure industry. In the words of Henri Raymond, Lefebvre's long-time collaborator, the "users" of tourist facilities expect a "somewhere else," a sphere beyond work. In a study about the French coast, Raymond argued that the sea and the beach are defined by symbolic practices of urban users: as both nonurban (the rhythms of leisure are opposed to the rhythms of work) and preurban (they symbolize nature). In order to produce this opposition, all technical means of the urban society need to be employed; in other words, the sea and the beach need to be completely urbanized in order to maintain their perceived, conceived, and lived opposition to urban space.[55]

For Lefebvre, spaces of leisure reveal the contradictions between abstract space and the possibility of its "other." He argued that they are sites where "the existing mode of production produces both its worst and its best."[56] Writing in 1973, the year of the oil crisis, and reflecting upon the modeling of economic and population growth scenarios with finite global resources in *The Limits to Growth* (1972), he saw spaces of leisure as exemplifying the technological capacities to make nature available for collective enjoyment and the destruction of nature by this very technology.[57] In his account, they are sites where the future is not yet decided and its various possibilities are taking shape; they share this potentiality with the street, the monument, but also the "urban" (the urban society) that, in a later text, Lefebvre would describe as "a sheaf of possibilities, the best and the worst."[58] Spaces of leisure are neither enclaves within the dominant mode of space production nor reflections of the interests of the dominant class; rather, they exacerbate the contradictions of the social totality, revealing the antagonistic forces operating within it. Spaces of leisure were for Lefebvre what the open-plan office was for Archizoom's "No-Stop City" (1968–71) or the Berlin Wall for Rem Koolhaas (1971): sites that condense the most extraordinary promises of modernity with the dangers of ultimate alienation.

If for Marx the past repeats itself as a farce, for Lefebvre the future is announced in a grotesque. Like the spaces of suburban houses examined by the ISU as an ironic answer to the demand for a sphere beyond work, in the tourist new towns the experience of the body beyond the division of labor is intermingled with its commodified images and fragmented gestures. The "total body" appears in a ridiculous, distorted, awkward form, as a part of "vacationland festivals" that "caricaturize the appropriation and reappropriation of space."[59] While Mario Gaviria was never tired of pointing out how traditional urban festivals become commodified by the tourist industry in Spain, he also pursued extensive research on the old center in Pamplona, the "space of festival and subversion," as a test case for the principles of the right to the city and the self-management of space by its residents.[60] In this sense, rather than contrasting "utopias" and "realities" in urban planning,[61] in Lefebvre's account utopia permeates tourist urbanism. As with Walter Benjamin's discovery that commodities convey the fantasy of social transformation in reified forms, the experience of spaces of leisure as detached from their conditions of possibility frees the references from their immediate context and reveals in the commodified images of the body, sun, and sea the promise of archaic symbols, at the same time illuminating the incompleteness of the social order.[62] Breaking away from the distribution of times and places that comes with the division of labor, in the landscapes of leisure "a pedagogy of space and time is beginning to take shape," writes Lefebvre, inspired by Jean-Antheleme Brillat-Savarin's egalitarian pedagogy of the sense of taste.[63]

The experience of spaces of leisure is hence not simply an instance of fetishism but conveys a hint of emancipation in the sense of overturning the social order that assigns groups to places of work and those of nonwork. In Lefebvre's view, this overturning is at the core of every "urban revolution," violent or not, including the 1936 electoral victory of the leftist Front Populaire, followed by the introduction of paid holidays that allowed for "the people of Paris and of France [to] discover nature, sea, mountains, and time that is available and free. They discover[ed] leisure and nonwork."[64] In this sense, spaces of leisure reveal a desire for another life and the anxiety never to live fully felt by those who are ready for it, and who have been ready for a long time. This anxiety, repressed in communist discourse, is what connects a worker locksmith writing in 1841 in a working-class newspaper that he would like to become a painter since, in spite of the respect for his profession, "he seems not to have found his vocation in hammering iron," and the inhabitant of a new town interviewed by Lefebvre in 1960, who cannot wait to abandon the boredom prevalent in Mourenx.[65]

Negation: Concrete Utopia

Lefebvre's theorizing of emancipation in terms of redrawing the borders that divide everyday life allows him to uncover the place of architectural work that, in his words, has been "forgotten" and "obliterated."[66] Within his general rethinking of Marxism, in *Toward an Architecture of Enjoyment* Lefebvre qualifies his earlier theorizing of architecture as a mere result, or an intermediate, of economic and urban planning defined as a "projection" of social relationships onto the territory.[67]

The latter position was conveyed by his critical accounts of architecture in many of his writings from the 1960s. For example, in Lefebvre's paper on Mourenx (1960), architecture appears as a transmitter of the division of labor in the factories and the respective social hierarchies: the management personnel would live in detached houses, the supervisors in towers, and the workers in blocks of flats. The doors and windows of white facades become dots and lines within a system of signs that make the socioprofessional status of the inhabitants transparent and commands their behavior.[68] Similarly, in his review of the new town in Furttal valley near Zurich (1961), Lefebvre saw architecture as reduced to one among many scales that are presumed to be vessels of preconceived social morphologies: the spatial sequence from the apartment to the city is isomorphic with the nested hierarchy of social bodies, starting with the family and ending with the urban community.[69]

The "forgetting and obliteration" of architecture as a self-sustained level of social practice in French postwar urbanization was a consequence, argued Lefebvre, of the principles of modernist architecture and functionalist urbanism and, in particular, of the "discovery" made by avant-garde architects of the 1920s that "(social) space is a (social) product."[70] While for late nineteenth-century psychologists and art historians, such as August Schmarsow, space was a result of a psychological process of associating the multiplicity of sensual impulses into an intentional object of aesthetic experience, the architects of the interwar period recognized in this labor of association a social and material process, rather than restricting it to a psychological one.[71] Read today, Lefebvre's attribution to modern architecture of an "abstract" concept of space, at the same time homogeneous and fragmented, geometric, visual, and phallic, appears characteristic for 1960s French architectural polemics in which "Le Corbusier," "Bauhaus," "modernism," and "machine for living" were often used interchangeably. This was only exacerbated by the Cold War discourse, evident in Lefebvre's sources,[72] that eclipsed "other" modernisms: those politically on the Left, geographically in the East, and formally heretic when measured according to Le Corbusier's "five points of modern architecture." In particular, this account did not reflect the multiplicity of the avant-gardes' sociospatial imaginations that shared the discourse on "space" without a consensus concerning its meaning; these "spaces" were so diverse in their philosophical and artistic sources, images, and political objectives that trying to find their common denominator seems to be an impossible task.[73]

Lefebvre suppressed this heterogeneity within his overarching argument about the redefinition of architecture in terms of space as the main contribution of the avant-gardes. He argued that this redefinition, which was launched as a progressive program of the production of a "second nature," in the course of the 1930s began to facilitate the modernization of capitalism and the emergence of abstract space as a "concrete abstraction": at the same time a universal medium of production, consumption, and distribution; and a commodity, itself produced, consumed, and distributed.[74] For Manfredo Tafuri, whose arguments informed Lefebvre more than he would be willing to admit, this abstraction of space displayed the most advanced critical procedure that capitalism appropriated in order to displace its contradictions to a higher level of historical development. In the context of the debates on workerism in 1960s Italy, Tafuri might have seen the contribution of these avant-garde architects as confirming the workerist premise about the primacy of living labor over capital, both as a decisive element in the capitalist model of development and as a subversive political force.[75] However, Lefebvre argued that the understanding of "architecture as space" was followed by the subordination of the architectural project to urbanism and planning, and this resulted in the active forgetting of architecture deplored at the beginning of *Toward an Architecture of Enjoyment*. Accordingly, Walter Gropius's vision of the architect "as a coordinator who would unify problems, proceeding from 'a functional study of the house to that of the street, from the street to the city, and finally to regional and national planning'" was reversed, wrote Lefebvre, and "structural planning subjected lower degrees and levels to its own constraints."[76]

The attempts to claim the concept of "architectural space" by postwar authors, from Bruno Zevi (*Architecture as Space*, 1948) to Christian Norberg-Schulz (*Existence, Space, and Architecture*, 1971), were a response to this subjugation and aimed at carving out a specific realm for architects.[77] Yet if there is any specific space of architecture, it is "a sheet of white paper," quipped Lefebvre in a 1972 debate with Tafuri; and in *The Production of Space* he argued that "[architects] raise the question of architecture's 'specificity' because they want to establish that trade's claim to legitimacy. Some of them then draw the conclusion that there are such things as 'architectural space' and 'architectural production' (specific, of course)."[78] However, these attempts only exacerbate the crisis of architectural discipline. On the one hand, if "architectural space" is one among many "spaces" produced by specific practices, their relationship reflects the power relations between their producers, and architecture is reduced to "one of the numerous socioeconomic products that were perpetuating the political status quo"—as it was put by the architect Bernard Tschumi in his 1975 reading of French urban sociology of the period.[79] On the other hand, if this "architectural space" is understood as somehow encompassing all others, subscribing to the vision of the architect as a "man of synthesis" connecting partial practices into temporary assemblages, architecture's disciplinary crisis is inevitable: since space is produced by many agents, architects arguably among the least influential, they will be held responsible for something they cannot control.[80]

Along these lines, Lefebvre's discourse was extended by many around 1968 in order to demonstrate the impotence of architects within the current social division of labor. A case in point was the discussion about "Architecture and Politics" organized in 1969 by the main French architectural journal, *L'architecture d'aujourd'hui*, with the participation of the architects Jean Deroche, Georges Loiseau, Jean Perrottet, and Pierre Riboulet and the editor-in-chief of the journal, Pierre Vago. Lefebvre's vocabulary suffused the intervention of Riboulet, a member of the Atelier de Montrouge. Positioning himself as a critic of the profession, Riboulet declared architecture a "projection of the society and its mode of production," deploring the loss of the "use value" of the city taken over by its "exchange value" and demanding the "right to the city" for the subjugated populations. Calling for a "political analysis of production of architecture" that would uncover architecture's implication into the material processes of economic production and social reproduction, Riboulet concluded that in order to change architecture it is necessary to change its mode of production.[81] "It would be illusory," he wrote in another text, "to imagine that architecture is done by architects."[82] While he admitted that the aesthetic concerns are specific for architecture, he refused to speculate about the possibilities of architecture after the social change since they are inconceivable with the conceptual and visual habitus of the current social regime; and hence he subscribed to the warning of Manfredo Tafuri not to anticipate an architecture for a "liberated society" but to introduce its class critique.[83]

In opposition to Tafuri—whose fierce critique of "architectural ideology" could hardly conceal his love for it—Lefebvre aimed at a different Marxist take on architecture. *Toward an Architecture of Enjoyment* and his later books open up a discussion of architecture not just as a "projection" of social relationships on the territory, but also as a medium by which the place of particular groups is defined, distinguished, and manifested within the social totality, and hence a site where collective subjectivities and their relative positions to capital and its various forms (financial, social, cultural) are negotiated. To envisage such repositioning is the task of an architectural imagination, developed from within the "near" order of everyday appropriation of space, which Lefebvre contrasted with the "distant" order of urbanism.[84]

In a 1967 debate with the architects and urban planners Michel Ecochard and Jean Balladur, Lefebvre compared the "macrosociological" perspective of urbanism to the "microsociological" one of architecture, which takes its clues from the practices of habitation.[85] The crux of this distinction is not the differentiation of scales, because just as architecture can be reduced to an instrument of urbanism, so is it also able to address a register stretching from furniture to gardens, parks, and landscape, writes Lefebvre.[86] (This is also how he theorized habitation in his reading of the ISU studies: as a practice reaching beyond the individual domicile toward the neighborhood and the urban territory.)[87] Rather, architecture and urbanism are distinguished by different modes of imagination: an opposition that comes to the fore in Lefebvre's distinction between "concrete" and "abstract" utopia.[88] While abstract utopia embraces current urbanization protocols and extends them into the future, concrete utopia "begins with jouissance and seeks to conceive of a new space, which can only be based on an architectural project."[89] Mixing admiration and sarcasm, Lefebvre illustrated abstract utopia with the example of the forest of Tronçais where Jean-Baptiste Colbert, the minister of Louis XIV, had oak trees planted in the year 1670 from which the French royal navy was to be built around 1900.[90] Lefebvre had much less sympathy for the abstract utopias of the postwar period, which he approximated with a "perfect city" of technocrats who believe in a possibility of a coherent and cohesive system of needs, services, and transportation.[91] One cannot help recalling the images published in 1967 by *Paris Match* about "Paris in 20 years," many of which became references in the architectural debates and a pool of raw materials for the subversive collages of the Utopie Group. They presented some sixty projects within the 1965 master plan of Paris showing the metropolitan territory extended by five new towns, connected by a rapid regional train network (RER), linked to large French cities (Le Havre, Orleans, Lyon, and Lille) by an "aérotrain," and embellished by the cultural center replacing the old market of Les Halles and by the "cybernetic tower" by Nicolas Schöffer paired with the Museum of the Twentieth Century designed by André Wogenscky based on sketches by Le Corbusier.[92]

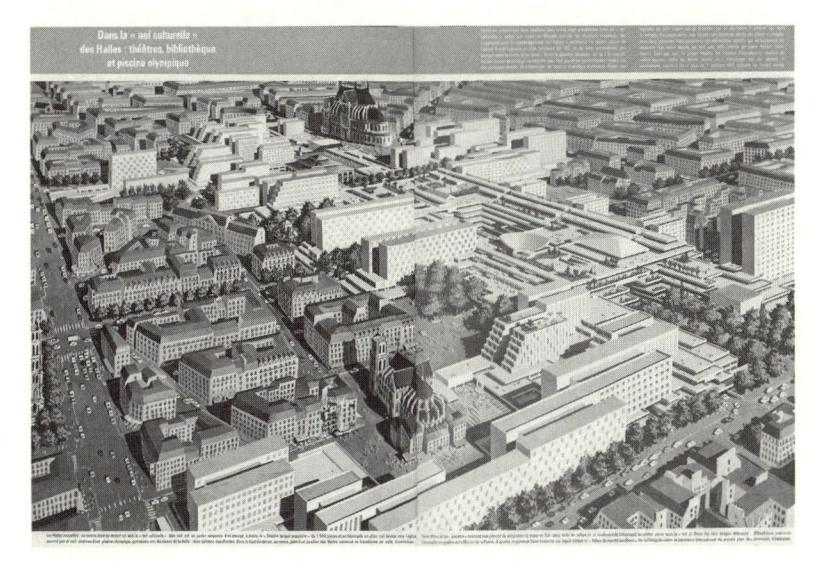

Proposal for the development of the site of Les Halles in Paris into a cultural center with theaters, library, and an Olympic-size swimming pool. From *Paris Match* 951 (1967): unpaginated. Courtesy of Hachette Filipacchi Associés.

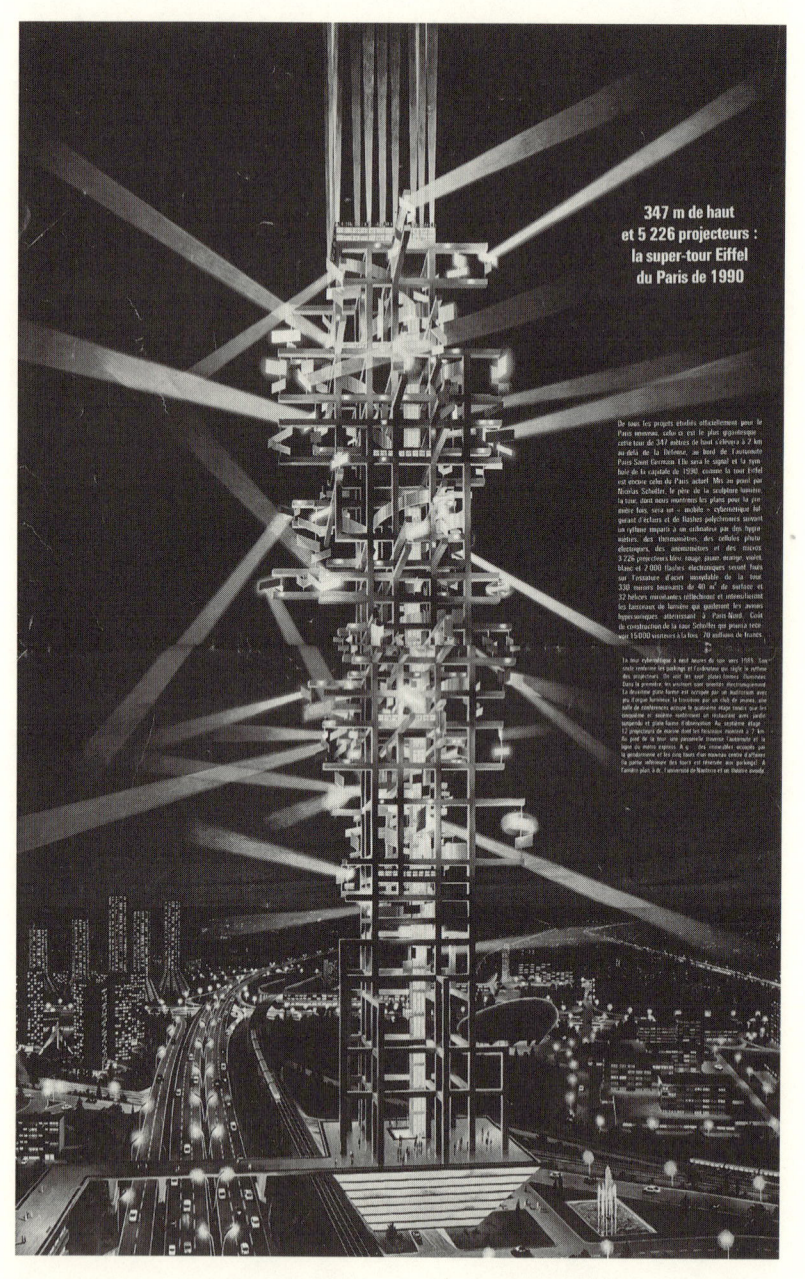

"Super Eiffel Tower of Paris in the year 1990," designed by Nicolas Schöffer. From *Paris Match* 952 (1967): unpaginated. Courtesy of Hachette Filipacchi Associés.

While abstract utopia is a "positive" extrapolation of the status quo, concrete utopia is "negative," that is to say it contradicts the premises of the current social order: the everyday defined by the division of labor, economy of exchange, and the state as the primary agent of economic regulation and political subjectivity.[93] This negativity is what Lefebvre found in the spaces of leisure that come with a hint of an everyday defined by nonwork rather than production, excess rather than accumulation, gift rather than exchange. But this was also the dynamics of habitation, studied by the ISU as a set of practices—sometimes material, sometimes discursive, sometimes imaginary—that appropriate everyday spaces by structuring them according to significant distinctions, in particular in opposition to the world of labor. While Lefebvre was among the first in France to show how everyday spaces become instrumental in capitalist reproduction, the studies by the ISU revealed to him that everyday habitation in the suburban house is lived "beyond" and "against" the routines of *métro–boulot–dodo* (commuting, working, sleeping).

Such understood practices of habitation are the starting point for Lefebvre's rethinking of architectural imagination. Like habitation, which the ISU studied as experienced beyond its socioeconomic conditions of possibility, in *Toward an Architecture of Enjoyment* Lefebvre argues for a procedure that "suspends by means of thought," literally "puts into parentheses," the powers that "subordinate" the architect to the execution of a program defined on the level of urbanism and planning.[94] He writes that only by postulating architecture's "relative autonomy" is it possible to open up the architectural imagination rather than repeating that "there is nothing to be done, nothing to be thought, because everything is 'blocked,' because 'capitalism' rules and co-opts everything, because the 'mode of production' exists as system and totality, to be rejected or accepted in accordance with the principle of 'all or nothing.'"[95] Lefebvre argues that this "parenthesizing" is a "dialectical reduction," which contrasts with philosophical reductivism, and follows the procedure of Marx to "reduce in order to situate and restore."[96] Rather than "putting everything into your system"—as Lefebvre polemically responded to Tafuri—he counted architecture among "open" totalities, semiautonomous subsystems, and nonsynchronicities within French postwar society.[97]

The "negativity" of the architectural imagination is hence not a project of an exception to capitalism, let alone resistance to it by architectural means. The "parenthesizing" Lefebvre postulated is an attempt to stake out a field of investigation for the architectural imagination,"to turn the world upside down using theory, the imaginary, and dream, to contribute to its multiform practical transformation, without being restricted to a limited form (political, 'cultural,' ideological, and, therefore, dogmatic)."[98] What appears as a withdrawal from a political engagement opens up a possibility of a political practice, since after the parentheses are lifted, the products of this investigation—concepts, images—would reenter social practice as projects and "counterprojects."[99]

Politics: Architecture of Habitation

The political dimension of Lefebvre's definition of architecture by means of habitation and the possibilities for a recalibration of the practices of architects along this definition become evident when *Toward an Architecture of Enjoyment* is read together with the Common Program: the coalition between the French Communist Party (PCF) and the Socialist Party (PS) signed in June 1972, thus around the time Lefebvre was beginning his work on the manuscript. In the context of the politicization of French urban sociology since the end of the 1960s and the introduction of questions of the city and urbanization into French politics, the Program posited habitation as the core of a comprehensive political project.

Many sections of the Common Program followed the postulates that Lefebvre had laid out for the PCF in the mid-1950s, and that had led to his suspension from the Party in 1958, followed by his exclusion. They entailed the demand of a collaboration among the Western European Left, learning from the Yugoslav experience of self-management, de-Stalinization, and a broad coalition of political actors gathered around the urban question.[100] The rapprochement of Lefebvre and the PCF began in the early 1970s, but direct exchanges did not happen until after the end of the Common Program in 1978 and the ascent to power of the socialist candidate François Mitterrand in 1981 ("on the ruins of its own ideology," as Lefebvre would comment).[101]

Without explicit references to Lefebvre's writings, the *Programme commun de gouvernement du Parti communiste français et du Parti socialiste (27 juin 1972)* (Common program of the government of the French Communist Party and the Socialist Party, June 27, 1972) included chapters on "urbanism, housing, and social facilities," "leisure," "urban planning," and "democratic planning," a concept that Lefebvre commented on in his 1961 review of Yugoslav planning.[102] Based on the demand of nationalization of financial institutions and major industry groups, and broader income redistribution, the Program postulated a "new urbanism" that aimed at the reduction of inequalities caused by excessive urban growth and the satisfaction of social needs by hierarchized and coordinated distribution of social facilities: "an urbanism for the people and not for profit of monopolies."[103] This required social control of the land market and speeding up of the construction of affordable housing (to seven hundred thousand units per year), which would include state-subsidized housing and renovations, integrated with places of work and leisure facilities. Under the broad concept of "advanced democracy," the Program postulated inhabitants' control over administrative councils of the public offices of subsidized housing (Habitation à Loyer Modéré, HLM) in which representatives of the collectives and tenants should be granted a voting majority. Much attention was given to transportation, socially managed and subsidized by the state and enterprises, but also to environmental issues, linking questions of ecological protection to the programming of free time. In general, the Common Program aimed at ameliorating the "environment of [everyday] life" *(cadre de vie)* within a vision of "unblocking" the human potential that is restrained in the current society; in the words of a historian, a "socialism of abundance and human self-realization" rather than a socialism of accumulation and austerity according to the Soviet model.[104]

The consequences of the Common Program for architecture and urbanism were advanced by two colloquia. The first ("Urbanisme monopoliste, urbanisme démocratique" [Monopolist urbanism, democratic urbanism], May 12–13, 1973), held in Paris, developed the discussion beyond repeating the commonplace that capitalist urbanization is motivated by profit and the reproduction of labor power. It reinterpreted the discourse on the "pauperization" of workers—promoted by the PCF leader Maurice Thorez and clearly out of sync with the increase in living standards in postwar France—into a "pauperization of time and space" caused by long commuting hours, minimal housing norms, and the absence of green spaces and playgrounds.[105]

The second colloquium "Pour un urbanisme..." (For an urbanism...) took place in the city of Grenoble (April 6–7, 1974) on the invitation of the socialist mayor, Hubert Dubedout. It was prepared by the

Party's journal *La nouvelle critique*, which published its results.[106] In contrast to the academic constituency of the previous debates, the colloquium gathered elected officials from many suburban municipalities and some working-class cities controlled by the PCF. Among the 1,200 participants were mayors from cities such as Le Havre, Dieppe, and Nanterre, elected officials, and Party functionaries, but also social scientists, architects, and planners active in France's "red belts" as well as architectural historians and critics, such as Bernard Huet, Claude Schnaidt, or Anatole Kopp.[107] The poster for the conference, designed by the French collective Grapus, linked the image of workers, evocative of Fernand Leger, with a photograph of students, by this conveying the main promise of the Common Program: solidarity between workers and intellectuals.

Lefebvre was absent from Grenoble, but many of his colleagues from the ISU were there, and so were his ideas. In particular, his discourse on habitation as a practice straddling all scales of urban reality was employed in order to discuss the controversies around the production of space in communist-controlled municipalities. Were they enclaves "in advance of the current mode of production," where "millions of people live their everyday in rupture with the dominant ideology," as some speakers asked in Grenoble?[108] Or, as others argued, were they the last instances of municipal communism, increasingly obsolete in view of the limitations imposed on urban design by the central government and new regimes of financial regulation of housing and social facilities?[109]

These questions reflected the experience of "red" municipalities in France, such as Ivry, Aubervilliers, and Le Havre. But cities abroad were also reflected upon in Grenoble, in particular the decentralization of communist-governed Bologna, which included, since 1956, the establishment of the district as the center of direct democracy, with broad participation of the inhabitants in decisions concerning planning, urban renewal, and housing policy.[110] Introducing an issue of the Italian architectural journal *Parametro* in 1977, Lefebvre stressed the constant negotiation between various scales of governance in Bologna: the neighborhood, the city, the region; this negotiation took place in Bologna's civic centers, the very nodes of political debate, decision making, and enjoyment.[111] This was a recurring theme in his texts, and in a discussion about the Paris Commune (1871), he argued that the urban problematic consists in finding spatial units that can be self-administered and self-managed in both economic and social terms.[112]

Poster for the colloquium "Pour un urbanisme..." (Grenoble, April 6–7, 1974), which gathered officials, administrators, architects, planners, and sociologists to discuss the consequences of the Common Program for the production of urban space. Poster by Grapus. Archives Municipales d'Aubervilliers, France. Courtesy of Jean-Paul Bachollet.

Scales of urban politics were heatedly debated during the colloquium, in reference to the ongoing research by Marxist urban sociologists and geographers. In particular, Manuel Castells and his team had been demonstrating since the late 1960s that the urban region is the basic entity of capitalist production and reproduction, and hence the everyday life of inhabitants, fragmented into work, housing, leisure, and commuting, can be neither understood nor organized at the level of a neighborhood or a municipality.[113] This was also the conclusion of the ISU research project on four suburban cities within the Parisian agglomeration: Argenteuil, Choisy-le-Roi, Suresnes, and Vitry-sur-Seine (1967). With the increased mobility of the population and the fact that the institutions that influenced the life of the inhabitants now operated on a larger scale, the authors concluded that the scale of the neighborhood "does not offer a sufficient basis for collective life."[114] Rather, they envisaged a network of architectural objects binding together an urban territory and offering reference points for the inhabitants.

The construction of urban space by means of an architecture of habitation was the focus of the renovation of Ivry-sur-Seine, a communist-governed municipality in the agglomeration of Paris, one of the most discussed examples during the Grenoble colloquium. The project was presented as granting the working class and employees (constituting 72 percent of the population of this municipality) the "right" to live and to work in the center of Ivry. ("To live in Paris is more and more a privilege," said Lefebvre at that time: a "privilege" that was denied to him in 1990 when he was forced to leave his apartment on rue Rambuteau, followed by his move to Navarrenx.)[115] The renovation of the urban fabric in Ivry (since 1969), which included housing as well as public spaces, shops, and offices, was based on a close collaboration between the architects (René Gailhoustet and Jean Renaudie), the municipality, and the inhabitants—thus giving a hint of a different organization of architectural labor, to be generalized after the means promised by the Common Program would be made available.[116] This included rethinking the relationships between individual and team work, forms of remuneration, and the division of labor within the architectural office. In the perspective offered by the Common Program, the participants challenged the hierarchies between intellectual and manual labor and imagined an alliance between architects, planners, and the working class—a postulate considered particularly urgent in view of the 1973 law on the architectural profession, privileging large offices and resulting in the fragmentation of the design process.[117]

Renaudie argued for the participation of inhabitants in design decisions: not as "users" (*utilisateurs*) but as interlocutors capable of experimenting, judging, critiquing.[118] Within the "new pedagogy" of the Common Program expected to create material and cultural conditions for the transformation of the society,[119] an architectural project could be perceived as a pedagogical experience for all those involved and required popular intervention at the level of programming, design, and realization. Hence, architects were supposed to transform their traditional competences, technical and cultural, and to renegotiate the understanding of the profession. What was at stake was less a new type of specialization, let alone a vision of architects as "specialists in the forms of jouissance" as mused by Paul Chemetov, but, rather, bridging the cultural gap between the architectural project and the population: this was the lesson to be learned from the aborted experience of the Soviet avant-gardes of the 1920s, as the editors of *La nouvelle critique* argued.[120] This pedagogical program might have motivated Lefebvre to postulate in *Toward an Architecture of Enjoyment* the employment by architects of a multiplicity of codes "without privileging any of them," in line with the recent discussions in the semiology of architecture and the city.[121] It might not be necessary, at the beginning at least, to realize the vision of Marx and "to hunt in the morning, fish in the afternoon, rear cattle in the evening, criticize after dinner,"[122] but everybody needs to be able to converse beyond their immediate professional interests.

The consequence of such pedagogy would be a radical change of the conditions of the architectural commission (*commande*) and its relationship to the social demand (*demande*). Clues came from institutional analysis, in particular that of Georges Lapassade, Lefebvre's colleague at Nanterre, and René Lourau, Lefebvre's doctoral student. In the course of the 1960s, Lapassade and Lourau carried out several analyses of institutions (enterprises, hospitals, universities) that, while commissioned by the management of the institution in question, were developed, primarily, as analyses of the commission itself, whether explicit or implicit. In contrast to the bureaucratized procedures of participation, which had become increasingly standardized in French urban planning during the 1960s,[123] the analysts aimed at creating self-managed situations in which the organization of time and space of the institution was decided together with every other aspect of the analytical situation, such as the schedule and the payment of the analysts (who thus accepted the risk of not being paid at all).[124] In the words of Félix Guattari, an active participant in the debate, such analysis accounts for various discourses, not only theoretical ones but also those about everyday life and spatial relationships, articulating them together, without homogenizing or unifying them, and making them "communicate transversally."[125] In this way, the analysts sought to "liberate the social energy in the group" and mobilize its collective activities, "to make it circulate and to furnish it with occasions of investment."[126]

Intensity of social exchange was also the ambition of the project in Ivry, characterized by a great mixture of functions, diversity of housing typologies, and combination of ownership structures.[127] In the view of Renaudie, the overlapping of dwellings and the visual contacts between the inhabitants were encouraging relationships between them and facilitated collective activities. Since each dwelling is different, no social norm or convention would emerge according to which individual uses of the apartments were to be judged; at the same time, the choice of the apartment went with a sense of responsibility—speculated Renaudie.[128]

Without subscribing to this belief about an unmediated agency of architectural forms, Lefebvre described the architecture of Gailhoustet and Renaudie as preventing the isolation of an architectural object. Writing in 1984, six years after the end of the Common Program, he speculated about an architecture of habitation that would open up everyday practices to social life and the urban society. Such architecture "treats space as an articulation of several levels: the organization of territory, the broadest level, that of the site; the urbanistic plan, that of the city; the architectural project, that of dwelling."[129] Architecture of habitation, argued Lefebvre, needs to stress the interconnections and relative autonomy of these levels, and this is why in *Toward an Architecture of Enjoyment* he opposed both the isolation of the bourgeois apartment, mocked as a small city (with the kitchen as a shopping center, the dining room as a restaurant, and the balcony as park), and the dependency of the Existenzminimum housing on external facilities, necessarily limited by the current mode of production.[130] Such understanding of habitation within the urban system implied a political program, that of urban self-management, as Henri Raymond pointed out in Grenoble.[131] This subscribed to Lefebvre's reinterpretation of the "right to the city" during the

"Ivry! Centre ville" (1977), on the foreground the complex of housing, shops, and offices "Jeanne Hachette," Ivry-sur-Seine, designed by René Gailhoustet and Jean Renaudie, 1969–75. Poster by Grapus. Archives Municipales d'Aubervilliers, France. Courtesy of Jean-Paul Bachollet.

1970s: not just the "right to dwelling" or the "right to social facilities" within the discussions about entitlements granted by the welfare state, but the "right to urban life" for those who inhabit, rather than for the global elite whose emergence Lefebvre sensed and whom he ironically called the "Olympians."[132]

Materiality: Spaces of Jouissance

"Cache-toi, objet" (object, hide yourself). When during May 1968 this graffito appeared in the stairwell of the Sorbonne, the architect Jean Aubert of the Utopie Group took it personally, as an attack on designers of objects: "we were the object, obviously."[133] The May uprisings originated at the campus of the university of Nanterre, and according to Lefebvre the university buildings were not only the site but also the target of the revolt.[134] This hostility toward the architectural object associated with the reproduction of social relationships was a constant reference in Lefebvre's work from this period, and it was reflected in much of the architectural experimentation around 1968. The possibility of an architectural practice that unleashes the flux of libidinal energy, rather than producing forms that ossify it, was sought by Constant Nieuwenhuys in his atmospheric New Babylon, drawn during his membership in the Internationale situationniste, and by Ricardo Bofill in the movie *Esquizo* (1970), which explored the production of space by means of transversal relationships between bodies, senses, emotions, and concepts.[135] This commitment to the ephemeral, buoyant, temporary, mobile was conveyed by Lefebvre's comments about the inflated structures of the Utopie Group, his account of the Montreal Expo 67, where the "everydayness was absorbed in festival," and his praise for the reappropriation of Les Halles in Paris, diverted (*détourné*) into a site of "permanent festival" during the three years before its demolition (1971).[136]

In these comments, Lefebvre seems to argue that the dynamics of the social production of space require a dissolution of architecture into a momentary enjoyment, a flash of desire, an ephemeral situation created by "activities of groups that are themselves ephemeral."[137] The consequences of such questioning of the ontology of architecture can be seen in the work of the Centre d'études, de recherches et de formation institutionnelles (CERFI), an extra-academic network of researchers and political activists, during its most active phase between the mid-1960s and

Graffiti on the wall of the staircase of the Sorbonne in 1968. In Jean-Louis Violeau, *Les architectes et mai 68* (Paris: Éditions Recherches, 2005), unpaginated.

the late 1970s, led by Félix Guattari and in exchange with Michel Foucault.[138] In spite of its polemics against Lefebvre,[139] CERFI shared his basic argument that the city cannot be conceived as a specific typology of settlement. Rather, the members of CERFI were convinced that the city is a metaphor. "When one speaks of the city, one speaks about something else," they wrote in the journal *Recherches*: about a process of gathering of heterogeneous, productive chains, including the knowledge of functionaries, the tools of artisans, the writing of the scribe, the spectacle of religion, exotic products, arms of the military apparatus, and so on.[140] Like Lefebvre, the cerfistes launched a critique of the concept of need, and in their numerous research projects on the genealogy of collective facilities since the eighteenth century they studied prisons, hospitals, schools, and housing not as satisfying a preexisting "need" (security, health, education, shelter) but, rather, as instruments of normalization of the population and its distribution throughout the territory.[141]

To this fiction of "need" CERFI opposed the reality of "desire." CERFI understood desire as a force working in the social and political domain, a flux between people and groups that is manifested in a negative way:

Still from *Esquizo*, 1970. Directed by Ricardo Bofill. Photograph by Taller de Arquitectura. Archive of Ricardo Bofill/Taller de Arquitectura, Barcelona, Spain. Courtesy of Ricardo Bofill.

as lapsus, revolt, refusal; but also as love, project, hope.[142] Desire was at the center of the work of CERFI starting with the first research projects of the group in the late 1960s, focused on the architecture of psychiatric hospitals and departing from Guattari's experience at the clinic of La Borde. Against the governmental proposal of gathering the patients of five Parisian new towns in one central psychiatric facility, the group recommended a network of smaller institutions and suggested reprogramming the relationship between the staff and the patients rather than focusing on the buildings. In a later contribution to the programming of the psychiatric institutions in the new towns of Évry and Marne-la-Vallée, the authors argued that a generic apartment of five rooms and a kitchen would be all that needed to be said in terms of the architecture of the envisaged facility.[143] It is this refusal to freeze the social dynamics by material forms that motivated CERFI to conceive public buildings or urban renewal projects as situations for the collective analysis of desire. In the introduction to the single published issue of the journal *Parallèles*, the editors called for an invention of "underground institutions" that would "reactivate the play of energies and collective knowledge," and thus the only architecture to be longed for is that "sweated by the body, continually disseminated by gestures, glances, and contacts."[144]

This view of architecture was conveyed by the most comprehensive engagement of CERFI: the rehabilitation of the Petit Seminaire (1975–86), a neighborhood in Marseille designed by the architectural partnership Candilis-Josic-Woods (1958–60). The researchers of CERFI-Sud (Marseille) mediated the process of redefining the boundary between private and public spaces, encouraged and sustained the speech of the inhabitants, and intervened on their behalf when the appointed technicians opposed design decisions collectively taken by the inhabitants.[145] The result was a modification of the layout of the apartments and a differentiation of the facades by means of decorative elements, which led both to their individuation and to the effacement of the original design, to the despair of architectural historians. Yet in retrospect, Anne Querrien, one of the leaders of CERFI, saw the failure of the project elsewhere: in the very fact of its ending and in the abandoning of the continuous programming of the social spaces in the neighborhood.[146] The colorful facades, the enhanced floor plans, even the arch dividing two rooms demanded by a Roma family that caused so much controversy[147] are all empty shells when they cease to spark interaction, debate, disagreement.

The experiments of CERFI shared the basic premise of Lefebvre's theory that social space is produced in social interaction. Yet they differed from it by contrasting this interaction with the material object, in particular the architectural object, seen as alienating, reifying, commodifying. Lefebvre resisted the Sorbonne slogan ("cache-toi, objet") from a materialist position and argued that material practices need to be analyzed as a part of the rhythmic continuum of the social production of space, including the slow rhythms of objects.[148] Slow, that is, in relationship to the body, which is the criterion for the rhythmanalysis of space. In line with the research of CERFI, which discussed the body between the extremes of discipline and transgression—the bodies of patients in a mental hospital, workers in miners' cities, or gay men cruising in the Jardin des Tuileries[149]—for Lefebvre the body is the very model of the production of space, at the same time material, experienced, represented, and imagined.

"To grasp a rhythm one needs to be grasped by it," and this is why rhythmanalysis begins with the individual experience of the body to be extended toward "enveloping spaces," "surroundings," and "landscapes."[150] Rhythmanalysis considers the body as an ensemble of rhythms traversing it: "the rhythms of my life, of night and day, of my fatigue and activity, individual, biological, and cosmic."[151] This is not a return to a supposed primordial authenticity of the body, but rather an attempt at grasping its social production by studying an interference of rhythms, whether cyclical or linear, repetitive or differentiated, singular or aggregated. It is the body that is the source of jouissance: "the body accumulates energy in order to discharge them explosively, by squandering, by a game, by a bursting; . . . the body disposes of an excess of energy in a useless expenditure that produces jouissance."[152]

This sense of orgasmic enjoyment, which is conveyed by *jouissance* in French, guided Lefebvre's analysis of the events of Nanterre in May 1968 and was captured in the title of his book about May: *The Explosion: Marxism and the French Revolution* (1968).[153] In direct relationship to Georges Bataille's description of Paris by the dynamics of repulsion and attraction, marked by the extremes of the abattoir and the museum, Lefebvre analyzed the performance of an architectural object in the urban territory as a dialectics of dispersion and gathering.[154] He argued that the "explosion" in Nanterre targeted the spatiotemporal distinctions on the campus, which were transformed into lived contradictions: between work, housing, and leisure, private and public spheres, male and female students. "The university community in which the 'function of living' becomes specialized and reduced to a bare minimum (the habitat)—while traditional separations between boys and girls, and between work and leisure and privacy, are maintained—this community becomes the focus of sexual aspirations and rebellions."[155] In a TV interview shot in his office in Nanterre, Lefebvre pointed out the composition of slabs and towers around the green center adjoining the shantytown housing immigrants and argued that "in order to answer the question why it started here one should look outside the window."[156] For Lefebvre, the target of the revolt was less a particular building and more the equilibrium maintained between bodies, objects, activities, genders by the spatial layout of the campus. This equilibrium, to Lefebvre, reflected the general design approach in postwar urbanism in which each element is defined by its difference from all others—just like, he argued, the Charter of Athens conceptualized the city as a closed system of flows between production (work) and reproduction (housing and leisure).

Much of Lefebvre's work since the 1960s was focused on debunking such understanding of society in terms of "systems of differences" posed by structuralist theorists, which he saw as subscribing to the capitalist exchange economy and, in particular, the "form of value" that, in the words of Marx, is never assumed by an isolated commodity, "but only when placed in a value or exchange relation with another commodity of a different kind."[157] It was against this reduction to the form of value of all levels of French postwar society—functionalist urbanism, modernist architecture, consumer culture, state bureaucracy—that the term *jouissance* was introduced in Lefebvre's book. Rather than being a technical concept clearly defined and consistently used throughout the text, *jouissance* is employed in order to lay out a broad field of investigation and is often used within and against a whole family of concepts such as *bonheur, plaisir, volupté*, and *joie*. The book is less a cumulative argument than a registration of a process of conceptual work in the course of which the relationships between jouissance, architectures, and spaces are approximated by a range of specific disciplinary discourses. This open-ended character of *jouissance* in Lefebvre's writings was conveyed in Donald Nicholson-Smith's 1991 translation of *The Production of Space*, where such concepts as *espace* and *architecture de la jouissance* were rendered as "space of gratification," "space of pleasure," "space," and "architecture of enjoyment";[158] in this volume Robert Bononno prefers the latter in most contexts. This variation captures the ambiguity and richness of the French *jouissance*, meaning enjoyment in the sense of a legal or social entitlement, pleasure, and, in particular, the pleasure of sexual climax, while the stress of the Dionysian, rather than Apollonian, character of jouissance remains a challenge for the English translation.[159]

When opposed to the economy of exchange, jouissance stands in Lefebvre's text for transgression, expenditure, and excess: "jouissance ... is merely a flash, a form of energy that is expended, wasted, destroying itself in the process."[160] This understanding of jouissance subscribed to the basic distinction in Lacanian psychoanalysis where jouissance is distinguished from both desire and pleasure: while desire is a fundamental lack, jouissance is a bodily experience of the limit point when pleasure stops being pleasure; it is a painful pleasure: "*jouissance* is suffering," writes Lacan.[161] In *Toward an Architecture of Enjoyment* this reference to psychoanalysis extends to Lefebvre's revisiting of other discourses, often alluding to the polemics developed in his other books.[162] He was inspired by the work of Roland Barthes, a close friend, and his description of the "text of bliss" (*texte de jouissance*) that "unsettles" the reader's historical, cultural, and psychological assumptions, the consistency of his tastes, values, and memories, and brings to a crisis his relation with language.[163] From anthropology Lefebvre takes the understanding of places as charged with affects, but such allocations never exhaust the meaning of these particular places, which are "overencoded" as semiologists would argue. The history of architecture and urban history clarify these experiences by focusing on the appropriation of space that is in excess over every specific practice and pertains to material practices as much as to imaginary and conceptual ones. One of the conclusions from Lefebvre's personal tour of Western philosophy is that joy, happiness, and jouissance, necessarily entangled with pain, cannot be produced like things. Consequently, architecture can neither produce nor signify jouissance; whenever architects functionalize the body in order to offer jouissance for consumption, they end up with such projects as the "center for sexual relaxation" by Nicolas Schöffer, which Lefebvre ridiculed as a fragment of a female body transformed into a technocratic machine of pleasure.[164]

Jouissance is not an "architectural effect";[165] architecture can at best sustain jouissance experienced by the body, and this is what guides Lefebvre through architectural precedence in *Toward an Architecture of*

Enjoyment. "I have always preserved a very strong sense of my own body," he wrote, and many pages in the book can be read as a registration of his travels through spaces of jouissance.[166] They included the visits to the Daisen-in temple in Kyoto, to the squares and palaces of Isfahan, and to the Alhambra and the Generalife gardens with Nicole,[167] but also oneiric journeys, triggered by images and texts by surrealist artists, science fiction novelists, and Renaissance writers, like François Rabelais and his description of the Abbey of Thelema, a community of people educated in pleasure, both carnal and intellectual.[168] While authors describing "queer space" defined it by the urban solitude of cruising,[169] Lefebvre is drawn to spaces where jouissance becomes a collective experience. This included an imaginary passage through the Baths of Diocletian in ancient Rome, seen as a "multifunctional architecture—polymorphous and polyvalent." The sequence of rooms serving the cultivation of body and spirit revealed a "space of jouissance" conveyed by the wealth of materials and finishing, architectural details, and works of art: a "luxury" from which "no one was excluded."[170] The baths prepared the body for an erotic experience, and Lefebvre goes on to describe the temples of Khajuraho in the Indian state of Madhya Pradesh and the caves of Ajanta in Maharashtra, "erotic cathedrals" as they were called by Octavio Paz.[171] They represent the path toward divine love through the culture of the "total body" whose natural beauty is enhanced by splendid clothes and jewelry: a body that makes love, dances, makes music, and only rarely works.[172] Lefebvre wrote that the reality of the body is that of neither an archaic past nor a future revolution, but the "now," the lived experience; in the words of Paz, "the body has never believed in progress; its religion is not the future but the present."[173] On this path, Lefebvre revisited reformist proposals of the late-eighteenth and early-nineteenth centuries: the Oikéma designed by Claude-Nicolas Ledoux as a part of the project of an ideal city in Chaux, and the project of the phalanstery by Charles Fourier, a "palace for the people" where different people would combine their passions and produce new constellations of love and labor.[174] (A photocopy of a phalanstery by Fourier was the only image attached to the manuscript.) Commenting on Fourier in a 1972 TV interview shot in the Palais-Royal in Paris, Lefebvre described the Palais as the model for the phalanstery: a place of theater, galleries, encounter, commerce, work, and leisure; he urged viewers to recognize in Fourier's dreams a "society of jouissance" becoming possible.[175]

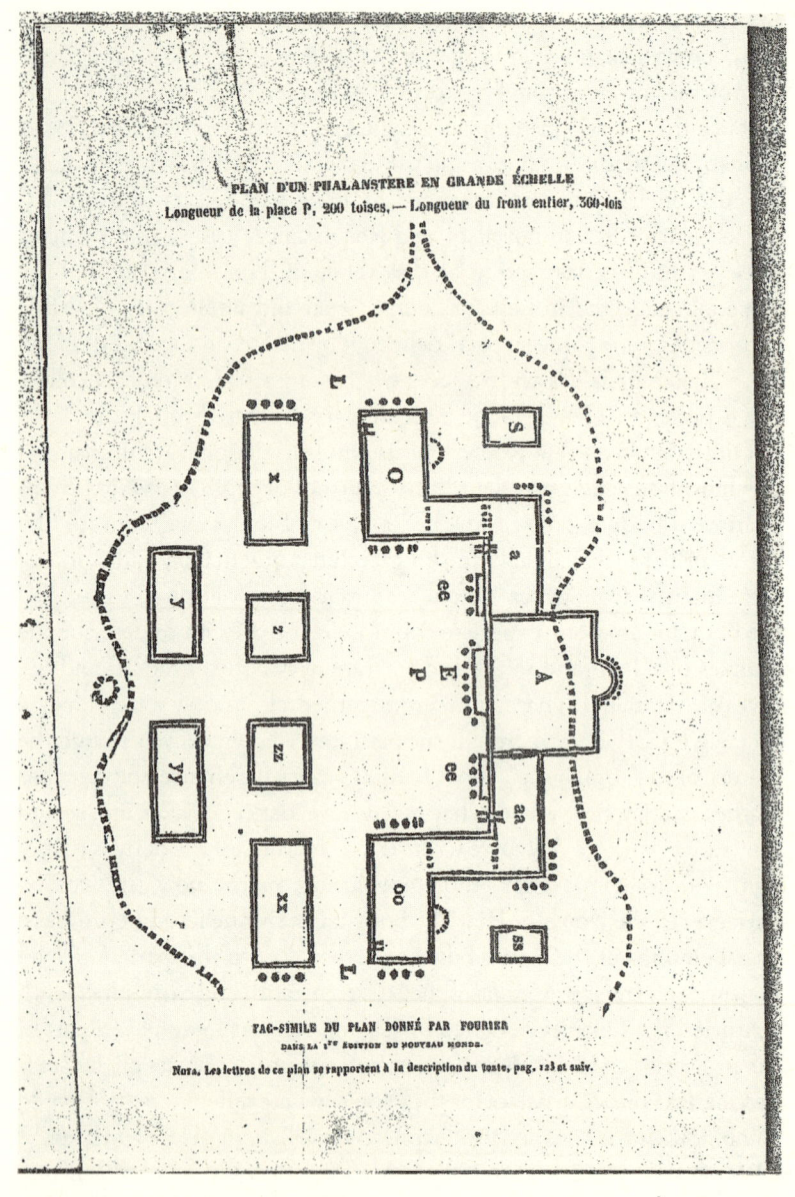

Photocopy of Fourier's plan of a phalanstery, attached to *Vers une architecture de la jouissance*. Originally published in Charles Fourier, *Le nouveau monde industriel et sociétaire: ou Invention du procédé d'industrie attrayante et naturelle distribuée en séries passionnées* (Paris: Bossange père, 1829), 146. Archive of Mario Gaviria, Saragossa, Spain. Courtesy of Mario Gaviria.

Toward an Architecture

Time to wake up. In *Toward an Architecture of Enjoyment* Lefebvre confessed that the popularity of Fourier makes him "suspicious": Lefebvre is wary of Fourier's productivist vision merging passion and labor; he reads Fourier's combinatorics of passions as coming dangerously close to Barthes's and Jean Baudrillard's descriptions of consumption as a "communication" between signs.[176] No less troubling is Lefebvre's own ahistorical narrative of the Roman thermae or temples in India, not accounting for the systemic violence on which these experiences were based, and his orientalist contrasts between the "West" and the "East" that haunt the book—in spite of his genuine admiration for non-European art. If these descriptions were in tune with the theorizing of the architectural experience conveyed by postwar phenomenology of architecture,[177] they demonstrate, first of all, the limits to Lefebvre's procedure of "parenthesizing." While this procedure allowed him to discover condensed energy where others saw dead labor, it is necessary to ask what happens when the "parentheses," which protected Lefebvre's argument, are lifted. In other words, how do we read *Toward an Architecture of Enjoyment*, an exercise in architectural imagination, together with *The Production of Space*, an analysis of space within the processes of capitalist reproduction, in which architects are assigned a restricted place?

Such reading needs to return to the status of *Toward an Architecture of Enjoyment* on the intellectual labor market: as a part of Gaviria's research report commissioned by the March Foundation. This status of commissioned research was shared with most of Lefebvre's empirical studies, which were commissioned by state planning institutions in France. Together with Gaviria, but also the members of CERFI and the institutional analysis group, since the late 1960s Lefebvre developed a range of strategies to deal with this changed position of critique resulting from processes of its normalization and institutionalization within the modernizing governance and economic systems of Western Europe. Hence, Gaviria's response to the research commission was a full-fledged critique of the capitalist production of tourist space, and the financing from the March Foundation was used to facilitate his activism against the construction of the highway at the Costa Blanca, a project in which the March Bank was an investor.[178] As for CERFI, the members of the group argued that in the wake of May 1968 the division between professional and militant life was intolerable. They strategically overidentified with capitalism and bureaucracy and accepted state research contracts in order "to use [this] money as an instrument and as a principle of reality that connects us to the real mechanisms of capitalist society." Such "collective analytical undertaking" was considered by the cerfistes to be the "new ingredient of the activist ideal, although this makes most leftist activists sneer."[179] Similarly, René Lourau and Georges Lapassade, when contracted to carry out an institutional analysis of private enterprises and public institutions, aimed at a collective re-creation of the crisis situations that had triggered the commission in the first place—a strategy that had a lot in common with Lefebvre's "internal analysis" of the PCF in the mid-1950s.[180] Lefebvre's own polemical style of writing, with concepts constantly changing hands and ideological demarcation lines being shifted, responded to the incorporation of critical concepts into the increasingly self-critical French state planning discourse, including concepts that he himself coined or shaped, such as "centrality," "everyday life," and "the right to the city."[181] In *Toward an Architecture of Enjoyment* this strategy resulted in his recourse to concepts that he took over from his opponents on the left and on the right: polemicizing with voices of imagined interlocutors and possible critics, mocking advertising discourse, and parodying the normalized jargon of urban sociologists, architects, and planners, which he introduced in quotation marks ("users," "needs," "participation").

In other words, Lefebvre's decision to speculate, against the advice of Manfredo Tafuri, about the possibility of an architectural imagination beyond the architects' position in the division of labor was followed by him critically engaging with this division from within his own research commissions; this contrasted with Tafuri's shunning from "the danger of entering into 'progressive' dialogue with the techniques for rationalizing the contradictions of capital."[182] Evidently, the responses by Lefebvre, CERFI, Lourau, and Lapassade cannot be repeated beyond their historical conjuncture, marked by the establishment of research contracts between French state institutions and its ideological opponents, an opening whose limitations soon became apparent and led to an end by the mid-1970s. (The seizure of CERFI's issue of *Recherches* titled "Trois milliards de pervers" [Three billion perverts, 1973], followed by the prosecution of Guattari in criminal court in 1974 are just some examples of the limits to this opening.)[183] Yet what architectural practices can learn from these experiences is how to formulate strategic interventions into processes of the production of space by responding to a specific commission while questioning the division of intellectual labor that this commission assumed. Read as a result and a notation of a co-opted research commission, *Toward an Architecture of Enjoyment* inspires us to rethink the place of architectural labor within the processes of spatial production, and to renegotiate it.

This negotiation is facilitated by Lefebvre's broad theorization of space in *The Production of Space*, which extends from material spaces to ways of use, representations, concepts, and experiences. Such perspective allows us to recognize architecture's instrumentality as perceived individually and collectively, experienced, interpreted, contested, and appropriated. Within Lefebvre's theory of space, architectural practices are to be conceptualized as transversal, that is to say cutting across ontological categories and contributing to all stages of the production of space, from formulating a demand to the phases of research, programming, designing, construction, and the continuous appropriation of buildings. Architects today contribute to these processes by mobilizing and aggregating spatial agents, activating or deactivating networks of resources, and analyzing their interrelations within the comprehensive system of the production of space by an application of architectural tools of research, recording, visualizing, and mapping.[184] Within the context of an antagonistic view of politics, Lefebvre's ideas on self-management and the right to the city are developed into a discussion on urban citizenship, radical democracy, urban commons, reappropriation of collective facilities, and redistribution of resources.[185] This perspective facilitates an extension of the traditional products of architectural labor toward research methods, program briefs, conventions of representation, educational tools, public pedagogy, regulatory proposals, and the reprogramming of buildings after their completion.

Architecture as space, again? A return to the modernist vision of architects as "producers of space"? The answer would be Lefebvre's typical "no and yes."

No, as far as this concept of space produced by multiple, heterogeneous, and often antagonistic practices has nothing to do with a modernist understanding of space as the privileged medium of architecture and a specific mode of aesthetic perception. As it was argued by Mary McLeod against the consolidation of the architectural star-system in the 1990s, Lefebvre's theory provides a powerful alternative not only to the "banality and mediocrity" of the generic built environment, but also to the modernist heroic discourse emulated by the neo-avant-garde.[186]

Yes, as far as Lefebvre believed in the progressive potential of the "discovery" that "instead of carrying on with the creation of isolated objects, separated from each other in space, modern society allows for the creation of space itself."[187] After attributing, once again, this "discovery" to the Bauhaus architects and Le Corbusier, in a 1972 interview in *Actuel*, he proposed "rationalizing this intuition and introducing the notion of the *production of space* as a fundamental concept." With the development of productive forces in the twentieth century it is possible to "take on and control consciously new forms of space production rather than getting locked in the repetition of mass social housing and highways."[188] In this sense, if the title of *Vers une architecture de la jouissance* appears at first glance as a polemical completion of Le Corbusier's 1923 manifesto (*Vers une architecture*), it can also be read as unforgetting the architectural imagination of the modern movement, which reconnects the means offered by technological modernization to political goals.[189]

Yet another of Lefebvre's definitions of *jouissance* as a "surplus" of use testifies to this complicated affinity with the ambitions of modern architecture.[190] Indebted both to the Marxist opposition between "exchange value" and "use value," as well as the juridical meaning of the French word *jouissance* as the "right to use,"[191] in *Vers une architecture de la jouissance* "use" is understood as a range of practices that assemble senses, forms, bodies, and images. Rather than subscribing to the functionalist understanding of use as a saturation of an isolated need, Lefebvre follows a different, more clandestine discourse on use in modernist authors, from Ernst Bloch's comments on "democratic luxury," through Le Corbusier's dialectics of architectural pleasure in *Une maison—un palais* (A house—a palace, 1928), to the understanding of luxury as an "excess in functionality" in Swedish modernism and as a "broadening of experience" by Siegfried Giedion.[192] In the course of the 1970s, such reading of modern architecture would reverberate with several younger architects, who discovered in this undercurrent a strategy for rescuing modern architecture from its reduction to the building production of the postwar welfare state. Hence, Rem Koolhaas recalled that within the "deep and fundamental hostility against modernity" emerging in the 1970s, he felt that "the only way in which modernity could even be recuperated was by insisting in a very progressive way about its other side, its *popularity*, its *vulgarity*, its *hedonism*."[193] And it was in the mid-1970s, with the first indicators of the waning of the Western European welfare state, that a new generation of Italian and French architectural historians launched a series of research projects on architecture and social democracy in interwar Europe, focusing on "collective luxury" as social bond in French garden cities and as compensation for the Existenzminimum apartments in social-democratic municipalities in interwar Austria and Germany.[194]

With modern architecture being the kernel of the worldwide techno-cultural *dispositif* of global urbanization,[195] the relevance of *Toward an Architecture of Enjoyment* today reaches far beyond discussions about the European welfare state and points to the centrality of jouissance in the social production of space. For architectural practices, this requires extending the struggles for the "right to the city" toward equal access not only to land, public transport, and infrastructure but also to spaces of education and enjoyment. From this perspective, equality in urban space is measured not by minimal standards everybody can afford but by aspirations everybody can share. The economy of social space, in this way, is an "economy of jouissance," a use economy: rather than destroyed by its consumption, the use value of social space is enhanced by its intense, differentiated, and unpredictable use.[196] There is no shortage of examples of such practices, many of which—both established and proven, as well as experimental and promising—were launched by municipalities in the Global South, making it evident that the geographies of authoritative knowledge about processes of urbanization are being recalibrated.[197] Bypassing the dichotomy between generic architectural production and iconic buildings, these projects depart from an understanding of urban space as an economic, cultural, and political resource.[198]

In this sense, *Toward an Architecture of Enjoyment* must be read together not only with *The Production of Space* but also with current experiences in architecture and urban design, which share Lefebvre's understanding that the paradigm of the production of space shifts from an "industrial" to an "urban" logic, that of habitation. To draw consequences from this shift is, in Lefebvre's words, architecture's "implicit" commission, delivered in spite of what is expected and sometimes against it—much like *Toward an Architecture of Enjoyment* itself.

TOWARD AN ARCHITECTURE OF ENJOYMENT

To Mario Gaviria, who inspired this investigation

"Trusting in absolute difference"
—Hegel, *The Phenomenology of Mind*

"Let us go, then! Off to see open spaces,
Where we may seek what is ours, distant, remote though it be!"
—Friedrich Hölderlin, "Bread and Wine," in *Poems and Fragments*

1

THE QUESTION

By "architecture" I understand neither the prestigious art of erecting monuments nor simply the professional's contribution to the indispensable activity of construction.[1] In the first sense, the architect elevates himself to the status of a demiurge; in the second, he responds to an external and higher command, which authorizes him to stand in for the engineer or the entrepreneur.

What I propose to understand by "architecture" is the production of space at a specific level, ranging from furniture to gardens and parks and extending even to landscapes. I exclude, however, urban planning and what is generally known as "land use planning."

This sense of the term corresponds to the way it has been used since the beginning of the twentieth century, which is to say since architects began to design furniture and to express their views and present their projects on what is commonly called "the environment"—although I shall be carefully avoiding this expression because it has no precise meaning and has been corrupted by abuse.

Why isolate the city, the urban, urbanism, and spatial planning in this way? Are questions concerning the various levels of spatial reality unimportant? Should we erase them from the map when it comes to architectonics? No! On the contrary, it is at these levels that certain agents and powers intervene that are quite capable of crushing architects and their work completely, if only by putting them in a subordinate position, by confining them to the mere execution of a program. And precisely because this is the way things are, the approach adopted in the present investigation will be designed to isolate those powers, at least conceptually, so as to define the place—the forgotten, obliterated location—of the architectonic work.

I repeat: This isolation is the only way forward toward clear thinking, the only way to avoid the incessant repetition of the idea that there is nothing to be done, nothing to be thought, because everything is "blocked," because "capitalism" rules and co-opts everything, because the "mode of production" exists as system and totality, to be rejected or accepted in accordance with the principle of "all or nothing." Any other approach can only incorporate the status quo, in other words the annihilation of thought—and hence of action—no matter the domain.

Try and think for a moment, with whatever degree of seriousness you like, of the nuclear threat or any of the mechanisms of planetary destruction (pollution, dwindling resources, etc.)—in short, anything that threatens the human race, with or without capitalism. How do you stop thinking about something like that? How is it possible ever to put the matter out of one's mind? Yet, inevitably, it is impossible to maintain one's focus on the subject. As soon as you think of something else, as soon as you choose to live, even for a moment or two, despite the danger, you effectively put the issue on hold, thus demonstrating the power of thought over the redoubtable forces of death. Does this mean that you deny the perils that lie in wait? No, not if you possess a modicum of perseverance.

Below, I present other arguments in support of this initial but not definitive reduction. Are they better? No. Different? Yes. And complementary.

Today, architecture implies social practice in two senses. In the first place, it implies the practice of *dwelling*, or *inhabiting* (the practice of an inhabitant or, to use a more problematic term, a *habitat*). Secondly, it implies the practice of the architect himself, a person who exercises a profession that has developed (like so many others) over the course of history, one with its own place (or perhaps without a place: this has yet to be verified) within the social division of labor; a profession that produces, or at least contributes to, the production of social space (if indeed it does have its own place in the production process). Engaged with practice in two ways, architecture operates on what I refer to as "the near order," in contradistinction to the "the distant order." Although the distinction is unavoidable, it has not always existed (the ancient or medieval city, for example), and is currently imposed by the mode of production or the political structure (the State).

But there is a paradox here. By setting aside the distant order, by clearly apprehending the link to practice, a consideration of the architectural work liberates the imaginary. Such thinking can approach utopian space by avoiding abstraction and underwriting in advance the concrete nature of that utopia (one that must and can reveal itself at every moment in its relation to practice and to *lived experience*).

Isn't there some risk in this approach? What illusion, what error! Any number of dangers haunt our progress along this slippery path. To take risks while avoiding accidents is a self-evident behavioral precept. For example, today, there are architects who assign a compensatory character to the space occupied by housing (the habitat). From their point of view, the (bourgeois) apartment becomes a microcosm. It tends to replace the city and the urban. A bar is installed to simulate the expansive sociability and conviviality of public places. The kitchen mimics the grocery store, the dining room replaces the restaurant, the terrace and balcony, with their flowers and plants, serve as an *analogon* (to put it in philosophical terms) of the countryside and nature. "Personalized" individual or family spaces, effectively subject to private ownership, imitate collective space, appropriated by an active and intense social life—confirmed by the most recent findings of advertising rhetoric. No longer do we sell only happiness, or a lifestyle, or a "turnkey" home; we exhort people, mistakenly appropriating the concept, "to live differently." In this way the bourgeois apartment and capitalist appropriation, by substituting the "private" character of space for its social and collective character, are established as criteria of difference. This is as true of a city or a vacation home as it is of a spacious and beautifully furnished apartment. We can extend this private/collective and individual/social opposition to the point of antagonism, even to the dissolution of the relationship between habitat and city, the dislocation of the social. But to what end? To provide the illusion of enjoyment, whereby "private" appropriation, in other words, the private ownership of space, is accompanied by the degradation of the real and social practice.

Proletarian housing, for its part, has the opposite characteristics. Reduced to a minimum, barely "vital," it depends on various "facilities," on the "environment," that is, on social space, even if this is not well maintained. There is no connection with enjoyment other than in and through external space, which remains one of social appropriation, even if that appropriation is realized only in terms of the restrictive norms and constraints of the existing mode of production. This is as true of hovels and new housing projects as it is of suburban detached homes occupied by workers forced to the outskirts of urban areas.

We can begin our inquiry with this spatial contradiction, which assumes its meaning only in comparison to some possible enjoyment of that social space, being careful not to elide or evade such contradiction (by setting it aside) because it defines the site, simultaneously practical and utopian, of that inquiry.

There was, and is, an architecture of death: tombs, the pyramids, the Taj Mahal, the Castel Sant'Angelo in Rome (subsequently used for other purposes), the Appian Way—imperishable masterpieces.

I can hear an objection, "No, an architecture of death doesn't exist, only an architecture of the rites of death. Those rites are social in origin, they arise in a particular society, which maintains a relationship with those who are no longer with them, their ancestors, and sometimes their founders. Inexpressible, irreversible, death creates nothing, does not allow us to construct anything. Funerary rites have a precise meaning. They prevent us from forgetting, but most importantly they ensure that the dead can do no harm and might even look upon us with favor. The dead are classified among the chthonic or cosmic powers, and as such they are potentially dangerous. They can seek vengeance for an injury or injustice experienced during their lifetime, for any insults that may have occurred after their death, and even the lack of remembrance, of veneration. Funerary rites protect the living; they exorcise the deceased and death in general. They depend on religion or magic or both. Architecture accommodates such gestures, rites, funeral ceremonies, processes, purifications, offenses. It provides them with a space and makes them possible."

Let us assume that funerary architecture arises from the contrast between the short life of the individual and the enduring life of societies, which use the disappearance of their members—individuals, families, generations—for their self-affirmation. Let us also assume that the funerary monument embodies gestures, offerings, processions, expiatory acts. It is true that those gestures alone allow us to understand the composition of monuments. It goes without saying that architectural masterpieces have staked their reputation on the appearance of the immortality of societies in order to transform that illusion into monumental beauty, into stone dreams. In this way the works survive the institutions that assert their eternity. And in this way as well they continue to speak to us about death; a metamorphosed death perhaps, but one whose tragic nature reappears, accentuated in the "immortal" work. Thus, the pharaoh, or the beautiful sultaness of the Taj Mahal, or Caecillia Metella:[2] stone dreams.

There are times when religious architecture does not turn away from the body. In the West, Christianity sometimes—rarely—rediscovers the body and its meaning, at least to some extent, in the resurrected Christ and the rather vague dogma of the resurrection of the flesh in eternal life. But concerning this flesh, its sex, for the Christian, remains unknown, and eternal life is analogous to that of the angels who sing of the Lord's glory without carnal desire. In general, in the West, religion and religious architecture assert the fact of transcendence and ensure that it is embodied in the material work, parish church or cathedral. This implies an apologia for death and mortal destiny: the flesh must die and will only be reborn in spirit. After they have been tested, the saved souls do not eat other than the bread of angels. They do not make love, even after they have regained their bodies. In this sense Roman art differs little from Gothic, although the latter has occasionally touched upon the theme of the physical resurrection of the flesh and the body as a whole.

In the East, the situation is quite different. There, divine transcendence doesn't necessarily destroy the body; the absolute doesn't abolish the relative; the infinite contains the finite and its sense of immanence. With the result that architecture *has* physical meanings, bodily symbolisms (it bears the perceptible signs of the body), and to a much greater extent than it *is* symbolic of the body in nature and in the divine, of the relative in the absolute, of the perceptible and the finite in the infinite. This embeds within material and natural elements the radical difference between East and West, one that does not predate their architectural expression.

Octavio Paz has written:

> Romanesque art links the ideas of order and rhythm. It conceives of the church as a space that is the sphere of the supernatural. But it is a space on this earth: the church does not seek to escape the earth; rather, it is the place where Presence manifests itself, a place laid out by reason and measured by rhythm.... In India, a strict and devastating rationality breaks through the limits between phenomenal reality and the absolute and recovers the sign *body*, which ceases to be the opposite of *non-body*. In the West reason traces the limits of the sacred space and constructs churches in the image of absolute perfection: it is the earthly dwelling place of the *non-body*.

> Gupta and post-Gupta art are the reverse image of the Gothic.... Gothic art is sublime: the cathedral is not the space visited by the divine Presence; rather, it ascends toward it. The sign *non-body* volatilizes the figures and the stone itself is overcome by a spiritual anguish. Gupta art is sensual even in its most spiritual expressions, such as the smiling, contemplative face of Vishnu or Buddha. The Gothic is an arrow or a tormented spiral; the Gupta style loves the curve that winds back upon itself or opens out and palpitates: fruits, hips, breasts. The post-Gupta sensual spirituality—such as we see it at Ajanta, Elephanta, and Mahabalipuram—is already so sophisticated a style that it soon leads to the Baroque: the immense phantasmagorical erotic cathedrals of Khajuraho and Konarak. The same thing happens in reverse with the flamboyant Gothic. In both styles the sinuous triumphs, and the line twists and untwists and twists again, creating a dense vegetation.[3]

Religious architecture, therefore, cannot be appreciated continuously and uniformly. In the West, it is apparent in funerary monuments. Every Catholic church contains an altar designed as the tomb of Christ and various relics, usually in the form of a reliquary, and therefore, a form of pluralized memory and commemoration; Christ is present because the tomb is also the site of resurrection, as well as the resting place of a saint, a witness of Christ, a martyr. If we consider religious architecture as a genre, in its totality, it is marked by an intense contradiction between what Paz refers to as the signs of the body and the signs of the nonbody. Even if these last signs lead to religiosity and religious sentiment.

A spatial contradiction? Or a contradiction within historical time and the social reality inscribed in a space? The majority of arguments support this last hypothesis. Can we formulate an acceptable argument about the contradictions of space before modernity, that is, before neocapitalism? Certainly not. However, in this sense—the contradiction of social time in space, of a materialized practice—the exposed contradiction should not be excluded from the considerations begun here. Why? Because of its harshness, because of the violence it implies and contains, because this opposition culminates in tragedy.

The Greek temple, however, is said to have escaped this spatiotemporal contradiction (that of a fissured time inscribed in religious space, that is, an absolute space or one assumed to be such). It does not bear the trace of intense conflict between body and nonbody. In it, it is said, all is measure, that is, harmony arranged spatially without transposition. Why? Because Greek religion was political, not in the modern understanding of the term—a State religion—but in the ancient sense: it was a religion of the city-state, accepted without conflict, by the citizens, and by "consensus." Which would make the temple always admirable.

> A building, a Greek temple portrays nothing. It simply stands there in the middle of the rocky, fissured valley. The building encloses the figure of a god and within this concealment, allows it to stand forth through the columned hall within the holy precinct. Through the temple, the god is present in the temple. This presence of the god is, in itself, the extension and delimitation of the precinct as something holy. The temple and its precinct do not, however, float off into the indefinite. It is the temple work that first structures and simultaneously gathers around itself the unity of those paths and relations in which birth and death, disaster and blessing, victory and disgrace, endurance and decline acquire for the human being the shape of its destiny.... Standing there, the temple work opens up a world while, at the same time, setting this world back on the earth which itself first comes forth as homeland [*heimatliche Grund*].... Standing there, the temple first gives to things their look, and to men their outlook on themselves.... The work is not a portrait intended to make it easier to recognize what the god looks like. It is, rather, a work which allows the god himself to presence and *is*, therefore, the god himself.[4]

It is a bit cruel to stick one's finger in the wound, to point out the fundamental failure of Heidegger's beautiful poetical-philosophical meditation. The illustrious philosopher overlooks sensuality and sensoriality, sexuality and pleasure. That Being is manifest simultaneously in the mind and in the Greek language is all that interests him. Only the singular game of hide and seek conducted between Being and its creatures grabs his attention: Being unveils itself while concealing itself, reveals itself while hiding itself, masks itself while revealing itself. There is no place for enjoyment. No question of pleasure. How can it be grasped, from whom? The philosopher comments at length and with obvious talent on these curious distractions of Being. No other movement disrupts the coy interplay of a being with being [*Seiende*]; for this Being, having neither sex, nor passion, nor life, nor warmth, participates in pure clarity and pure shadow. This chaste relationship between Being and beings is even somewhat comical.

Why these premature comments? Because Heidegger's ascetic considerations of habitation, building, and inhabiting, examined in greater detail below, will serve as a means to highlight our own thoughts on the matter. Not alone, but accompanied by several other intense formulations, metaphysical and scientific, so unlike poetic practice that they stand in opposition to it. Such poetic practice transfigures the quotidian, transforms the residues left behind by knowledge, without any other assumptions than the ability to grasp lived experience in itself in order to overcome it.

Lived experience is the sensory and the sensual, pain and pleasure, anguish and joy. *Overcoming* it implies that we can get beyond the ambiguity, uncertainty, and blindness of lived experience. That such practice can be defined only by moving closer to music, poetry, architecture, or theater—to the imaginary—while moving away from verbalized knowledge, will be shown in the appropriate time and place. Architecture, examined on its own, will benefit from this reconciliation. Under the best of circumstances, philosophical asceticism reveals a form of spirituality that has nothing to do with a sensory and sensual work; it merely adds enjoyment to certain activities (to a "function" or to several "functions," to use the jargon of scientism, which ideology overloads with a meaning sometimes favorable, sometimes pejorative, without ever bothering to investigate the validity of concepts and their limits to its conclusion).

Religious architecture is not limited to temples, churches, basilicas, or cathedrals. There are also monasteries. And not only Western convents, and not necessarily Catholic either, but Buddhist monasteries. Neither absolute space nor space of death, contemplation has resulted in an architectural genre and specific spaces. For example, is the cloister a place of contemplation? Not exactly, for contemplation takes place within us, and if it does assume objective reality, it takes the form of the monastic cell. The cloister allows these contemplatives to meet one another without losing the meaning of their life, reinforcing it through their encounters. This space is measured in terms of bodies and gestures: the monks walk around while conversing (if the rule of the order authorizes them to speak). Although the meaning of the space is to contain bodies in motion and their movements, those bodies are barely physical; as bodies they lack passion, their measured gestures determine the exact measurements of the cloister, a rectangular (never circular) path that may be filled with symbolic objects, small columns with sculpted capitals, slender (ogival) arches. Around those bodies, metamorphosed into walkers of pure spirit, the signs of the nonbody are multiplied. In the cloister, contemplation is protected and affirmed, affirmed as a society of contemplatives.

In the most beautiful cloisters (what does the word "beautiful" mean?), space is so finely balanced that even today the visitor, the tourist, feels simultaneously captive and liberated. Something is adjusted to each body, precisely to the extent required. Space speaks and does what it says. Is it the human being present in such a place who receives a message from that space appropriate to its meaning—contemplation? On the contrary, wouldn't it be space that receives the perpetually confused message of the human being in search of life and truth, and that reflects it back upon him, or restores it clarified and intensified? What does the term "beauty" mean if not such interaction, such effect? The one who gives himself over to a life of contemplation discovers in the cloister the difference between contemplation and observation. He is no longer a spectator. What is there for him to see? Almost nothing. The contemplative perceives a handful of objects in the center of the square or rectangle, a few plants. He takes little interest in what he perceives, his only interest being in the absolute. The contemplative turns away from aesthetics, where he would run the risk of losing himself in art; and yet support of the aesthetic order inclines him to cross the (fictional) barrier separating the sensory from the intellectual and the mystical. He frees himself of his body by placing it—to some extent—into the action, onto the stage. The aimless promenade that takes place between the hours of prayer and spiritual exercise (or labor) reinforces the effects of the austerity of monastic life. The cloister resembles a desert in its silence and by the overwhelming presence of stone. Here, worldy chatter has ceased. Like the philosopher, although somewhat differently, the contemplative needs to venerate objects that are calm and cold, which he warms in passing by lending them some of his burning soul. Without this, contemplation exhausts itself in pointless discourse. Here, in the rhythm of the promenade, the search for the absolute is resumed. Listen to the sound of your footsteps, the muffled timbre of voices that accentuates the slightest intonation, the intensity of birdsong, the sound of the bells, the odor of the earth, the grass, the rain within the space of the cloister. There is something to be learned here, even for those of you in the twentieth century: this space, oriented toward disembodied purity, is nonetheless complete.

I have an image, a memory (specifically, a postcard and a trace of nostalgia) of the "garden of dry ocean" at the Daisen-in temple in Kyoto. What delicacy, what sober elegance in the construction surrounding the garden. It is almost forgettable. It is said that the contemplatives in search of the eternal who live around the periphery of the garden occasionally open the sliding wall of their compartments. Their object of contemplation is then the garden. What do they perceive in the sand streaked with spiral grooves, in those two small mounds? Certainly not what the Western observer, no matter how attentive, might see. Perhaps an emergence, a growth. Perhaps the least important of possible objects, which nonetheless bears the vision, the least signification denoting the greatest, the least uncertainty the greatest certainty, and the smallest pleasure the greatest joy possible. That there exists a contemplative enjoyment, purified, nearly evanescent, at the uncertain boundary between pleasure and physical syncope (although that is not how the contemplative experiences it), there is no doubt.

As for the very famous "dry landscape garden," the analytic Western mind would say it is open to multiple "readings." Microcosm, very sensory, barely sensual, land or landscape of miniature mountains whose meaning has been accentuated, this bed of dry sand suggests the river of time, from its origin on high to its disturbing and barely discernable disappearance. Time descends from its peak; the river bypasses terrible obstacles, blockages, a path littered with impediments. And yet there are not that many objects gathered in the garden, and their variety is not very great. It is the way they are assembled that creates their ability to stimulate. This bridge, a footbridge made of a broad, long stone—what does it cross? To whom, or what, does it lead? To nothing or to everything?

Of course, the Oriental initiate doesn't grasp these meanings by separating them. In its own way, isn't the garden an ideogram with multiple and indistinct meanings, inseparable from the sensible in terms of its meaning? For the initiate it may have other meanings inaccessible to the Westerner;[5] and within the sensible it appears as a privileged work, a complete image of the world.

In short, can I claim that this impoverished "signifier"—sand and stone—contains an indefinite wealth of "signifieds"? A wealth that is in keeping with its (apparent) poverty? I can, yes. But what does this abstract formalization add to perceived or unperceived form? Not much, except for the fact that the signifieds reside in the one who perceives; he perceives himself in what he perceives, but he contains the referent, the reserve or resource, especially when those signifieds provide pleasure or joy. And these signifiers do not float, they are not separated from their signifieds, a confused or too surprising message. On the contrary, these signifieds, although they differ from their signifier and have no relationship to it that could be determined by a single code or by various well-defined codes, are no less present and presented. Art (a certain art) consists in a choice of such signifiers, assuming that the distinction between signifier and signified is here relevant and sufficiently informative. The poverty of the *perceived* is merely apparent and leads to a poverty of the *conceived*, suggestive (initiatory) of an extreme diversity of presences (not representations).

There is no need to belabor the point that there exists an architecture of power alongside religious architecture, often associated with it but nonetheless distinct. Political architecture includes military architecture just as religious architecture includes the architecture of contemplation. Fortresses, palaces, and castles go together. Power always attempts to present itself and represent itself in the eternal, through imperishable architectural symbols and works. Power is exercised on a space, which it dominates and protects; there, it plants its symbols and its instruments, which are inseparable. The keep has both a symbolic and a practical relationship to the surrounding land, which it dominates and penetrates. It surveys space; it possesses nature the way a male warrior possesses the woman he has conquered and holds captive, partly through violence and partly through protection. At the same time, the keep or the watchtower pays homage to what it holds; it remains there, enduring, like a desire that will never fade. Below, in the underground vaults, the conqueror guards his prisoners and his treasure; above, the scouts, the watchmen ... it is as much a question of power and violence as it is happiness and enjoyment.

The architecture of power doesn't hesitate to make use of cruelty, as if power found in it a source of enjoyment. Octavio Paz has shown how the Aztec pyramids combine politics, religion, enjoyment, and cruelty. To the ancient Aztecs, dancing was synonymous with penitence. The equation dance = sacrifice is echoed in the pyramids. The upper platform represents the sacred space where the dance of the gods takes place, a creative play of movement and, through movement, time. The place of the dance is, by the same logic of analogy and correspondence, the place of sacrifice. Yet for the Aztecs, the political world wasn't distinct from the religious world: the celestial dance, creative destruction, will, in the same way, become a cosmic war. The pyramid, petrified time, place of divine sacrifice, is thus the image of the Aztec state and its mission: to ensure the continuity of the solar religion, source of universal life, through the sacrifice of prisoners of war. The Mexican people identified with the solar religion: its domination is similar to that of the sun, which each day is born, goes into battle, dies, and is reborn. The pyramid is the world, and the world is Mexico-Tenochtitlan.[6]

I would go so far as to speak of a tragic architecture, one that can be treated as tragedy. What is it that gives it its strength? Catharsis (purification of the passions) or, on the contrary, intensification. Tragic architecture dramatizes the sacrifice of man. It lends itself to the most intense dramatization: a death that is expected, prepared, consented to (so it would seem), and even demanded by the victim, in the extreme, almost erotic, almost voluptuous (or more than voluptuous) tension shared by executioner and victim alike. A simple platform, offered to the sun, at the top of a series of ascending and descending steps.... Here, the ritual gestures of human (inhuman, too human) sacrifice unfold.

In contrast to this political architecture, which openly states its reason and its function—domination—and which therefore draws its power from its meaning, stands oneiric architecture. It exists. The castles of our dreams have no function; perhaps they were never inhabited because they are uninhabitable. They do not so much make us dream as partake of the realized dream, truer than the real. But this dream is not harmless or anodyne. Far from it. In the châteaus of Louis of Bavaria, there is something terrifying, violent, monstrous, as in the famous sacred wood of Bomarro.[7] Here, horror seeks its fulfillment by becoming fictive-real, whereas in the Aztec pyramid the horror architecturally denoted and allowed became effective. Fear and terror, provoked as in a dream by images, by bizarre figures, provide a strange sense of enjoyment. The poet Ariosto excelled in voluptuous and cruel descriptions, and every amateur of such sensations, including Louis II of Bavaria, was (it seems) a reader of *Orlando Furioso*, although they ignored Sade.[8] No doubt because Ariosto himself, attentive to space, described places as well as people and actions, and because Sade, more analytical and less of a poet, doesn't go as far in the direction of voluptuous horror. I cannot help but think that the princes who were able to afford such sumptuous toys were also immature. They cultivated their childhood. If the dream castles speak of the disarray of an era, they also speak of the vanity of a power—that of princes and kings—that has abandoned reason and seeks alibis and substitutes. Those princes, Louis II of Bavaria and Charles III of Sicily, Prince Orsini, played at frightening themselves, played at taking pleasure in horror and (feigned) terror and (postponed) destruction. Why not? The most sensual objects to depict enjoyment in the architecture of dreams are the frequent abductions. A beautiful, naked woman, a Sabine, Dejanira, collapses into the arms of a centaur or a powerful warrior, who carries her off for his own enjoyment. No doubt there are compensations. Here, the signified overcomes the signifier, and therefore, something brutal, limited, slightly vulgar, but effective in its own way.

But desire is also punished. Acteon, guilty of having surprised Diana at her bath, was changed into a stag and torn apart by dogs. The theme is as common as the abduction of the beautiful woman. Equally cruel and voluptuously ambiguous is the contradiction of desire and refusal. The intensity of the contradiction, the violence of the action, expresses the strength of desire and counterdesire. The explosive energy of the act is frozen in a momentary gesture whose beauty exorcises the horror just as the architectural beauty of the tomb exorcises death. There are sculptures, often found in gardens, that narrate an abduction that leads to a cruel voluptuousness as well as beauty: objects not constructions. Will pleasure, desire, and enjoyment escape architecture?

Yet there are places where space has overcome sensoriality to achieve a deeper sensuality, where enjoyment (refined, sophisticated, no doubt sublimated with respect to desire) flourishes. This is the throne of the mad king, the virgin king, the Wagnerian and Nietzschean hero, Louis II of Bavaria, his throne crowned with glass peacocks with their wings extended, fantasy and enchantment augmented by a sumptuous irony.

Then there is the garden of the Palazzo Borromeo on Isola Bella. Concerning the palace itself, I don't believe its effect is anything but sensory: in spite of the pleasing diversity of its lines and the objects on view, Stendhal was right when he found the palace to be "as dry for the heart" as Versailles.[9] But in the gardens, with their grottos and their water lilies, something else arises, seeks to materialize. Is it the architecture? Yes, in the broad sense. How can we separate the parks, the gardens, the surroundings, the landscape itself, from the buildings?

After lengthy examination, the investigation reached maturity. It begins thus: "Since there were architectural works devoted to death, to violence, to the celestial beyond or terrestrial power, do we find among such works a counterpart, an architecture devoted to life, to happiness, to voluptuousness, to joy? In a word to enjoyment, understood in the broad sense, the way we are said to 'enjoy life'?" It's a dangerous question, whose interrogative stance consolidates the previous hesitancies, motivated by an examination of architectural works. Yes, many palaces and castles provide wealth and power something more than an external frame, something better than a work of art occupying a corner of space: an objective realization of their enjoyment. But what did they enjoy, the wealthy and the powerful?

The powerful take pleasure in crushing the weak and defeating an adversary whose power is equal to or greater than their own. Once victory has been obtained, the enemy (of caste or class) crushed, power becomes dejection. How many palaces and castles provide no more than a painful impression of a heavy mass, of dull ennui. Sadism, with its masochist implications, often associated with obscure unconscious motivations, can only be understood in terms of the will to power. This will is exercised or realized as best it can, for or against things, when earthly creatures and celestial fictions escape its grasp. But the will to power insists on the violence of its actions: to crush, to break. Once the act has been accomplished, it perseveres mindlessly and without purpose; it lives on. Any number of monuments declare victory, but they also speak of sorrow. Rich with meaning, those monuments, palaces, and cities have little to say about joy.

Can we, in the so-called modern world, discover an architecture of enjoyment? This incongruous question contains its ironic response. What do we see around us? Monotonously reproduced habitats, with miniscule variations presented as if they were profound differences whose appearance is at once dissolved by our gaze and by our other senses. Monotony, boredom, combinations of repetitive elements whose variations obstinately call to mind some fundamental identity. Asceticism is the dominant emotion, a cult of intellectualized sensoriality and abstraction made tangible. Thought and gaze oscillate between two entities: the "unconscious" (inaccessible by definition) and "culture" (banalized by definition), both of which are equally dry and devoid of sensual life, each reflecting the other in a play of mirrors, a revolving door. And this is as true of architecture (reduced to construction) as it is of the other arts, and philosophism and scientism, the ultimate rationalizations.

Accident? Circumstance? Hardly. In this asceticism we find manifested a contradiction of the contemporary world in its developed forms, that of the large industrial countries: on the one hand abundance, waste, an almost extreme productivity, and on the other uneasiness, insecurity, anxiety. The conflict between (an elusive) satisfaction and dissatisfaction (which is all we ever encounter) becomes aggravated in every aspect of life. The intellectualizing asceticism of art echoes this uneasiness and dissatisfaction, while scientism declares its satisfaction and the triumph of productivity. But art like science, literature like philosophy are joined beneath the banner of a carefully determined category: the *interesting*. Not enjoyment.

In all fields of what is generally referred to as art, ever since the nineteenth century, the tendency to the baroque, to the fantastic, to symbolism has remained marginal, aberrant, dominated by an intellectualizing asceticism or soon co-opted. This includes surrealism. This asceticism, occasionally disguised (pop art confronted with a fully disembodied op art), has experienced success and even received the stamp of officialdom. It reflects the dominant ideology (sometimes disguised as protest) and incorporates it in the tangible (reduced to its simplest expression). Would this be the occasion to get to the bottom of things, as we say, by admitting that there is a bottom of things?

In the nineteenth century, the building dethroned the monument. I contrast the two terms, with their content and their meaning, by clearly defining them, for there has been, and still is, some confusion about them. The monument passes for a building because it is built (constructed). In the seventeenth century (1624), the English architect Henry Wotton defined architecture by writing: "Well building hath three conditions: commodity, firmness, and delight,"[10] a definition that has remained celebrated.

It was during the nineteenth century that the building became distinct from the monument, a distinction that slowly entered architectural terminology. Monuments are characterized by their affectation or aesthetic pretension, their official or public character, and the influence exercised on their surroundings, while buildings are defined by their private function, the preoccupation with technique, their placement in a prescribed space. The architect came to be seen as an artist devoted to the construction of monuments, and there was a question of whether buildings were a part of architecture at all.

There was a terrible loss of meaning that followed the extensive promotion of the building and the degradation of the monument. The monumental was rich from every point of view: rich with meaning, the sensible expression of richness. These meanings died over the course of the century. We may deplore the loss, but why return to the past? Negative utopia, a form of nostalgia motivated by a rejection of the contemporary, has no more value than its antithesis, technological utopia, which claims to accentuate what is new about the contemporary by focusing on a "positive" factor, technique.

The meaning ascribed to monuments disappeared in the wake of a revolution that had multiple aspects: *political* (the bourgeois democratic revolution, for which the revolution of 1789–93 provided the model), *economic* (industrialization and capitalism), and *social* (the extension of the city, the quantitative and qualitative rise of the working class). The demise of the monument and the rise of the building resulted from this series of cyclical events, from this conjunction of causes and reasons.

The monument possessed meaning. Not only did it *have* meaning, it *was* meaning: strength and power. Those meanings have perished. The building has no meaning; the building has a *signification*. An enormous literature claiming to be of linguistic or semantic origin is now seen as derisively ideological for its failure to observe this elementary distinction between signification and meaning. A word has signification; a work (at the very least a succession of signs and significations, a literature, a succession of sentences) has meaning. As everyone knows, the most elementary sign, letter, syllable, phoneme has no signification until it becomes part of a larger unit, becomes part of a larger structure.

The destruction of meaning, a democratic as well as an industrial revolution, engendered an abstract interest in significations. Paradoxically, and yet quite rationally, the promotion of the building was accompanied by a promotion of signs, words, and speech, which erupted together with the significations to which they corresponded. The power of the thing and the sign, which complement one another, replaced the ancient potencies, endowed with the ability to make themselves perceptible and acceptable through the symbols of kings, princes, and the aristocracy. This does not imply, however, that political power disappeared; it was simply transferred to an abstraction, the State.

The complementary powers of the thing and the sign are incorporated into concrete, which is twofold in its nature, if we can still continue to employ the word: a brutal thing among things, a materialized abstraction and abstract matter. Simultaneously—synchronically, I should say—architectural discourse, highly pertinent, filled with significations, has supplanted architectural production (the production of a space rich with meaning). And the abstract and flawed signs of happiness, of beauty, proliferate among concrete cubes and rectangles.

Buildings are no longer the abodes of gods—or kings. They are no longer the symbolic embodiment of the macrocosm. They have become bourgeois, but the process includes a certain amount of democratization. Need I point out the bourgeois democratic character of the great French revolution, the most successful until a new order of revolution arrives? The event pointed to a deep contradiction, which grew more intense and was laid bare during the nineteenth and twentieth centuries, when the bourgeois slowly, but powerfully, took precedence over the democratic. During this process, with State power asserting itself and even rising above society, the monumental reappears, with a deliberately political signification. But that is another story.

The destruction of meaning, this practical reduction, left a vacuum in its wake. Who would fill it? Nothing and no one. It would have been preferable had the (democratic) revolution made a clean sweep of the past to leave room for happiness and joy, and their conditions. This was, and remains, the philosophical utopia of democrats, a utopia that would be neither negative nor positivist (technocratic). Unfortunately, what occurred bore no relation to that great hope. The insistence on efficiency and profit that had supplanted luxury and the festival; the demand that capitalism (mode of production and the power of money) should dominate the global market; that in the market for space, the developer or banker who provides financing had subjugated the architect, and architecture—these are all inseparable aspects of the same question.

Function dominates, asserts itself, is on display; it is function that signifies. The signification of the building is its functionality. Period. Shapes become fixed: boxes that are stacked and assembled. Structure is simplified, tethered to the notion of an inside and an outside. The monument became associated with certitudes: religious, political, moral. An illusory certitude? Perishable? Yes, clearly, but those who held such views were unaware of their fragility. "Safety/anxiety" replaced lost certainties.

"Satisfaction/unease" replaced the older sense of the festival in cities historically associated with monumentality. Conflicting pairs, it is true, but the misunderstood contradiction became unconscious.

The monument exposed an absolute: religious and moral values concealed beneath aesthetic values. Within the plurality of meanings that arose with *the seen, the known, the lived* there appeared sexuality, violence, cruelty. Duration, which is to say, eternity (represented as possible), shared power (that of a caste or a community, the city), strength, and knowledge (celebrating their union) were offered to the people. What did monuments continue to express? The transcendence of power, its divine character, the omnipotent, signified by the ability to kill; war, sacrifice, judgment, execution. But also unity, that of a community kept and maintained on the land.

The palace and the castle asserted, physically incorporated, materially realized that power over the territory; they made it acceptable and accepted by the people whom they protected and dominated.

The building is poor. It is solely poverty, built by and for the poor, mental poverty addressing social poverty. Even wealth took on the appearance of poverty. The destruction of meaning and values, having no valid substitute, left behind only what was derisive: poor spaces for poverty, spaces that, nonetheless, had a revolutionary element: scorched earth, a tabula rasa for what was possible or impossible. But we are still waiting, and the loss of meaning grew into the loss of identity.

Otherwise, how can we understand the contemporary obsession with poverty? The poorest appears to be the richest. *In a sense*, it is, because it possesses and retains *meaning*. It is not poverty that we consider interesting, not even the facile comparison between comfort and consumption on the one hand and unfulfilled aspiration on the other. Neighborhoods, cities, and old villages are emptied of their inhabitants, who leave for modernity and profitability; others come to take their place, to live in their empty shells: intellectuals, the liberal bourgeoisie, artists. What do they find in those empty shells? The picturesqueness of poverty and its attractions require an explanation. Why do crowds of tourists and the curious invade the world's primitive regions? Why the devouring rush into the old neighborhoods, the ruined villages? The consumption, or, rather, *use*, even caricatural, of works and spaces must provide enjoyment. There is, in such places, something—a quality—to see, to grasp, to feel, and then, to devour, over and above the customary consumption of industrial products. What then? In the most recent works, appropriated space, monuments, homes (peasant or aristocratic) reveal the sense of something lost. The dream, utopia, the imaginary, the consumption of symbols and works, and finally tourism reinforce one another. *Arte povera* continues to experience a well-merited success. Destitute spaces maintain the obsession with poverty and direct us to other spaces where the poverty of objects does not exclude the richness of space. "Culture" and impoverishing cultural consumption reflect another, more nourishing form of consumption; an obsessed poverty spreads to the poorest locations for its enjoyment. Where then is the architecture of enjoyment?

Is this a reason—theoretical, followed by spatial and architectural practice—to return to the past, to the palaces and châteaus, to the agora and forum of the city, to the peasant home as a "dwelling"? After a lengthy detour, we would have come full circle to the philosophy of the Prix de Rome, or almost. No. The regional, peasant home (so-called vernacular architecture) was adapted to a spontaneous (organic) practice (a way of life) tied to the land, inscribed in a site and the surrounding landscape. The list of its virtues and qualities, those associated with its space and its appropriation of space, could be extended: balance, health, a certain comfort, some beauty in the best of cases, an activity governed by the length of the day and the seasons, fulfilled by a certain level of abundance. A trace of happiness, but no trace of enjoyment.

The demystification of the erudite monumental architecture that had barely gotten underway extends to immediate architecture, popular and spontaneous, which stands in contrast to it throughout historical time. The château, the fortress, the city ramparts, the watchtower that monitors a space filled with villages, huts, cabins, and sometimes houses constructed for successive generations bear witness to the enrichment and consolidation of well-to-do peasants (the laborers of the earth, conquered or purchased). On either side, lords and vassals, the home reflects the will to endure; victory is experienced in the future; joy, well-being, pleasure are obtained only with perseverance and are dependent upon it: rare are the festivals that suspend the strict order of labor and the workday; marriage is a once-in-a-lifetime affair.

A mystification: the Château d'Anet. In Paris everyone—architect, urbanist, sociologist—exclaims, "You seek the architecture of enjoyment in vain, in the Orient, in Spain, while it can be found just outside Paris:

in Anet. The Renaissance, the most sensual kings of France, Diane de Poitiers, Philibert de l'Orme."

Because King Henri II offered the château to his mistress, the illustrious Diane, who was said to have lost her virginity to François I, father of the reigning king, because Philibert de l'Orme placed his architectural genius at the service of royal fantasy, the structure is assumed to be the seat of pleasure. This is how artistic mystification is constructed, an illusory reputation.

Diane de Poitiers, Duchesse de Valentinois, was identified with the pagan divinity whose name she bore: Diana, the virgin goddess of the hunt, symbolized by the moon, upon which the ingenious symbolism of the three interlaced crescents is based. Over the monumental portal is a statue of Diana, a long, graceful but sturdy body in the style of Fontainebleau, inspired by the owner's mistress, nudity of the purest kind. With her right arm, the goddess embraces the neck of a large stag, and at the top of the portal, the stag, horns erect, is surrounded by four large dogs who are preparing to attack. The noble and pure construction of the portal presents these figures to those entering and leaving the château.

Pleasure? Enjoyment? Purity and cruelty! Which harmonizes well with what we know of the beautiful Diane—the king alone could profane the goddess, transgress the law that protected her. She was twenty years older than her royal lover, who took his revenge by raping young Italian girls during his campaigns. More ambitious than sensual, Diane was the goddess of frigidity: a cold, lunar divinity. Her symbols—frigidity and purity—are interwoven with great virtuosity on the roofs and walls, an echo of the hunt and chastity.

In truth, by examining the architectural horizon from all sides, only a single case, a single example legitimates this search: Grenada, the Alhambra, the palace and gardens of Generalife. Even so, this example does not go unchallenged. The Alhambra does not exist in its original state. In our imagination it is covered with rugs and couches, perfumed, populated with birds and fountains and the beauties of the *Thousand and One Nights*. But what did the arabesque mean to the Arabs—was it the reason for sensuality or reason in sensuality? Its limit or its cause? Or a warning of the end, for the supple line separates and defines as much as it unites and mimes the most graceful movements of life? Does it prescribe pleasure? For us, twentieth-century westerners, it suggests it, but for others, perhaps, it may have evoked serenity more than passion. Yet the existence alone of the Alhambra would justify our inquiry. Joy, serenity, sensuality, happiness? They are of little importance. I decide to assign it the + sign. And our question then becomes: "Why do neutral constructions or those strongly marked by the − sign, the sign of suffering, of anguish, of cruelty, of power, cover the inhabited earth, while its opposite, the + sign, is rare, so rare that until we have further information, a single example is offered for our examination? Does this situation have a meaning? If so, what is it? What can we predict? What can we conclude for the future? Can this situation be reversed, overturned, upended? How and when, and under what conditions?"

2

THE SCOPE OF THE INQUIRY

This inquiry is not limited to specialized or technical questions about architecture. Its scope is broader than a purely aesthetic analysis. To use a common expression, we could say that it is philosophical, except that philosophical reflection or meditation is centered on the philosopher's proof (experience), whereas here it is a question of social practice.

The classical philosopher, whenever he subjects productive or creative activity to analysis—art, science, work—begins by establishing the terrain of philosophy, the scope of his inquiry, its fundamental methods and concepts. He does not examine philosophical activity in itself. He is seduced by it, by hypothesis. Here, nothing of the sort takes place. Lived experience, practice are reflected upon, not to reduce them but to comprehend them in themselves; criticism of knowledge demonstrates that this act of comprehension modifies and, sometimes, transforms them, thereby dissolving a more profound metamorphosis.

Inquiry resists all efforts to reduce it. Architecture can be defined by ambiguity, by availability: space and the architecture of contemplation—the cloister, the monastery—do not determine the conscience of the contemplative, that is, they leave him with the benefit of the decision. Is he released from the world, emptied, to achieve a state close to nothingness (nirvana)? Is he penetrated, filled with content and knowledge, presentations and representations? How? Why? To achieve what kind of plenitude? The goal and meaning of the architecture and space of contemplation may be to be forgotten by being associated with some "other thing," some "elsewhere." The mausoleum repudiates or denies death; it transcends it in a way that is both fictional and real, rather than presenting it as an absolute, but does it leave uncertain what subsequent analysis separates into two opposite certainties, mortal end and immortal survival? Let us assume that is the case. But what architecture allows us the choice between pleasure and nonpleasure, between joy and sorrow? None. No architecture allows itself to be forgotten in the face of joy, in the face of sensuality, except for some brief, special moment, one that is the most neutral, the most anodyne. Apparently, no architecture is *nonsignifying* with respect to happiness, while being profoundly *signifying*: it is charged with signifieds—in the "positive" sense described above.

If this inquiry seeks to challenge anything it is power and its essence. The will to power, normal and profound, which shares with sadism and the pathological solely the ability to provoke them, provides enjoyment. The morality used by the will to power proscribes pleasure, something the masters of that big-hearted but unenlightened servant known as morality do not deprive themselves of. The energy they are able to accumulate is expended explosively, with a shudder and a groan. They take great pleasure in conquering an adversary, bringing him to his knees. But their victory is short-lived, even when it's sexual—for it's over in a flash and the bitterness seeps out unabated. Is there an original sin for every activity? An ontological finitude? A historical or social limit resulting from the division of labor? The cause is of little importance. The work that would eternalize the moment is nothing and speaks nothing more than shadow. It does not present, it represents, this confusion being part of aesthetic illusion. The monuments to victory, the triumphal arches, as ponderous and sorrowful as certain sculptures representing rape or abduction, an impassioned coupling, have merely a distant analogical relationship with the moment of glory they commemorate. The will to power as a source of sensuality is expressed in an act, and the memory of that act, because of its vanity, is demoralizing. Which means that nothing is erected by the will to power or by power other than that which serves its interests. The architecture of power—palaces and castles—most often bears the signs of a power without joy, or happiness, or sensuality.

It is the essence of power, then, that is being questioned, together with its means, as well as the essence of knowledge and the system of knowledge. Understanding too brings joy, but this joy destroys itself. Source, resource, the turn to philosophy, the joy of knowing (said to be the only joy by the Socratic philosophers of antiquity, followed by Renaissance thinkers such as Petrarch in a celebrated text, and by the philosophy of the Cartesian Logos) exhausts itself, contradicts itself. Is there anything more austere than the concept, aside from political power and the State? Anything drier than this core of knowledge? The joy of knowing grows desiccated once acquired knowledge is defined and taught and becomes an institution. Likewise, the joy of power grows cold, except when it embraces obscenity by exhibiting itself, by putting itself on display; and obscenity and its trappings cannot preserve it for long from such aridity, such glaciation. The work of Hegel and Nietzsche reveals how this culminates in the foundation of a radical critique that demolishes such monuments, the theoretical analogues of palaces and castles: systems, the philosophical system of knowledge, and the political system of the State, rely on one another, one against the other. The joy of pure knowledge is as short-lived as the impure pleasure of power; it wants to endure, to persevere in being, to renew itself. But to do so it requires new acts, new conquests, without end. Understanding progresses only when it becomes passion, but when the passion for understanding reigns supreme, the joy of knowing turns into anxiety and pain. And only then does it recognize its vanity. What good does it do to know everything, asked Faust, before summoning the devil?

The monument promises the continuation of finite joy, of short-lived pleasure, but it doesn't keep its promises. The monument strikes out: it is the failure of monumentality across all orders, levels, and domains. But who or what will replace it?

The above concerns only the sensuality of the warrior—the joy of wisdom that is separate from struggle. Does claiming that such joy and pleasure are brief, finite, and marked by finitude, bittersweet, that they wish only to continue, to prolong themselves; that the powerful and the wise have invented art by welcoming artists; that architecture and painting and sculpture are to be understood in this way, condemn ipso facto both the search for happiness and a place to welcome it? If we are dissatisfied with the word "happiness," we can replace it with the word "enjoyment" in the broad sense: to take pleasure in this body, in nature, or in discovery and creation, to enjoy life.

In what way does "gay science" differ from "sad science"? Nietzsche himself was unable to answer the question he himself proposed. Wouldn't the difference arise from the fact that a gay science might renew the joy of lived experience rather than setting it aside? And that rather than creating an abstract framework, it would soon procure, invent, create, a sensible, sensory, and sensual entourage?

But this hypothesis reveals another perspective, one of radical subversion: turning the world upside down exposes a new pathway; it means stripping power and knowledge (associated or dissociated) of their privileges. Among others these include that of modeling space as they wish, of building according to their various interests, from the most superficial to the most essential, the greatest being that of enduring, of continuing in being: to maintain—half fiction, half reality—the impression and expression of their duration.

Could we refer to such a transformation of the building as an architectural revolution? Why not? It goes without saying that this project alone is incapable of changing the world. Setting aside the relationships of production doesn't change them; on the contrary, it highlights their role, their importance. The same holds true for political institutions and the role of the State, capitalist or otherwise. The architectural revolution will not replace other forms of upheaval and subversion.

But how can another life, another world arise when what are referred to by so many with an impoverished vocabulary and inadequate terminology as "the environment of everyday life," or "decor," or the "morphological" have not changed? Can change occur without expectation, without exploration of the possible and the impossible? Must we wait forever, claiming that the present is stalled and the real (unbearable) is as full as an egg? The architectural revolution can only be defined as a parcel of the immense global upheaval that everyone knows they are pursuing in different ways, violent or nonviolent, bloody or peaceful, political or nonpolitical. The architectural project, when placed alongside other projects, whether or not it competes with them, has a life of its own, part and parcel of the whole movement but endowed with relative autonomy.

On the other hand, it is far too easy to label as "revolutionary" any empirically motivated project, and advertising rhetoric takes full advantage of this, adding the most audacious connotations to the most common denotations (to once again employ the jargon of scientism and the sad science). Here, the term "project" is understood in the strongest sense. It implies an appeal to utopia and the imaginary. Not in just any way, in the disorder of an unguided approach. Thought has cleared a path through the rubble and the available materials, through whatever obstacles lie in its way, in its own manner, theoretical and practical (associated with a practice and its difficulties and struggles).

Politically speaking, the architectural revolution can be viewed as having completed the democratic revolution that destroyed monumentality and as having surpassed the bourgeois era that merely multiplied the number of buildings. This brought about a limited transcendence of politics as such, necessary but not sufficient.

To turn the world upside down using theory, the imaginary, and dream, to contribute to its multiform practical transformation, without being restricted to a limited form (political, "cultural," ideological, and, therefore, dogmatic), in this way the meaning of our initiative is given.

If we are to acknowledge the failure of this initiative, we must also draw the resulting conclusions. These can take us far afield as failure consists in a negative response, a nonresponse, a disappointing response.

It will perhaps be shown that nothing can disturb the will to power using the effects and works of power. The new ever since Marx (not from his perspective necessarily but critical of the State) has become the discovery and analysis of the will to power. I suspend it by an act of thought, in my head, which may appear to be a case of simple reflection or profound meditation but is already part of the imaginary. At once, power and the will to power reestablish their rights in practice. My imagination—and everyone else's—is powerless against them, as is the imaginary and the appeal to creativity. Why? Because the omnipresent will to power is also within me, in the act of thinking, which attempts to contest a weak will deprived of sufficient means (that of an "intellectual" in the words of certain malicious French technicians). Therefore, there is nothing to disturb it other than a pure act, purified and purifying, purely poetic, that transcends it subjectively. An act that Nietzsche realizes when he abandons the gay science to leap into the abyss that separates the human from the Superhuman, not confronted, and nonconfrontable, by a social practice. So, while the gay science confronted the real and the actual by singing, dancing, laughing, or shouting, even analyzing and inventing architecture, Zarathustra, all grandeur and vastness, cosmic and worldly, chose, from among the infinity of possible interpretations and outlooks, an infinity that defined the prospective nature of existence, a new infinity that makes us shiver, that exalts the new joy.[1] Only with Zarathustra does the "tragic vision" attributed to Nietzsche's thought gain consistency, while the gay science can be summarized in the advice to learn to love—for which we must learn to hate.[2]

Here, too, one outlook—open because deliberately chosen—intersects another, which seeks a radical modification of social relations and the mode of production. This convergence is defined for a terrain or, rather, defines a terrain: space itself and, primarily, the space of habitation (the near order). If power alone (political power) could and can still become tangible, can materialize itself by realizing meaning, through the canny use of social relations, if this convergence fails, what fails along with it? The idea of total revolution? That is one perspective. A philosopher might be tempted to claim: perhaps Europe and the Logos, perhaps the West, perhaps the human species. For the human, all too human, will have lost the capacity to identify a path to the possible, to reconstruct itself by projecting the construction of novel forms. Lacking this capacity, consciousness and humanity are merely errors of nature, and life itself a disease, a flaw; this is assumed by pessimism and asserted by nihilism, whether European or religious, it makes no difference. The architect (demiurge or hack) and the limits of architecture (as specialized activity, aesthetic or technical) are secondary. It is a question of "mankind" and its future.

"Nothing is true, therefore everything is permitted." "God is dead, therefore everything is possible."[3] These words were written by Dostoyevsky and Nietzsche, almost at the same time. A short while earlier, Hegel had written, "Everything is true because everything that exists is both real and true. The true is fulfilled, everything is consumed, the whole is completed in its truth, the State." Marx: "No, the truth has not been fulfilled, a path has opened, the path to the possible, that of the working class, which implies and stimulates both economic growth and the development of society." A statement both realistic and critical, harboring highly concrete promises.

Where does this leave us? How much has transpired, or hasn't transpired, as if Hegel were right: blockage, fulfillment of the real in spite of its dramatic failures, nothing more than details to be added to the picture of the world, technical and political. Bet on the working class? How many disappointments, past, present, and future, for someone who has gambled his life on this! But over the long term, "historically," as is said in common parlance, perhaps.

To what extent have the will to power and political power used the proletariat to construct an apparatus of domination and spread across a given space? What consciousness or knowledge does the global working class have of this? For, everything is permitted: any use, or abuse, of violence. God is dead, but the State, which has replaced him, is not. So, what then is possible?

Defeat would mean a return to the monument and monumentality for anything in society that depends on the State, directly or not, the State apparatus, the so-called public power held by its employees, or the will to power. This monumentality, deprived of its older meanings—cosmic, religious, aesthetic—will rise in all its rigidity. It has already done so, has risen up as a tangible expression of that which rises above society: the State.

This implies that art in general, and the art of building in particular, would become an official expression of power. Which they were at a time when power legitimized, religiously and cosmologically, its exorbitant capabilities: to kill, to humiliate, to oppress, to exploit. Failure means the proliferation of interchangeable structures (buildings), the continuation of architecture reduced to communication, within a well-defined framework, that of a space produced for the purpose of exchange (buying and selling). Under cover of State power, we find the dictatorship of things and signs, in other words, money, capital, and merchandise; for the products delivered to the marketplace are cloaked in the signs of the work, of art, of "style," even of happiness. In other words, endless habitable boxes for obedient tenants who give birth to children to sustain the labor force.

Such failure also means the failure of democracy, because failure is able to conceal itself behind the facade of democratism and liberalism—the right to housing, access to property, increased construction (by and for speculation), even the "participation" of users in these programs. This can sometimes result in an obscure synthesis between the building, plagued with an excess of vulgarity, and the monument, rising in its arrogance. But neither participation nor synthesis will provide architecture with the dignity of bearing the + sign, that of joy, happiness, enjoyment, or sensuality—the sign of *life*.

The above comments should be added to the previous considerations, which emphasize the radical critique—Marxist and Nietzschean—of the State, of political power, and of the will to power. In more strictly Marxist terms, Marx never separated growth (economic, quantitative) from the development (qualitative) of society. He did, however, acknowledge the existence of a discrepancy, a "distortion" (a term borrowed from modern scientism), between growth and development, that is, the lag between them. According to Marx, superstructures (political and ideological) generally slow down productive forces (base) and the social relationships of production and ownership (structure). Under capitalism, this delay would be overcome through revolution.

Our situation is more complex. Significant economic growth has taken place and productive forces have expanded (technology, the destructive control of nature) without disturbing the social relationships of production. To the point that politicians have gambled everything on unending growth without concerning themselves with development. With time, this strategy has begun to appear increasingly strange. Superstructures have failed to overcome their lag. Development hasn't kept pace across the board. And this results in the magnitude of the inequality of growth and development.

Yet space has a relationship with all levels of social reality: productive forces (base), the social relationships of production and ownership (structure), political and ideological forms (superstructure). The organization and production of space give rise to new contradictions. Architecture, buildings, monuments, their contradictions can thus be connected to this relatively new ensemble of inequality and conflict. Does the concept of inequality enter into that of contradiction or, on the contrary, does it subordinate it? Logically, this would not appear to be the case. It develops and amplifies it but doesn't entail the classical (Hegelian) notion of dialectical movement.

The approach taken here will attempt to help thought and imagination close the gap; to compensate for the void resulting from the disparities within a body of interlocking conflicts.

3

THE QUEST

The doorway to dreams lies ajar, a sinuous road passes through. What will I find on the other side, where, with a shiver of fear, the bold would confront monsters? The void? A voyage through the interplanetary vacuum or monsters in a land of marvels? To discover the place of enjoyment, we must enter the dream because the real has betrayed joy.

This departure is like many others: initiatory voyages, Alice in Wonderland, Wilhelm Meister (a dangerous analogy but Wilhelm crossed the theatrical imaginary before completing his personal education). What is specific to my case is that, from the outset, I know what I'm looking for: not happiness, or delight, or joy, or sensuality, but the place where I would like to experience them, the place where I can linger in one of those felicitous encounters. This is not as absurd as it sounds. There exist places of contemplation, of serenity, of power and cruelty. So, is what I am looking for, once awakened near the doorway to dreams, simply beauty? Yes, if beauty is the "promise of happiness."[1]

I've prepared a long time for this trip. Over the course of years, I've attempted to cultivate and educate (problematic words: "culture," "cultivate," "education") my body, to provide it with a sense of space. But this complicates the situation, for in order to discover or construct the space of enjoyment, mustn't we enjoy space and, therefore, have learned it the way a child learns to walk? I've asked a great number of people and have come to the conclusion that none of them strongly experienced his body in space, the relationship of his body to his surroundings. Was this informative? A charming Brazilian, A., long and lithe as a vine, said to me, shortly after his arrival in Paris, "This space is no good for me. I've lost the dancing gait I had back home. I'm stiff. My walk is uncertain. These walls are like a vice, the angles are cruel instruments."

It is obvious that most people experience their body only through the words that identify and separate the parts of that body, that the body is dispersed in their conscious mind through its fragmentation. It is also true that those same people have only a narcissistic perception of themselves, reduced to the skin, the face (understood in terms of beauty and ugliness), the eyes—to a handful of privileged locations. Is there a reason for this? Language, perhaps? The mirror? The unconscious? No. Rather, it is Western culture, more barbarous than the barbarians, that misunderstands the body. It is the ideology of imagery and language, the Jewish and Christian tradition of contempt for the flesh, aggravated by the reign of advertising rhetoric, signs and significations, in a social space in which references to the body have disappeared, supplanted or replaced by the reference to speech alone.

This return to the body does not imply a return to the body of old, when the child, the adolescent, the adult obtained from their environment the indispensible elements that enabled them to experience their body without leading it astray. A tree? Consider the *uses* for the body and the gifts that this creature of nature, so easily within our reach, showers upon us. The tree remains upright, tall and calm, from its roots to its uppermost leaves. The child turns around the tree, climbs upon it, hides in it, and his body uses it as a model, taking the measure of this enracinated being, solid and erect, rising to its full height. Likewise, from the most delicate blade of grass to the most stable rock, nature provides the lesson of living things; they have nothing in common with the abstract thing, the fearful thing, the sign-thing, the coin, the banknote, the wallet and portfolio, the electric light, a Gillette or Philips razor, gadgets and kitsch. In all these objects, there is nothing that offers our senses (the organs and our awareness) the body entire. All are fragmented and dispersed, degrading and extrapolating the body's perceptions and its lived experience (through a process of metaphorization).

Most people ignore their body and misunderstand it. Some, caught up in the division of labor, only make use of the gestures of fragmented labor, gestures that have an influence outside work and shape the body and daily life. Others, including our "elites," are consumed by images, narcissism, abstraction. Abstract social space contains this unrecognized (diabolical) paradox. It is homogeneous because subject to general norms and constraints (political power, the economic domination of money) and divided (broken up into parcels, lots, plots, crumbs).

The reduction of the body followed that of "meaning" (religious and other values). The organs followed space, and its deterioration determined their degradation. Reduction and destruction of lived experience by a form of knowledge, by a space of sign-things, substitution of the dust of signification (of signifiers) for the signifieds of the body, the substitution of the natural by words (culture)—this is what confronts us. What does it mean to "inhabit" a modern building? The body has no point of reference. Even children, when we set aside a space where they can play, find in it and bring to it few if any sign-toys: miniature rifles and revolvers, a ladder, a merry-go-round. A more concrete object, a pile of sand, is a kind of marvel (and in the *banlieu* as great a marvel as the Buddhist temple in Kyoto).

It is impossible to return to this natural body, to this natural space, to this natural education by living, natural beings in nature. It is not a question of returning to nature, to the original and the spontaneous that irresistibly distance themselves from us. The argument that a state of grace is to be found in the state of nature, which humanity might rediscover, is a critique offered by naive humanism. But the body is there: mine, yours, ours. A kind of pedagogy of the body, its rhythms, a kind of teaching, will fill the enormous gap. But such unpleasant words: pedagogy, teaching, fill! Of course, the body cannot be appropriated with speech, and references to language fall on their own at the appropriate moment. What is needed is a practice, addressed to lived experience, to lead it to the level of the perceived world. How can we reeducate bodies for space? Sport is inadequate (although the body of a soccer goalkeeper admirably appropriates its space and is perfectly suitable for it) as is what is known as physical expression, mimetic learning. These are merely the indicators of a need, of an appeal. If the space of nature can no longer play its part, let constrained space supplant it, through the use of knowledge.

For reasons I am unaware of, I have always preserved a very strong sense of my own body. Stronger than the majority of those I have questioned. It is inspired by a kind of wisdom that can only be called instinctive or organic. My body knows what it wants, what it needs (even in love, although here the causes of the disturbance pile up—which could be said to be alienating). I know which boundaries mustn't be pushed through work or fatigue, and the stress from eating and drinking. When I exceed these bounds, it's because something is not right: I want to punish myself, destroy myself. It is to my fortunate bodily makeup that I owe my unshakable health and vitality. Neither my lucidity nor my thoughts are foreign to this body; it is my body that reflects, that tries one thing or another, not an "I," a "cogito," a "subject," a cerebrality lodged in my brain. Philosophically, this practical experience is similar to Spinoza's arguments concerning the unity of space and thought, and the materialist statements found in Marx's *Economic and Philosophic Manuscripts of 1844* and Nietzsche's aphorisms in *The Gay Science*.[2]

I owe to this attitude not only a kind of solidity through the labyrinth of contradictions but also an absolute resistance to the external causes of destruction and degradation. This is part of physical and mental health. I believe that it is to this that I owe my long-standing interest in space, an interest whose conceptual and theoretical formulation has taken shape very slowly, but that cannot be reduced to that formulation. There is also a poetic side to this, and a poetic practice, that attempts to vivify the entire body with all its rhythms and senses (it is not a question of giving in to a nostalgia for nature or of emphasizing the use of one of our senses—sight, for example—or of exalting the sensory organs in general). In almost methodical fashion, although there is no method in the strict sense of the term, what I refer to as "poetic practice" intensifies lived experience by associating it with the perceived world, by accelerating the interactions and interferences of the body and its surroundings: roads and streets, countryside and cityscape, forests and metal, lakes and streams, and stones.

How many times, since I was a child, have I played at walking with my eyes closed or blindfold. "I'm blind! They've poked out my eyes! I'm walking through a crowd of people and things and will find my adversary, the enemy, and will take my revenge. I'll kill him by feel. I'll know where to plant the knife. I'll know where to strike. Everything has an echo. The contours of objects can be felt by the skin, heard by the ear. I can move around obstacles without fear.

"One night, I'll fly like those nocturnal birds equipped with nature's radar. I'll be like the blind samurai in that popular Japanese film, who can cut an annoying wasp in two with his sword merely by the sound it makes."

I have diversified and multiplied these experiences for no reason other than one of "aesthetics" in the archaic sense of the word: to heighten senses and sensations and thereby take pleasure in them. Unsuspectingly, I became more sensitive to painting, to sculpture, to music itself, without managing to find something that would have satisfied my expectations: the entire body being moved and moving in the dance. One day, sooner or later, you reach the limits of your experience, and you pay for your initial mistakes or failures. You never fully overcome the faults of your origin, of your childhood, your traditions, your religion, and so on. You will never achieve the total body and the thought that knows it (recognizes it). Nevertheless, along this pathway to physical and practical truth, you manage to take a few steps.

I'd prefer if the sensory experience of space provided an opportunity for inspired and precise narratives, for protocols. Like dream narratives or those of psychoanalysis and psychiatry. The way that André Breton—but with a very different goal and a very different subject in mind—felt that "medical observation" could be used as a model for reports of surrealist initiation: "with no incident omitted, no name altered" so that the "strict authenticity of the document" would be assured.[3]

Might this reference imply a type of acceptance (posthumous or parodic) of the surrealist method or an homage to the enduring work and memory of the lost poet (ignoring the disagreements for now)? Neither. Everything that has attempted to overcome or avoid the real, the existent here assumes new meaning and is enlisted to assist the quest, everything except the archaic return to nature, to the original, to the ontological, to an outmoded absolute: we find this in Breton's work as well as, although to a lesser degree, that of Nietzsche (someone for whom Breton had little use, even though he would reference Hegel, an easily comprehensible misunderstanding).

Shall I take as my guide this slender volume of *Mad Love*, more seductive than profound? Perhaps. Especially as it narrates the expectation and then the attainment of total love, and the search for places where the inseparable joy of pleasure could be found.

> The peak of the Teide in Tenerife is made from the sparks glancing off the little play dagger that the pretty Toldedan ladies keep day and night against their breasts.[4]

When you are cast into the spiral of the island shell so as to see only the three or four first great twistings, it seems to split in two so as to present itself in section with one half standing, the other oscillating in even beat upon the dazzling base of the sea. Here, in the brief succeeding intervals of the superb milk hydras, the last houses grouped in the sun, with their stucco façades of colors unknown in Europe, like a deck of cards with the backs marvelously dissimilar and nevertheless bathed in the same light, uniformly discolored by all the time for which the pack has been shuffled.[5]

At the foot of Teide and under the watch of the greatest dracaena in the world, the Orotova valley reflects in a pearl sky the whole treasure of vegetal life, otherwise sparse between regions.[6]

Because it is here, on this side of the ocean, within the confines of a park, in a relatively closed vessel (if I judge by the outside) but set on the slope of an endless hope as soon as I entered there with you—as if I had just been transported to the very heart of the world—not only have the natural and artificial succeeded in finding a perfect equilibrium, but in addition, there are electively united all the conditions of free extension and mutual tolerance that permit the harmonious gathering of individuals of a whole kingdom.... Orpheus has passed this way.[7]

The perfect self-sufficiency that love between two beings tends to cause finds no obstacle at this moment. The sociologist should perhaps pay it some notice, he who, under Europe's sky, only goes so far as to turn his gaze, fogged in by the smoky and roaring mouth of factories, toward the fearfully obstinate peace of the fields.[8]

But have I substituted for my departure, my voyage to the possible and the impossible, the amorous peregrination of a poet who invents the path of love, who creates the time and place of a total act that overcomes action and passion, banal pleasure and common suffering? No. His somewhat precious quest can be summarized as the "golden age" he discovers in the Canary Islands. He's right, of course, to discover a place where "the great moral and other constructions of grown men, founded as they are on the glorification of effort, of heavy labor are endangered" so that the "livelihood we call 'earned' returns to the aspect it had for us in childhood: it takes on once more the character of a life *wasted*. Wasted for

games, wasted for love. What is required most earnestly to keep up this sort of life loses all its value at the passage of the great dream trees."[9]

And where is this place of delight? A place of passage, of steps, a spectacle for a passerby, a landscape. An ephemeral rarity. Would the problem be resolved by the "transition from subjectivity to objectivity"?[10] But saying is not doing, and I am surprised to discover that an *image* shown on a suitable screen—the sea, a cloud, a few words spoken off screen, a sentence—can realize this transition, provide objectivity. This fails to satisfy me, even though the powers of objective chance are involved. Even though there appear on screen in letters of fire what a man wants to know, in letters of desire. Such a statement is far too close, for my taste, to the purely visual exercise of what is sometimes referred to as a "paranoid" characteristic (what bothers me: the visual not to say the paranoid). "Desire, the only motive of the world, desire, the only rigor humans must be acquainted with, where could I be better situated to adore it than on the inside of the cloud?"[11] "We will never have done with sensation. All rationalist systems will prove one day to be indefensible to the extent that they try, if not to reduce it to the extreme, at least not to consider it in its so-called exaggerations."[12]

Yes, but what sensation? What exaggerations? Is the image betrayed by the sensate? One argument, widely held and briefly but adamantly expressed by Marx, holds that all social forms that have succeeded in civil life (society) were first experimented with in the military. Paid labor experienced its first success, so to speak, in the army. Large-scale commerce as well. Naturally, the warrior has a sense of his own body as well as those of his enemies and the surrounding environment. Especially when fighting with a heavy sword or an épée, or a knife. Unfortunately, it is difficult to refer to this rich experience of space, which is somewhat specialized and restricted, especially in the West. In the East, physical practice still owes a great deal to the martial arts. However, I'll leave such questions aside.

My guide sits before me on the table, and I read it the way we read a travel guide before a visit to a foreign country: to learn something about what we're likely to encounter. After absentmindedly flipping through the book, out of fear of neutralizing the charm of the journey, we would do well to leave it behind.

The guide is Brillat-Savarin and his *Physiology of Taste*. The work is wrongly considered trivial and difficult, a pedantic philosophy of food.

Its author was a philosopher, an heir and follower of the sensualist empiricists (Condillac) contemporary with those "ideologues" whose historical mission no one any longer challenges: the theory of education and the practical realization of scientific institutions that arose after the French Revolution (science and technology and the École polytechnique, the generalization of the teaching of mathematics, the concept of the secular university, and so on). The ideologues studied the formation of ideas that, as far as they were concerned, derived from the senses (individual). Their teaching would enable everyone (children, adolescents, adults) to comprehend the most abstract ideas—mathematical and philosophical—starting from sensory experience.

From this point of view (need it be repeated?), the term "ideologue" assumes a positive meaning, unlike the pejorative sense given to it by Marx. Ideology contains within it a pedagogy that is far from scholarly, but assumes a practical orientation (it cannot be called "social," for French ideologues were fierce individualists).

Brillat-Savarin (I dare you, I challenge you, Mister Censor, whether on the left or the right; and I scoff at you a little, leaping from André Breton to Nietzsche, then to the philosopher of the kitchen, but this leap has a meaning, I'm warning you)—Brillat-Savarin turns to food as his subject matter only after considerable reflection. He wants to raise this practice to the rank of one of the fine arts, the way sad and gentle Thomas De Quincey in London did for murder. Because taste lags behind the other senses, Brillat-Savarin, more of a bon-vivant than De Quincey, satisfied himself with cooking. *The Physiology of Taste* provides a method for cultivating, for guiding the organ of taste to the level of aesthetic taste, which can judge, appreciate, or depreciate rather than swallow whole everything that comes before it. Physiology, then in fashion, extended ideology by applying to the living organism the assumption that a natural element (see Balzac and Saint-Simon) could undergo a form of subtle development. Taste, for Brillat-Savarin, was as discriminating as sight and hearing and could comprehend objects as complex as those found in painting or music.

In one of his first meditations, he writes: "The flood of time, rolling over centuries of mankind"—this philosopher, who has no concept of history and replaces them with trite metaphors—"brought endless new perfections"—introduces into his language the idea of general progress, even in the field of the sensory and the sensual—"whose genesis, always active although almost unperceived, is found in the progress of our senses, which, over and over, demand their satisfaction"[13]—a sensualist theory of progress, somewhat weak, but agreeable—the senses demand it. But there are inequalities and, therefore, a form of injustice in the development of the senses: "It must be noted, however, that although touch has made great progress as a muscular power, civilization has done almost nothing with it as a sensitive apparatus; but we must not despair, remembering that mankind is still very young."[14] The philosopher's heightened critical faculty doesn't guard him against optimism. These considerations remind us that he wrote shortly before Fourier, who, in comparison to Brillat-Savarin, comes off as an ascetic intellectual, for he appeals to the combinatory passions—the composite, the cabalistic, the ephemeral— more than the pleasures of the senses. Their proximity is even more remarkable and interesting when the author comments: "For instance, it is but some four hundred years ago that harmony was discovered, that celestial science, which is to sound what painting is to colors."[15] This enabled sounds to overcome the distance that separated them from forms and colors, enabled music to measure up to painting. In this way, we can hope for a leap forward, ahead of the other senses: "who can say if the sense of touch will not be next. . . . Such a thing is more than likely, since the tactile sense exists on every surface of the body."[16]

The general, or generic, stimulus is the genetic, that is to say, desire (sexual, naturally). "We said before that physical desire had invaded the workings of all the other senses; no less strongly has it influenced all our sciences" (a fortunate era, that of the Revolution inspired by the eighteenth century, when a philosopher could believe that progress would take the shortest path, with knowledge and social practice reunited, to pleasure!), "and on looking at them closely it will be seen that everything subtle and ingenious about them is due to this sixth sense, to the desire, the hope, the gratitude that spring from sexual union."[17] Here we find a more direct apology for desire than any modernist lucubration: desire, that monstrous beast hovering in the shadows of the unconscious, obsessional, filled with anxiety and unexpressed violence, never possesses this subtle and ingenious character; desire, according to the critical disciples of psychoanalysis, more closely resembles the rutting Cro-Magnon than the voluptuary rites found in a civilization of pleasure. This bestiality closely resembles the brutality of labor imposed by capitalist society, its hidden side, although ideologues confuse it with what they take to be a form of radical critique. The machinery of production is tethered to the desiring machine!

In his second meditation, Brillat-Savarin analyzes the sensation of taste and identifies three "moments" (the term is not his): the *direct* (immediate), the *complete* (when the organ appreciates the object, grasps its taste and scent), and the *reflective* (when judgment and appreciation alone come into play). These different moments are combined and distinguished by and in the total sensation, positively when we taste a good wine and negatively when a sick man is forced to swallow a foul-tasting medicine. Taste, which is initially less endowed than hearing or sight, shares in its complexity: taste (objectively), aftertastes, perfumes, fragrances, that is, a first-, second-, and even third-degree impression.

Is mankind designed for pain rather than pleasure? Brillat-Savarin feels this is the case, although art can modify and transform this troublesome disposition. Today, Brillat-Savarin's classic analysis appears *revisionist*. Sight has achieved such a degree of sophistication that it provides more uneasiness than pleasure. Having been brought to this degree of cultural sophistication, the other senses no longer seem indispensable. It would be more appropriate to direct our sight from spectacle and image to physical truth. As for sexuality and desire, their function as an engine of the drives has been extensively utilized. Whether in the discursive mode, with the literary fetishism of Eros, or the sophistic mode, with its active eroticism, sexuality has reached the metaphoric or, rather, anamorphic stage where it exceeds its virtualities. As with sex so with the eye, it is time to rediscover the meaning of the total body.

Is it possible to apply to space the procedure invented by this "ideological" philosopher, that is, a pedagogy of refinement in the field of sensation, to raise this aesthetic (aesthesis, sensation) to the highly developed level of art?

Why not? The sense of space associated with the body (which is an occupied space, which *has* a surrounding space) is rudimentary. Our relationship to our body coincides with our relationship to space but is not identified in the discourse on space. The spatial relationship reunites, no less strongly than sex and sexual relations, all the sensations; it degenerates within a falsified space and in a false discursive awareness of the surroundings. Poorly developed, atrophied, this sense of space can be refined by avoiding the sophistications of aestheticism. It can then reach the aesthetic level of architecture, which is also based (rather badly) on the sensation and perception of space (on lived experience and the perception of bodies in space; on the conception of space and the discourse concerning it).

But now, let us cast the book aside. It doesn't aim very high or very deep. It drags along upon the surface of things, which isn't all that bad because it marks, it labels the border between the sensory and the sensual. Let us abandon books for now and take flight. Climb onto the magic carpet, the flying carpet of the imagination. Where would you like to go? You can cross continents, travel through time.

Imagination: images-memories-dreams and sometimes meditations and the trace of our thoughts. A flash. As in a science fiction novel. I move from one space-time loop to another, through hyperspace or the continuum. Where am I? Have I gone back before the time of capitalism or even Judeo-Christianity? To an original time before sin? That's what happens when we go too fast. We return to the Earthly Paradise. Inhabited shells, girl-flowers, animated plants and fruits, lovers, naked in a crystal bubble. What! Am I face-to-face with the Lord? Or am I going to meet the Serpent? What's going to happen to me? Might as well accept it. Unfortunately, I've wandered into a Bosch-like landscape. Let's get out of here: there is no architecture—I knew that—no houses, no clothing in Paradise. I carefully avoid a space created by Patinir:[18] on the left he depicts the joys of Paradise, on the right majestic homes and a burning city, besieged by all the demons of Hell. The oneiric quest is not without its risks. Another flash. Here I am in the charming Ali Qapu palace, overlooking the magnificent square of Isfahan. I recognize the source of my confusion: there is something exquisite and subtle in the lightness of the columns, the arches, the vaults. Unfortunately, specialists were slowly and carefully removing the coating on the frescos intended, or so it seems, to suggest pleasure, but that revealed only fleeting fragments. Now, I remember. Here it is—a perfect balcony, surmounted by a lightweight structure for shade, a mosaic floor. What for? To linger for a while, to wait. Wait for what? For everything, maybe for nothing. He who waits, waits without boredom in this place not designed for waiting. "Do you know," the Iranian who was accompanying me said somewhat mockingly, "do you know that this charming palace is said to have been built by pederasts for pederasts?"

"Dear friend, whenever asceticism gets the upper hand in society, Christian or Islamic, only deviants understand the meaning of pleasure and the body—prostitutes and courtesans, dancers, clowns, mimes, drug users, pederasts. I almost forgot pickpockets, thieves, and pilferers."

(I interrupt my oneiric quest to turn toward you, Mister Censor. From here I can see your frowning face, which speaks volumes about your uncongenial interpretation. However, you are mistaken and that is unfortunate, for so many things, so many impressions and sensations and pleasures will have escaped me, including this one, and I too may disappear without having experienced it. And if the homosexual component is awakened, it's a bit like a swelling that ceases, better late than never, Mister Censor. And where does this strange discomfort before the beauty of bodies come from? This anxiety in the face of nudity? This absurd fear of contact and odor, and subsequent flight? One part of the body freezes, another dries up, one organ swells in size, another atrophies, and the entire body is broken, gripped by the cold icy sun. Do you not see, Sir, that we struggle, offering any number of excellent reasons, against the damned and the wrongdoers; we protect the well-meaning against crime, against evil; and behold, little by little, the body, my body, yours, those of your sons and daughters, begins to crumble and crack, frozen, a body foreign to itself, to its space, to the space around it, to pleasure, to joy.)

Enough with the Censor. Salut! Adios! Ciao to Ali Qapu and proud Isfahan. A flash. Between Haguenau and Bitche, not far from Reischoffen, how they overwhelmed our childhood (the cavalry, 1890, how far it all seems). And here's the Castle of Falkenstein! A château if you prefer. Immense rocks linked by walkways and stairways, supporting walls and towers. Below, there are grottos, their sandy soil dry and white. Up above, there are passageways in the rocks, some in their natural state, others changed into rooms, with chimneys, seats cut into the rock. Everywhere, there are plants, grasses, bushes, trees. Mineral and vegetal, natural and built, mixed like the pieces of a puzzle, and we can run from one to the other, mixing them up until they are indistinguishable. We run, we meet, we build a fire in a medieval chimney, we jump from rock to rock, avoiding the walkways.

Beware the pitfalls of the dream. Falkenstein is a space for games, a castle of dreams. In my opinion, it is more wonderful than the castles of Louis of Bavaria. Enjoyment? Yes, one certain, the other uncertain. A kind of fairy tale more than a setting for sensuality. Architecture? No doubt. One indication can be found in the fact that the transitions provide greater enjoyment, pleasure, and joy, are more generous than carefully defined states. And the poorly delineated elements more than the precise and all too clear combinations that are addressed to the intellect rather than the senses, sensations, and sentiments. Nonetheless, Falkenstein failed to convince me. Let's move on, then, let's move on.

But where? Nature is an illusion. The picture-perfect landscape is a trap. A work that predates products and, therefore, capitalism. Long live the countryside, then, up to a certain point. Down with nature, naturism, naturalism, the return to spontaneity, to barbarism, even when qualified by the words of the savage (savage architecture). Nature? Phusis? Perpetual birth and ceaseless death. Rising up, as they say, and falling back down. Youth and old age. One and the other, one in the other. Contrasts, ambiguity, transitions. What can be said, no, what can be *presented* in a place? But which place? The Zen gardens of Kyoto? Yes, but we must be cautious of gelid simulacra, which the firstcomer will fabricate out of four rocks and a bag of sand. We must avoid replacing nature by the stillborn signs of nature.

The tall belfry on a church battered by the wind. Beneath the roof, alongside the bells, is a platform, a ladder. A girl, naked beneath her coat, cries out, weeps, leans forward. A priest and another young man, the girl's lover and brother of the priest, whom the priest has been pursuing, cursing him all the while; the two brothers extend their arms to the girl, a prostitute. The scene is erotically charged. The place? The eroticism is doubly, triply sacrilegious. The place has not been prepared for pleasure. Quite the contrary (the scene is found in Bataille's *L'Abbé C*).[19]

The palaces unfurl before us: Pitti, Ca' d'Oro, Borghese—the Incas, Angkor Wat, Tokyo, Negoya—palaces, castles! Far from the quotidian, the sovereign gods lead an inhuman and human life. Cosmos, sovereignty, transcendence. The palace exercises power: it is a mediator between man and the divine man. In the palace, the theocrat sighs with boredom, is forced to undergo interminable ceremonies, accept a rigorous etiquette, his every action carefully monitored by the priests. The relations of force and power are so tight-knit, so ritualized, that the slightest misstep (whether too much or too little) will lead to his downfall: the end. Such tact! Such poise! Imagine the fatigue of it all. Let us set sail, then, upon the wings of the dream, on our magic carpet.

L'Ile Verte, the Isle of Joy, the perfect utopia, is situated in the No-Where: not nowhere, no, everywhere. At the conclusion of Chrétien de

Troyes's *Erec and Enide*, Brandigan builds a city on the Isle of Joy, surrounded by walls that overlook a river and its estuary. Joy requires an orchard filled with fruit and a marvelous tree populated with singing birds.[20] We should remember this. In Erec's garden is a path that rises in a luminous spiral to the sanctuary in which a great silver couch is found. Flowing water, abundant and clear, flows from the source of life.

The garden contains the tree that lifts the curse, not the tree of science but the tree of life. The sanctuary, an otherwise concealed central location, is found, in Erec's garden, at the summit; after the initiatory climb to the statues marked by the rites of sensuality, it turns out to be a bed. The message of the medieval storyteller is contrary to that offered by Christianity: the climb to Golgotha is reversed in the ritual of pleasure.

"Pretty! Pretty!" Is it true, as Henry Cabin and Pierre Gallain claim, that medieval storytellers discovered the notion of pleasure in Oriental tales, some of which can be found in the great compilation of *The Thousand and One Nights*, and especially the Shiite tale "in the land of hidden love"? Does the fantastic castle in the Grail story become the Château de Brandigan? I would be happy if this were the case. And if the path of asceticism had given rise to its opposite, its parody, just as the Grail quest gives rise to its parodic opposite in the quest for the "Dive Bouteille" in Rabelais. And it pleases me even more that the Orient has taught the Occident during its own decline that someone (who? you, him, me) could do "tot el," quite differently than the others and earlier.

But architecture? Erec's garden, to my mind, is more subtle than the Garden of Eden. A joyous island, a town ... and, yet, the garden alone provides pleasure. But architecture? The town? The Blessed Isles are nowhere to be found.

A flash. The magic carpet is surrounded by fog. I land in the midst of a crowd but am invisible. I walk around. Massive palaces, the sober architecture characteristic of an imperial power. My wish was to visit the town, and my obedient fantasy at once did my bidding. Where am I in space-time? Can this be Trentor, the capital of the galaxy? No. "One night of partial fog." Phrases whispered in my ears, some I recognize; others are strange, foreign. "There must have been days when we searched for one another at the same moment in the powerful labyrinth." London! London! "Perhaps, only a few feet from one another, such a thin barrier became an eternal separation."[21] At this moment, I follow De Quincey, the opium eater, gentle and chaste, [as] his poor soul went dreaming. London was then covered with a thick fog. The anxiety of the city, "alphabet of unknown symbols, infinite." Secret hieroglyphs. Silence, violence. Fleeting languages. Imminence (of what?) and suspense (of what?). Endless flight and pursuit. The smallest thing mirrors the greatest: the city in the pavement, a puddle of water, traces. The obscure sublime: a light in the fog. I cry out for help. I'm afraid. I was wise to avoid the city and urban life.

Dizziness. Another flash. Halfway between a thick book and the image it describes. Not exactly an illustration, however, something more. I can hear the text. I know what it's saying. How astonishing! But I am not yet convinced. It says: *How the abbey of the Thelemites was built and endowed.*

> The architecture was in a figure hexagonal, and in such a fashion that in every one of the six corners there was built a great round tower of threescore foot in diameter, and were all of a like form and bigness. Upon the north side ran along the river of Loire, . . . Every tower was distant from the other the space of three hundred and twelve paces. The whole edifice was everywhere six stories high, reckoning the cellars underground for one. The second was arched after the fashion of a basket-handle; the rest were ceiled with pure wainscot, flourished with Flanders fretwork, in the form of the foot of a lamp, and covered above with fine slates, with an endorsement of lead, carrying the antique figures of little puppets and animals of all sorts, notably well suited to one another. . . .
>
> This same building was a hundred times more sumptuous and magnificent than ever was Bonnivet, Chambourg, or Chantilly; for there were in it nine thousand, three hundred and two-and-thirty chambers, every one whereof had a withdrawing-room, a handsome closet, a wardrobe, an oratory, and neat passage, leading into a great and spacious hall. Between every tower in the midst of the said body of building there was a pair of winding, such as we now call lantern stairs, whereof the steps were part of porphyry, which is a dark red marble spotted with white, part of Numidian stone, which is a kind of yellowishly-streaked marble upon various colors, and part of serpentine marble, with light spots on a dark green ground, each of those steps being two-and-twenty foot in length and three fingers thick, and the just number of twelve betwixt every rest, or, as we now term it, landing-place. In every resting-place were two fair antique arches where the light came in: and by those they went into a cabinet, made even with and of the breadth of the said winding, and the reascending above the roofs of

the house ended conically in a pavilion. By that vise or winding they entered on every side into a great hall, and from the halls into the chambers. From the Arctic tower unto the Criere were the fair great libraries.... In the midst there was a wonderful scalier or winding-stair.... It was made in such symmetry and largeness that six men-at-arms with their lances in their rests might together in a breast ride all up to the very top of all the palace.[22]

Very well, but the Abbey of Thelema was nothing more and nothing other than a medieval castle that had been diverted from its military use to something more agreeable. Of course, that's not so bad, but it requires some explanation. The impatient reader may say to himself that the road sometimes runs through the imaginary, sometimes through the analytic, and sometimes through their fusion or confusion, and that the road is sinuous, even tortuous. He feels the author is going round in circles. Common sense is talking to me, my common sense. And how right it is! But I still don't know where it is, the center of this circle. "You're looking for an invisible enemy," my common sense adds. How right you are! But I happen to know this invisible enemy. Invisible because omnipresent. This enemy is the real, a tough nut to crack. It is power, heavier than air, everywhere active, as invisible as air, or a violent wind.

As we make our way (I love this expression, which says exactly what it has to say: I, we make, invent, produce the way) there are a number of ideas, a number of topics to keep in mind, and last of all, the appropriation (of a space, of a preexisting architecture). At one time, water and grass, contrasting values were important: nature and antinature, birth and death. As were transactions, passages, distances traveled (not just from one place to another but from one act to another, one state to another). This gave rise to the primary meaning of the labyrinth, the grotto, the terrace, various markings, then, those curious concepts integral to architectural discourse but possibly useful: the underlayer of a discreetly effective architecture within a highly complex space. Believe me when I tell you (reader or censor, whether or not you are one and the same) that I would never have dreamed of interrupting the dream to establish a reckoning if my common sense hadn't told me to do so, on your behalf, most definitely. Such impulsive common sense, what obligates me to listen to you?

Having said this, and this being the case, I find the description of the Abbey of Thelema convincing now that Rabelais has excluded the bigots and hypocrites and welcomed the comely ladies of shapely profile.

Architecture? The towers seem to me severe, copied from buildings of power; and the superb staircases are incapable of changing such masses into a place of enjoyment. Nonetheless, the intention and the project have a certain value, and Thelema a date. The Renaissance, in France, only summoned the past to its aid—Greece, ancient Rome, Jerusalem, and papal Rome—to invest (as we would say) in pleasure. By metamorphosing that glorious past.

A flash. What do I see along the horizon? A woman's breast, cut clean, sitting on the ground like an overturned bowl on a base. What is this? An image? A memory? A nightmare? A text? The text is projected onto a vast screen: "Center for Sexual Relaxation." We're a long way from the city of labor. Curving lines dominate in the design of the building, located in the center of a park, resembling the shape of a swollen breast placed on a base. A broad, gentle slope, spiraling down, through a parade of abstract forms.

No, no! This would at best be a form of architectural discourse, and good intentions. We're confusing signifier and signified, and assigning the signified the role of signifier of art. The technocrat pictures himself producing enjoyment the way we produce steel or concrete. A fragment of the (female) body is transformed into a pleasure machine, whereas the absence of pleasure results from the disintegration of the body, the fragmentation of desire. All of this wrapped up in a form of extreme, but exhausted, visualization.

The magic carpet has already carried me away, and I fly past embankments and beaches. From high above, like a stripe, a thin ribbon of sand. But near at hand the beach. The elements are there: earth, air, the sun's fire, water. The "fourfold" as a Heidegerrian would say, referring to the elements, the cardinal points (but what do we learn by referring to them as the "fourfold," other than an appearance of knowledge, of lengthy disquisition, with a somewhat solemn insistence, a bit like that of a priest).

Here, the elements meet, but their intersection signals the demise of each in the other. The earth culminates in the sea; the sky dissolves into the earth and the water. This surface of encounters is one of interference: the fine sand, its delicious fluidity. Here, bodies no longer experience water alone or earth alone, or air and sun in isolation—I almost said, abstractly. Each element plays a role, receives the others and protects itself from them by sheltering living bodies; water protects the sun and the sandy earth from the assaults of the sun, the waves (such a beautiful name, the waves, always repeated, always different, uncertain, unambiguous, individual, caressing, violent). Fire burns and consumes by its own force, water engulfs, and the air sweeps away and dries. Where they end, the beach begins. Transition, passages, encounters. A space of enjoyment.

Formed and deformed by the motions of labor, bodies assume a certain plenitude here. Nudity is not uncommon: sheltered from the elements, through their encounter. A kind of physical culture, however awkward, takes shape. Children discover a form of perfect pleasure. And not only children. The sensual and the sensory meet as well. Who has never wanted to make love on a bed of sand or beneath the caress of waves? The total body begins to appear. Until quite recently, a sense of fear was associated with beaches, which were given over to fishermen, peasants, collectors of kelp to fertilize fields, pillagers of shipwrecks. The modern era discovered them as a space of enjoyment that could be used by everyone, all class distinctions being dissolved in a strip of land near the sea. At least in Europe. Unfortunately, beaches can support no constructions other than those that are forgotten. Anything more and the structure would obliterate the space of enjoyment, in the process destroying its most characteristic feature: fluidity, transition.

And architecture?

4

OBJECTIONS

The imaginary voyage and the oneiric exploration of the possible have turned out to be disappointing. The ability to make our way appears to have been less useful than presumed. What now? The moment has come to seriously examine the objections. Whether by order of increasing or decreasing gravity hardly matters. This moment could have come earlier; the objections could have been addressed from the start. However, they first had to be identified. Our path has led us around and over those obstacles. But now the obstacles stand before us; we must tackle them head on.

The first objection is philosophical. Pleasure, joy, enjoyment, sensuality vanish as soon as we (human beings) pursue them. They are gifts, opportunities—psychologists refer to them as "gratifications." Whatever was hypothetically (arbitrarily) marked with a + sign has something spontaneous, wild about it. Joy? Happiness? Pleasure? They come from us; they have their source in our internal attitudes and, consequently, in our subjectivity. Whether it's a question of thought or passion, they are indifferent to external realities, the frame, the setting. There is no code for pleasure.

For better or worse: pleasure and pain are obscurely related, which provides little purchase for knowledge, for technique. Pain, whether endured or inflicted, yields strange pleasures. As does the nearness, the proximity, or the remoteness of death. If we are to believe Robert Jaulin, death deferred along the pathway of death is the West, and its sole pleasure. "The individual references life essentially with respect to his death, and the Western privilege of the individual is nothing more than the privilege of death, that is, the West's orientation toward death. Of course, such a proposition is not metaphysical in nature; I'm speaking of urbanism, the solitude of cages—apartments, the disappearance of streets, squares, fields in which one can wander, glean; I'm referring to forms of speech."[1] Just how far will the West's nostalgia, nihilism, and self-destruction go? It's a serious objection. It bears on the essence of pleasure and joy, on the one hand, and productive and creative activity, on the other. Humans together can produce the real, needs and satisfaction, things, as well as saturation, boredom, suffering imposed by instruments of torture (material or spiritual). But never pleasure or joy or enjoyment. Such rewards cannot be provided by production or knowledge or planning. They arise from nature. Jaulin's remarkable book shows that "savages," "primitives," for all their poverty and deprivation, have incomparably greater pleasure and joy in their lives than modern Europeans. Ethnology and anthropology take this argument even further, going so far as to invoke a radical criticism of the society that engendered their research, their knowledge, their pursuit. Such "primitives" are not only exemplars of a disappearing human species, possessing a certain conceptual, linguistic, mental, and mythical baggage that would have to be quickly invented before its end. They have more to teach us, especially the fact that they are not obsessed with death, in spite of the dangers they experience, and that by exterminating them, the West has signed its own death warrant. The madness of the Western Logos surpasses the extreme limits it could have established to avoid its self-destruction.

To respond to this, we need to appeal to philosophy as a whole. And examine the mode of existence of the acts and states under consideration. In what do pleasure, joy, enjoyment, happiness, sensuality consist? Accident? Luck? Unforeseen, minimal, or noble rewards? What differentiates them from satisfaction, comfort, well-being, and saturation? From the overexcitement resulting from the reliance on death, suffering, or torment (material or spiritual)?

There is no certainty that the response will be favorable, but it has not been proven in advance that pleasure and joy are governed by no law, other than suffering, lassitude, and the decomposition of the grave.

A second objection relates not to "human nature" but to architecture, to architectural production and practice. The limits of architecture and the architect are of little importance. The "built domain," constructions and buildings, results from a wide range of elements and factors. The morphology of a given society, the territory of its space, the forms of daily life have much greater influence than the talent (or lack of it) of architects.

Little by little, within the context of modern societies (industrial, capitalist, organized into nation-states, etc.), an *architectural rationality* has been defined. An integral part of the dominant rationality, it falls within the domain of social practice. It constructs public buildings that dominate or are dominated (governed by economic requirements, by political institutions) within an existing space. This rationality covers all aspects of construction, from final ends to means and conditions (that is, from the acquisition of land to the functions of public and private buildings, from the use of materials to the instruments and tools of construction). To pursue the symbolic, the oneiric, is to ignore social practice, to set it aside rather than promote the concept itself.

Besides, "people" know that objects are important for their enjoyment: furniture, the instruments of everyday life, miscellaneous facilities. Comfort is the first thing they introduce into their surroundings. Once the necessities have been taken care of, the rest is superfluous; comfort is followed by pleasure, then luxury. For most people, enjoyment is associated with luxury: furs, rugs, jewelry. However, any location can serve as a site for pleasure and joy once it has become occupied, once its intended use has been hijacked, as in the case of a warehouse that becomes a ballroom or theater. The architectural effect, to the extent that it exists, does not necessarily arouse joy or pleasure. We can provide people with certain conditions of existence, but not the meaning of their existence. However, it is important that we not confuse the enjoyment of a space (a park, a stadium, a well-designed apartment building) and the space of enjoyment. Every well-arranged space, appropriated to some extent, provides enjoyment. But doesn't seeing it as a space of enjoyment require extrapolation, an approach mistaken from the start?

The very narrow limits assigned to "architectural effect" by "architectural rationality" are, however, quite surprising. It's true that modern art has experienced a similar reduction—it has become decorative, we find it interesting or amusing. It appears to have given up trying to provide pleasure, enjoyment, joy; yet, among other effects, goals, ends, and meanings, hasn't the work of art always tried to please, that is, provide pleasure? Are pleasure, enjoyment, and joy incompatible, even though the differences between them are more than a matter of degree or intensity? The greatest works of art have not only been able to serve as decoration, to amuse or distract us, but to delight as well, to provide (produce?) enjoyment and joy, inexhaustibly. Of course, no one inhabits a painting, a sculpture, or a poem. Nor can we reside there, visit them, enter and leave. Not to focus on the architect's ancient, demiurgic vocation, his magnificently artistic mission, or to suggest that architecture should follow a monumental model, but it is worth remembering that aesthetic effects are deeper than simple visual or auditory delight.

To respond to this objection, we must examine art and its destiny, aesthetics and its scope. "When architecture acquires the place belonging to it in accordance with its own essential nature, its productions are subservient to an end and a meaning not immanent in itself."[2] To what end? Hegel has thought a great deal about architecture. He characterizes it both by its independence, wherein he sees it as an autonomous sphere distinct from any practical aims, and its finality, wherein it is subordinated to "something" outside itself and that gives it meaning. Is it impossible for this finality, once known as beauty, or truth, to be given new names: joy, happiness, pleasure?

The modern world would be governed by communication, by the trend toward legibility, communicability, and, therefore, transparency. Architecture would be no exception. It is a form of communication. It has an architectural message and a code or codes to decipher it. An architecture can be compared to a language and the act of dwelling to speech. The institution, the social reality, is realized in an event, but that event exists only in and through that reality.

This realist objection, relying as it does on a form of resolute scientificity, is, in fact, very widespread, even when those who acknowledge it ignore the "positive" or pertinent element of support. The desire for communicability, for effective communication, would be sufficient to alter social relationships; mass media are changing the world. This summary ideology is that of Marshall McLuhan. He has done us a great service in formulating it, for a diffuse ideology has provided a kind of influential (guaranteed success) philosophy of the mass media, although somewhat simplistic and even vulgar.

To address this, we must turn our attention to semiology and contemporary semantics. However, an initial response has already been provided. When discussing architecture, is the transmitter, the one who sends a message, the structure or the building? We need to reverse this point of view. The message arises from human acts, and the message is chaotic, dramatic, emotional, filled with redundancies and unforeseen surprises.

The built, the constructed, provide a sense of order. They do not receive a decoded message but refract practical recommendations, gestures, acts, and rhythms back to the transmitter. Communication doesn't cover all of social practice; it is but a moment. And the criterion of "legibility," of "transparency," is especially deceptive, for it tends to reduce lived experience in practice.

Then there are the political objections. It's unclear which are the most serious. Some claim that the search, the pursuit of a dream, goes beyond simple reformism. Wouldn't such a project, with its postrevolutionary appearance and intent, be counterrevolutionary when expressed in a prerevolutionary manner? To suspend, by an intellectual act, the mode of production, the State, social relationships and their totality, does not mean these can be sidestepped or transcended. Only philosophical naïveté assumes this to be possible. Under the existing mode of production, there is a division of labor. Architectural production or, quite simply, the production of buildings, has its place in this division of labor. Moreover, it is unclear that it occupies a greater place than the production of steel or sugar; construction is merely one branch of industry among many others. As totality, as system, the mode of production comprises productive forms of labor distributed according to an internal law; its presence is such that any project that is successfully brought to fruition can, consequently, be co-opted, and sooner or later will be.

A response concerning the merits of this vehement accusation has already been provided, and has been given so often that only the tenacity of dogmatism can explain such an objection. The concept of a closed totality, a closed system, subject to an absolute law, which can, therefore, only continue or collapse, this desperate concept helps explain the thought that conceived it. Where do words come from? Concepts? The possibilities of detachment, of a critical distance capable of grasping this totality? How can a member, a part, a detail, an element comprehend the whole? Although the "whole" in such a totality is dependent on it, that totality also controls ideas, representations, knowledge, science. How could a society consisting of a base on which structures and superstructures are built—or, in a different formulation, one consisting of a practice whose representations, rationalizations, and theorizations can be comprehended—be formed, be subject to a single logic? Institutions and politicians struggle to achieve this without ever succeeding. Old contradictions are reborn; new ones come into being. This is not to say that, totally exposed, society has no consistency, no cohesion, and stands defenseless before deft or spontaneous initiatives. It means that inroads can be attempted here and there, taking advantage of fissures, cracks, faults, and weaknesses, in other words, contradictions, some of which are latent and some of which are openly subject to hostile pressure. Isn't the theoretical thought that manages to define the "real," the existent (society, the mode of production), already a kind of incursion? It crosses the "real" from end to end, from its origin to its possible disappearance.

Co-optation? Reintegration? No doubt, but also incursion by means of the *imagination*, which can put an end to the pseudoblockage of thought, to the paralysis of practical initiatives. Either we manage, by this means, to come into conflict with the real, which should explode any contradictions, or we reach a kind of compatibility, which cannot fail to clarify this real.

The danger is that the project that believes itself to be freed of the real will expose itself as being inspired by this reality (capitalist, statist, technicist, and technocratic). But it is up to censorship to demonstrate this.

Of course, what purpose does it serve to investigate enjoyment and a suitable morphology when we know that between now and the end of the century, millions, tens of millions of homes, the humblest, the simplest shelters, will be needed around the world? Of course! What good is poetry or what is still referred to as art?

Nevertheless, questions need answers: Who will build the architecture of enjoyment, assuming it is possible? For whom and with what means? What networks, what techniques will be used? Will it be an apartment building, a public building, a village, a château, a town? A "folly," as the eighteenth century was fond of saying? We cannot continue for long to set aside social needs and demands. Are such questions harmful, however? Initially decisive? If the architecture of enjoyment is possible, the demand is implicit.

In my opinion, the most serious objection is political in nature, although not associated with any particular political strategy. On the contrary, its wording alone implies a (theoretically formulated) reticence in the face of politics as such. It runs something like this: "There is an internal connection between architecture, monumentality, political power, and the will to power. Doesn't architecture retain this meaning still? To serve power. The will to power with its various means is concealed and, at the same time, conspicuous in the architectural work. It assumes a practical existence without which it would be reduced to ideology. Government buildings contain more than the expression of power, more than the rituals of its manifestation. They are its instruments. There is no army without its fortresses and barracks. Every legal system, every tax system, every public figure has its corresponding morphology, which has little to do with joy, or enjoyment. In present-day society, the technological discipline and gaudy structures on display fail to conceal the concern for yield and profit, the implacable exploitation of taxpayers, users, and consumers. At best, one exploits oneself. Joy? Pleasure? The portion of space assigned to them and the sites devoted to them require that they remain humble and hidden, that they reside in the cracks.

"From the point of view of society—and, therefore, politically—these individual intentions hardly differentiate themselves from the crimes tracked by ideological and police repression. A society that would leave room for the inclinations of its members, for their pleasure, would disappear after a period of decadence. Power provides true pleasure. The only kind. Look around you at the people you cherish. What is the greatest source of pleasure? To be served. There may be no servants, but husbands have wives, and parents have children. Omnipresent, the will to power in everyday life has only an indirect relationship with the frame and its decor. The only thing that counts is subjectivity, personal relationships."

Such objections deserve a response. And yet, we might ask if each of them individually and collectively might not be part of what they denounce. We must treat them "symptomatically." Moreover, their effect on thought and practical activity is *reductive*.

The question has been raised, here and elsewhere, concerning the (methodological) concepts of reduction and reductivism. Asking the question does not provide clarification; at present the issue is clouded by confusion. What is needed is to distinguish dialectical reduction from logical reduction—methodological, theoretical, ideological, practical (effective).

Logical reduction is also a reduction to logic. Thought decides (an act that does not appear to be a decision but a necessity) to set aside contradictions, to examine only cohesion and coherence, systems and subsystems, equilibria actualized for the possible. The only method is logic, considered sometimes as an operation on symbols and signs and sometimes as an operation on "realities."

Dialectical reduction, the approach followed here, sets aside a number of elements, aspects, moments of the real, in order to rediscover them. It could be summarized as follows: reduce in order to situate and restore. This is the approach taken by Marx, who temporarily ignored needs and the materiality of products in order to define the exchange of material goods in terms of exchange value. These disregarded moments were then restored to their place in the sequence: labor, money, the relations of production, capital, and so on. The sequence of arguments obeys formal logic, incorporated into a dialectical progression.

Dialectical reduction differs from phenomenological reduction, an approach used by philosophers who temporarily set aside the world to focus on philosophical subjectivity, the thinking "subject" defined as subjectivity. This approach carefully avoids dialectical methodology, even though subjectivity as moment cannot and should not be eliminated, which leads to some confusion.

Theoretical and ideological reduction give rise to reductivism. This incorporates an attitude, (conscious and unconscious) bias, misunderstandings, concerning certain ignored moments, which thought refuses to take into consideration and which it consequently logically denies and eliminates, although this does not fail to serve certain practical plans, certain strategies. Most strategies assume reductive operations at the outset, which action then tries to realize. To reduce, first by ideology, then through violence, classes and peoples, their aspirations and differences, is a conscious operation. Using this approach, thought moves from knowledge to ideology. Reductivism is an ideology, grafted onto the legitimate movement of thought. It is important to note, however, that reductivism cannot avoid the trap of dogmatism. It becomes dogmatic through its constitutive approach; it tends toward a system, inevitably seeking to form a whole, deeming invalid that which it refuses to accept. And by this we make the transition from theoretical and ideological reduction to effective reduction.

What constitutes the semantic reduction whose initial expression is attributed to Saussure? Is this a methodical and legitimate reduction to language of the chaos of social and linguistic facts, gradually eliminating successive layers, including that of speech? Or would this be an (improper) reduction of facts by language?

To whom, or what, should we impute the loss of meaning experienced by architecture with the decline of monumentality? Is this a (legitimate) reduction of the meanings applied to public buildings by aristocrats fallen from power? Or is it the dramatic disappearance of meaning, a restriction of signification, a form of disenchantment, as claimed by sociologists such as Max Weber?

Who then is responsible for this reductivism? When did it begin? Where will it end? Did it start with abstraction's reduction of the spontaneous, the organic, and the natural, the same reductivism that religion seems to have assumed at the time of its origins? And which is more efficient? Merchandise and money, through their establishment of historic space? Industry viewed as an autonomous factor? Capitalism, based on industrialism in a determinate framework, societal relations, and modes of production? The bourgeoisie as a class, endowed with particular "tastes" and "needs," good or bad, and ideologies commonly referred to as culture? The destructive revolutions of the past, initially democratic-bourgeois, then democratic–working class, at least in principle? The novel and its abstraction, which reductively promote concepts and the products of conceptualization rather than lived experience? Modernity, with its specific accents of spectacle, mass media, and technicity? Or political power as such, with the State and its various instruments, constraint and persuasion? Given the loss of meaning and in spite of lost meanings, how can political power again make use of monumentality for its own purposes? How can the architectural work preserve its affective and symbolic charge? How can active power impose new signifieds for old signifiers, by appropriating them, while using the "open work," transparent, human, and all too human, for its own ends? For appropriation has contradictory results; it isn't always realized by and for "progress." Would this mean dramatizing, or theatricalizing, the situation when it would be better, tactically, to minimize it? No, because the entire meaning of the situation must be revealed, must burst apart.

Is reductivism, whether semantic or not, the cause, or the effect, or both? Doesn't it occur simultaneously—theoretically, through knowledge, and practically, through power? If so, would the association of power and knowledge be situated at the center of this reductivism? And just how far does it extend? Does it extend, little by little, from the meaning, or meanings, of lived experience, from lived experience to the entire body, and therefore, to pleasure, joy, or enjoyment?

We can assume that capacities and reductive powers form a unified whole, an enormous whole. Colossal! Objections are an integral but unconscious component of this whole, individually and in their totality. They play a reductive role by accepting, by endorsing, the reduction. They aggravate the weight of the whole by demonstrating that it cannot be undermined. They conceal the extent of the threat (no longer a threat but "reality" itself). The objections help shape the reasons and causes for failure into a unified block.

The situation, however, isn't improving. This enormous block comprises everything. What it weighs upon is weightless, but it crushes what it rests upon: the body, the everyday, usage and wear, symbols of depression, femininity. Bound to pleasure and the body, humiliated like them, overwhelmed, exploited, reduced by the many stratagems of false praise, femininity cannot even be defined. Faced with a condition of endemic revolt and vain rebellion, its cries of suffering and calls for help are lost in the clamor raised by violence and the oppression of the unified block. A full-scale revolution would be needed to overturn it.

That there is no architecture or, to put it in simpler terms, that there exists no morphology of enjoyment, that it is barely conceivable and almost unimaginable, is terrifying. Especially given that this is not an isolated finding but connected to other facts. And in this way, the petty and perfidious interrogation of architecture, insignificant in appearance, assumes its full scope.

To one side, the heavy, powerful, destructive side, lies knowledge—and power, persuasion, and violence, economic and political. Which very clearly indicates the self-destruction of the species. On the other side is nothing but the old despondency, the interminable complaint of history, the tears of the humiliated, the exploited, the oppressed.

Before giving in and acknowledging defeat and its consequences (wait for the block to crumble and fall or admit the failure of the human species), we must question philosophy, art, architecture itself. Pepper them with questions that are increasingly specific.

5

PHILOSOPHY

Philosophers have distinguished the nuances of affective tonalities with the utmost finesse: pleasure, sensuality, happiness, satisfaction. Every great philosopher has focused on one such quality and given it a particular meaning. Before delving further, we might ask ourselves if the philosophical breakdown of what we have referred to with a single "positive" word—enjoyment—doesn't contain an error of some sort, that of philosophy itself.

Spinoza inquired into the secret and meaning of joy. It arises from understanding, the highest form, that which grasps the (divine) substance in its unity and totality and that consequently is eternalized the moment it rises to this sublime degree of understanding, the "intellectual *gaudium*" that does not transcend the body and space but comprises them as such and accepts them. Nature (causal), which is grasped in the human being, consists of knowledge. Spinoza's theory of joy never condescends to a preoccupation with the particularity of the body and space, the humble need for shelter or a physical expression of the totality of art.

Satisfaction? Hegel determined its essential qualities, and it assumes a primordial function in his system. A need is satisfied when it encounters the object that corresponds to it, which it destroys while preserving. It disappears momentarily and returns if the need is genuine. The needs of humans living in rationally organized societies are never isolated; they constitute a system, the system of needs, that appears as a subsystem in the social totality. The State, which actualizes this totality, is composed of subsystems; it contains them and holds them within itself. The objects that satisfy needs are the result of socially divided labor. To the system of needs there corresponds a system of labor: each need corresponds to the labor that produces the object intended to satisfy that need. The system of needs and the system of labor adjust to one another like two parts of the State machine (the total system, philosophical and political). Out of the interplay of objects (produced and consumed), needs (satisfied and, therefore, momentarily abolished, then resurgent), and labor (executed according to a rigorous finality), life results, the internal mobility of a society.

It goes without saying that needs and labor change, that they have a history and participate in history. Moreover, architecture is part of the whole; it satisfies needs in practice, which does not prevent it from also being an art (satisfying very subtle needs) and, in this sense, being included in an aesthetics.

But where does happiness fit in? There is little doubt that it was with Aristotle that philosophical thought attempted most forcefully to understand it. For Aristotle, the essence of the human being finds its fulfillment in happiness, which consists in living according to reason (Logos) within the perfect framework of the polis. The nature of man, the political animal, expands and is fulfilled within this frame.

The Greek city assured its citizen-inhabitants of the exercise of all their activities and faculties: the body in the stadium, the intellect in the agora, the heart and the family home, thought in the temple of the city's divinity. Aggression and combativeness were to be found there as well, and the taste for the *agon*, or the warfare of violent games. Out of these activities, each of which was exercised in its own time and place, arose a plenitude. This is the teaching of the *Nicomachean Ethics*.[1] In this prestigious analysis, and even though Aristotle doesn't insist on this point, which he finds obvious, the harmony among times, places, actions, and objects is part of the rational unity of the polis.

Enjoyment? The concept, in the broad sense, seems modern. It arises in medieval thought and the idea of the "fruitio" (from *frui, fructus*) of an object, especially an object created for such use by nature. Intentional activity has general scope. The medieval meaning persists in the willfully archaic language of the law. For example, jurists distinguish enjoyment and usufruct from an ownership right (a person can enjoy an asset without possessing it, while someone else may have "bare ownership" of that asset). The term refers, therefore, to the relationship of need and even desire to the object, emphasizing the act rather than the result, as we find in Hegel (satisfaction, momentary disappearance of a tendency).

No longer limited to legal language, the term is found today in everyday use. However, its absolute sense (to enjoy, to obtain pleasure) connotes an egocentric tendency and implies a curious schizophrenia that abstracts the object (sexual or otherwise) to insist on its status. The materialist and Marxist current (from La Mettrie to Pierre Naville, by way of Brillat-Savarin, Fourier, and Lafargue) contributes to this resurgence of a word, a symptomatic resurgence. But when the question of pleasure arises, the situation becomes complicated, and a careful and detailed analysis is needed.

Until a new order arises, one characteristic appears to be obvious. Joy, happiness, enjoyment are not produced the way things and objects are. They are not results that we can obtain from an exchange (at least, outside of the sex trade). The satisfaction associated with the accumulation of money or goods shifts whatever it is that objects provide toward abstraction. No activity targets happiness as such, or joy, or enjoyment, all of which are obtained as a kind of surplus. They arise from the use, the encounter with an object, as a reward for the activity that discovered that object. The relationship to an object is not an object! To seek such states, to suggest that we can produce them as "realities," is to invite disappointment. Joy, enjoyment, happiness, therefore, arise from nature and usage. They have conditions, but the connection between those conditions and what they yield when transformed is not easily understood. No form of logical determination is involved, no causal sequence; yet some form of finality is implied. But as we all know, nothing is more obscure than "finality." More specifically, the concept of a "final cause," which seemed clear in a limited context, with well-defined references (the polis for the Greek philosophers), has deteriorated and become obscure with the advent of modernity.

The great tradition of Greek thought, that of the pre-Socratics, doesn't yet differentiate knowledge from wisdom, poetry from politics. Within a living totality, simultaneously intuitive and conceptualized, the division of labor has not yet resulted in separation. With incomparable power, the pre-Socratics perceived the primary areas to which specialized philosophers would later turn their attention, much to their detriment; it was they who developed the important notion of intelligibility through stability (Parmenides and the Eleatics) as opposed to intelligibility through movement (Heraclitus).

They didn't concern themselves with details. Individual fate was of no concern to them. That fate became a problem only during the decline of the polis, characterized by the shift in Greek tragedy from Aeschylus to Euripides. Consequently, there is little point in questioning the great pre-Socratics about pleasure or happiness. Once the polis ceased to be a natural, rational framework, a source of activity and happiness, an obvious supreme good, there arose the problem of nature, happiness and misfortune, destiny and individual freedom, suffering and pleasure.

Make no mistake, these problems emerged only with the decline of Greece and the period of decadence. Its creative power had disappeared. Either the acme had already been passed, or the finitude of that power had become manifest and Greece would have failed to reach its acme (which was Nietzsche's opinion in his *Das Philosophen-Buch*).[2] The age of heroic tension, of tragedy, concluded with the victory over the Persians. Everything that, a thousand years later, was taken to be miraculous—logic, the fetishism of the concept, philosophy, "pure" knowledge—and that would be transmitted by circumventing the West was nothing but the work of the decadents.

Aristippus and his school, the Cyrenaics, introduced new areas of research, that of pleasure primarily. In this sense, in terms of opening up a new perspective, Aristippus can be considered one of the last great anti-Socratic thinkers. He was also the leading Socratic, for he worked hard to identify the concept of pleasure and its conditions. He attempted to define, and, consequently, to conceptualize, that which by definition escapes the concept: the most fleeting, the most uncertain form of lived experience. It shouldn't come as any surprise that Nietzsche barely mentions him among the great thinkers, for those men did not reflect the leading tendency among the Greeks to focus on life's new pleasures. In contrast, they reflected (to the extent that there was a reflection) the tensions that their internal struggles and war against the Persians would give rise to, in spite of themselves, among the citizens of their cities. This led to the severity we find in the work of Pythagoras, Empedocles, and Anaximander; the enthusiasm for the true as opposed to the Greek tendency toward stratagems and lies (Odysseus); and a Heraclitean pride and solitude diametrically opposed to Athenian sociability.

At a given moment, following the victory, there arose the infamous claim to happiness, and the philosopher's state of mind becomes the center around which the world revolves. The Socratic misunderstanding of the Apollonian "know thyself" resulted in the separation of science and wisdom, music and philosophy, poetry and politics.

According to Aristippus, whom we know through Xenophon, Plato, Aristotle, and Epicurus, pleasure is the supreme good. There is only one good among the various forms of good and that is pleasure, for either those goods provide pleasure or they are not truly good. Philosophy consists in this form of practical wisdom alone. For the Cyrenaics, that pleasure would assume this value and cease to be was a certitude, one that comes to be associated with this characteristic as soon as it is no longer concealed beneath absurdities. The identity of the supreme good with pleasure cannot be demonstrated; it is not the result of argument; it has no relationship with reason (the Logos). It is a fact of nature. Pleasure possesses a vital or experienced obviousness; it bears no relationship to pain. Pain replaces pleasure when pleasure is no more; the two can never be comingled; they confront one another in an opposition that in no way resembles their coexistence in thought, for consciousness. Pleasure and pain have nothing in common with compatible objects. In modern terms, they are existentially incompatible. Once a philosopher has expounded this truth, he has said all there is to say. All that is left is to live: to seek pleasure. Only Aristippus offered as a precept, a maxim, the notion that we should seek out and desire pleasure.

Aristippus's thesis, therefore, has the frankness, almost the brutality, of unreserved affirmation. No libertine or anarchist philosophy would possess this powerful simplicity. Pleasure defines—because it is—the absolute. Or conversely, if you prefer. In the search for knowledge (theoretical) and wisdom (practical), there is but a single response, a single word: pleasure.

"Take pleasure when and where you can." This the Cyrenaic did with the courtesan Loïs. After him, no one was able to maintain this line of thought; they turned instead to the conditions of pleasure, its limits and consequences. There were increasingly subtle disagreements in the interpretation of hedonism. It was expressed in negative—"the desire to avoid pain"—rather than positive terms. In a later age, Schopenhauer would reduce pleasure to the absence of suffering, to the cessation of the most fundamental pain, the pain of existence.

What do we get from pleasure, movement, or rest? Stated this way, drily and coldly, the question—that of the objective and subjective conditions of pleasure—preoccupied Plato and Aristotle. They did not challenge the importance of pleasure but its conditions or, rather, their absence. Aristippus disdained subtlety. For him, pleasure can arise at any moment, we need simply extend our hand. It exists everywhere and always. There are no special places assigned to pleasure. It has no need of preparation, of effort, of some prior activity. But according to Plato, who was followed by Aristotle, this was incorrect, for pleasure originates in an act and in movement. This movement must have a meaning, a goal. Without a goal, deprived of meaning, the pleasure that arises from some poorly oriented impulse is merely ambiguous, mixed with pain, sullied with illusions. If the philosopher Aristippus took pleasure with the courtesan Loïs, it was because Loïs was beautiful and Aristippus desired her. According to Plato, movement is nothing like mere agitation; it has an end: its goal, its meaning, its finality, and its completion. For him, the meaning and end of the movement of desire is beauty. More profoundly, desire wants to create in beauty, wants to create a new beauty. Unalloyed pleasure, so close to joy, comes from the Beautiful. The presence of beauty, participation in beauty, possession of the beloved being for her beauty—pleasure is complete only when true, and it is true only through beauty. Of course, it is good and, therefore, is part of the "good," but as a consequence or an implication. Can we attribute to it an inherent and, therefore, autonomous essence? Can we treat pleasure as the center or foundation of a philosophy? No. But what is beauty? The absolute, Plato affirms, transcending with a speculative leap relativism, perspectivism, and historicity, on behalf of an immense nostalgia.

But what about movement and effort? Of course, says Aristotle. Toward Beauty? The realist, the scientist, the positivist smiles ironically. The end of activity—its goal—is civic and political. Pleasure is added to activity as the flower of youth is added to youth, when activity is employed according to its models and its goal, when a free man acts in the polis, according to its laws. Pleasure can no more be disassociated from society, from the norm, than it can from the act, as a form of compensation. It is part of happiness. The pleasure that comes from activity, then, accompanies the repose in which movement is concluded.

The philosophy of pleasure as an immediate and proximate absolute bursts apart. It cannot be sustained. It is reduced to mere prattling about pleasure, which becomes relativized. We discover that it has certain conditions, that it cannot simply come about in any manner or in any place.

And at the same time, because of this, the philosopher submits pleasure to his conditions, to his knowledge, to his definitions. Pursuing their research on the sources of pleasure, philosophers have recourse to nature (doubly determined: outside "man," without him, before him) or, rather, a certain human nature. "Sequere naturam" the philosophers obstinately repeat, stoics and epicures. But what is nature? Is it sufficient to determine the supreme good, they ask, about which each has his own idea?

By a surprising reversal (one of those highly frequent reversals of meaning), the search for pleasure turns into asceticism. A particular but robust asceticism. Diogenes the Cynic dismisses the beautiful courtesan who comes to seduce him. Diogenes has no need of her: he is self-sufficient in his barrel. The philosopher depends on no one, he holds wisdom within him together with the principle of its pleasure. Masturbation replaces love. Whatever is strictly necessary is sufficient. There is no need for the superfluous world. The most humble spot (in the sun), the most modest nourishment are all he needs. No activity, no desire, no goal. A kind of nirvana that is achieved through the cult of pleasure. The pursuit of pleasure tends to free itself of all external conditions, of space and time. What good is philosophy? To learn to be dependent on no one. It cuts, without the advancement of freedom; it liberates at one stroke. A deceptive liberation I might add. Would Diogenes the Cynic have found pleasure in his barrel if he hadn't rolled down the streets of the city? If he hadn't chased Alexander from his place in the sun? If he hadn't scandalized the polis and all of Greece when he dissociated himself from civic life?

Purified, sophisticated, asceticism returns with Epicurus. Human nature, the stoics claim, is reason, the Logos. Epicurus, however, claims that it is the body. And the supreme good, that of the body, is health, equilibrium. What is my body? A bag of atoms. Violent pleasures, love, wine, and drunkenness, rashly upset this bag and risk disturbing the particles.

Fresh water is worth more than the finest wine for the body, and the same holds true for taste: someone who is able to appreciate water finds in it qualities that are more refined than those found in wine. A calm garden is worth more for the body than a palace. The supreme good is pleasure, but what sort of pleasure attains perfection? Rest, when there is a certainty of not being dependent on anything else. What about the rational autonomy of the Stoics, the rejection of passion? No, it is serenity, the serenity of the Epicurean gods, who reside in the interworlds:

they too are composed of atoms but are sheltered from disturbances, among the stars, which are in no sense divine.

What lies at the top of the hierarchy of pleasures proposed by epicurean philosophy? Tranquility, indifference (ataraxy) almost, a state not so unlike the stoic precept of abstention.

Philosophical writing since Hegel illustrates the surprising destiny of *nature* (concept and reality). The keystone of ancient philosophical thought, and possibly the modern world as well, the notion lost its coherence because, like "reality," it is subject to any number of contradictory interpretations and incompatible viewpoints. To the question "what is nature?" the philosophers respond by proposing their own interpretation and outlook, which they assume to be obvious and proven.

The nature of pleasure seems obvious only to intentional pleasure seekers, hedonists or cynics, who have no relationship to the philosophical schools that bore those names. Such pleasure seekers toyed with society, with its values and morality: they were libertines, sophisticates. For the ancients, pleasure was such that it could support no logic, no rule, no ethic. What can we conclude except that logic and ethics, values and morality, addressed pleasure reductively. From antiquity, logic and morality, knowledge and values struggled against pleasure, seeking to reduce and destroy an irreducible and indestructible lived experience, which continuously reaffirmed itself in that it alone allowed life to go on, bodies to survive. Philosophy, seen in terms of this relentless negation, is not the least effective instrument. Pleasure protests. If there are conditions for pleasure, the body, the organs, needs and desires, and pleasures are also a condition of life; without pleasure, the body and its organs, its needs, will atrophy and degenerate, will deviate from their course. In what language can pleasure, allied to desire, protest? Not that of the philosophers; rather, it must engage the language of poetry—or music or dance. Sometimes voiceless, humbly but inevitably associated with the revenge of the oppressed—women, children, slaves, deviants, outsiders. All are deprived of pleasure and, by a (dialectical) reversal of situations, are the only ones capable of experiencing it intensely. For the masters and the powerful soon lost the source of enjoyment—vitality.

To revitalize this source, to give pleasure its revenge, festivals disrupted the order of antienjoyment. Festivals have been extensively analyzed by identifying sociologically and philosophically noteworthy features: the unmitigated waste, the sudden eruption of anything that "normal" life dissimulates and spurns, everything that ordinary (face-to-face) communication rejects. All that remains is to reveal this clear and brutal moment: no one, not the oppressors, not the oppressed, can live without pleasure; it was necessary for society's armature to crack so that, violent and, at times, bloody, enjoyment might emerge. Philosophy, including logic and ethics, was suspended.

Like the monuments of architecture, those of philosophy misunderstand enjoyment. All of these constructions, of course, present a utopia. The philosopher believes he can change the world with his system, although he merely interprets it, as Marx and Nietzsche noted. This utopia is not one of enjoyment, however. To the utopias of power, which see themselves reflected in a monumental eternity, correspond utopias of knowledge, a melancholy and bitter knowledge.

Spinoza himself does not hide the fact that modern philosophy, evolving out of Cartesianism, misunderstands enjoyment. It is not that intellectual leftism lacks grandeur, but the definition of passion (and, therefore, of love and sensuality) owes its celebrity to its exquisite naïveté. "Amor est titillatio, concomitante idea causae externae."[3] Ostensibly, philosophy does not approve of such agitation. To its credit, we can acknowledge the ambiguous charm of the word "titillation" and the idea of the object, which is essential to pleasure, something later ignored by theories of narcissism, revolutionary spontaneity, and onanism that would claim, explicitly or implicitly, that pleasure has no need of an object. "Object, hide yourself!" are the words written on walls by contemporary anarcho-situationists. Much earlier, Jean-Jacques Rousseau informed his readers that he had had much pleasure but few possessions.

The intellectual asceticism of the Cartesian tradition and the European Logos follows from the definition of the "subject." It thinks, it exists as a thinking being; its connection with space and, therefore, with the object can be summarized in a concept. As center, the cogito in no way resembles a burning hearth. The philosophy of knowledge detests the imaginary as well as the emotive and focuses on the act of understanding (judgment, logic, deduction, concept), repudiating other emotive, and therefore passive, activities.

Diderot, alone among philosophers, escapes this vulgar classification of the passive and emotive in contrast to the active nature of knowledge.

With a titanic—promethean—effort he pushed European thought beyond its limitations, beyond its dryness, beyond its rationalist abstraction. While La Mettrie, a somewhat mechanistic materialist, wrote *L'art de jouir*,[4] Diderot put it into practice, with all that pleasure implies: art as opposed to abstract knowledge, especially music, the rehabilitation of women and femininity, the restoration of the sensible and the total body, that is, all the senses. The gay science of the eighteenth century was spoken, and sung, through his joyful prose.

Utilitarianism, the calculation of pleasure based on English empiricism, has nothing in common with Diderot's generosity. Utilitarianism assumes that pleasure and enjoyment unfold and develop according to a program. It mechanizes the essence of pleasure by quantifying it.

The Logos culminates in Kant. Prudent and subtle, philosophy surpasses the absolute. Logic turns to science. Morality formulates the categorical imperative. Kant cleared the way for the rise of the bourgeoisie, which would struggle between the need to economize in order to invest and the penchant for enjoyment (Marx). The solution to this great and unfortunate problem was hypocrisy. Pleasure would be reserved for certain moments—youth, with its excess, and maturity, when our fortune and career are safely behind us, with its little lies, the brothel or mistress, the midlife crisis. But for the public, for the facade, for the masses, there was morality, the imperative.

We had to wait for Hegel before enjoyment officially became a part of philosophy. But with what restrictions! The triad of "need, labor, and enjoyment" plays a determining role in the Hegelian construction of society and the State. Enjoyment has to be earned through productive labor, as a form of compensation for one's activity. But what activity? Not that of the free citizen of the polis but of a responsible member of a nation-state, the activity of labor useful to the collectivity. His is a specific, rational form of enjoyment, limited to objects produced within a familial, professional, or national context. It has nothing in common with the romantic and fictional pursuit of love, which is expressly criticized by Hegel. His is a rationalized, normative, moralistic enjoyment. From any point of view we choose to adopt, it is that of the paterfamilias, the functionary fulfilling his duties, precisely and punctually.

Enjoyment in the Occidental Logos is further deflected from the gay science to become satisfaction. Needs are classified, objects stamped, work organized, thereby resulting in a form of widespread satisfaction within the State, a sovereign entity that brings about a contentment that is freely granted to all its members. It follows that satisfaction has no assigned place or time—it derives from the State, always and everywhere.

In the deadly struggle between master and slave, what pushes the master toward his own destruction? Enjoyment. He is devoted to pleasure, thereby losing contact with the real, with knowledge, and with work—benefits that accrue to the slave. This results in a dialectical reversal. Hegel, the philosopher of history and historian of philosophy, never loses sight of the Roman Empire and its decadence. He wants to ensure that the modern nation-state can avoid this. He cautions the masters, the politicians, away from enjoyment; he recommends morality.

Nietzsche understood that the masters lost their sense of enjoyment because they were fixated on the attitudes and values of power, and he exposed the very foundations (the root, Marx would say, using a naturalist metaphor) of power and the will to power. To continue to dominate those he humiliates, oppresses, and exploits, the master must exhibit himself, must strut about, wear masks in worldly masquerades, perform, observe a rigid etiquette. The dominator is imprisoned in his domination in order to maintain its conditions and components. He loses his reason for existence, enjoyment, if he does not renew it by means of cruel new inventions whose effectiveness is quickly exhausted. Only the people—the humiliated, the oppressed, the exploited—retain a vital, explosive energy, the energy of enjoyment—expended in festivals and revolutions.

What does Marx have to contribute to the theory of enjoyment? Not much but a great deal. Not much because the Hegelian triad of need-labor-enjoyment remains at the center of his thought, his project, as clearly demonstrated by the *Manuscripts of 1844*.[5] Additionally, although Marx, especially as concerns the State, is strongly opposed to Hegel, on this important point he extends his argument. And yet, he adds a great deal to theory. Why would the working class assume control of society unless it were to achieve the enjoyment it is denied by the bourgeoisie, which owns the means of production and manages society in its own class interests? When workers achieve this enjoyment simultaneously with power (political), it will be the first moment of their and the world's transformation of society and social relations. The second moment is the negation of labor itself through automation of the production process. This misunderstood aspect of Marxist thought was not revealed until recently with the growth of technical progress, partial automation, and the new contradictions that subsequently appeared. For Marx, only the working class can lead total revolution to its conclusion and, consequently, lead society as a whole into an age of enjoyment. Naturally, there will be difficulties. These arise not only from politics but from the requirement of a generalized transcendence, including the transcendence of politics. The working class has as its mission to transcend the theoretical and practical situation of existing society (capitalist in terms of the relations of production, bourgeois in terms of the dominant economic and political subject) by transcending itself. It is the workers' task to repudiate themselves as such in order to transcend themselves. They can do this, Marx claims, whereas bourgeois domination, prisoner of the mode of production, established and maintained by it, oscillates between economy (savings, financing for production) and waste, but without much enjoyment.

As for Fourier, we should be suspicious of his recent success. To what does it owe its origins? He is thought to have provided a code of pleasure: a vocabulary of passion. The essential passions, the second-level passions—the Cabalist, the Butterfly (or variety), the Composite—obligate the first-level passions to change, to combine with one another. Just as harmony can be used to vary the combinations obtained with the intervals between sounds by making use of different timbres. The "female" passions assume an emotional content (desires, ambitions, intrigues) that can lead to a kind of infinite production—the production of emotional discourse.

But aside from these arguments concerning harmony, the Fourierist system, which is highly overrated, proposes nothing more than continuous labor and, consequently, a form of communal ascesis. A day in the phalanstery requires the continuous efforts of members of the phalange. If we pursue the musical analogy, based on the same terms as this apparently libidinous and libidinal utopia, in the phalansterian opera, labor would correspond to words, the passions to song, and the emotional composite to the patterns of the ballet. Where is the harmony, then? On this point, which is not without interest, Fourier leaves us in the dark. Utopian socialism merely projects a utopian enjoyment. It only overcomes the division of labor by means of continuous labor without division, because it is overdivided.

For Hegel, however, satisfaction is associated with destruction. This diabolic, negative side of his positive construction is sometimes dominant. Need destroys the object (consumes it) and is destroyed as it is satisfied. It disappears temporarily as a need. Desire does play a role in the *Phenomenology*, and more than one modernist consideration of desire follows from it, although the result is eclectic: a little materialism, a little Hegelianism, and a pinch of Nietzscheanism.[6] In the *Phenomenology*, desire appears only to immediately disappear. It is immediately destroyed, either by becoming a need or by taking hold of an object that is no longer in touch with its social conditions—labor, ethics, political discipline—and so, desire dies from a disorderly, delirious enjoyment. It self-destructs.

Although Schopenhauer was violently opposed to Hegelianism, the idea of the self-destruction of desire can be found in his work. The will to live is only manifested through its self-denial. The world of representations obeys a principle of sufficient reason, whereas the interior world, that of the will to live, blind, unconscious, has no law other than its violence. The will to live denies itself by giving rise to representations (the illusory diversity of living beings, things, and objects). It is further denied in art, where it is separated from itself when it presents the illusion of beautiful appearances. And it is totally denied in contemplation and ascesis, and, finally, in the cosmic suicide that Schopenhauer claims will culminate in the will to live.

The will to being experiences self-enjoyment only in the will to nonbeing: destruction, self-destruction, and so on. Essentially and completely violent, the will to live turns its violence against itself; anxiety and suffering become ecstasy. The explosion of the will frees it in a deadly burst of pleasure.

Some might find it surprising to mention Nietzsche in this context, given his asceticism, the heroic rise toward the Superhuman, and Zarathustra's solitude in his cave. Moreover, Nietzsche's ideas are often viewed as a means of countering Marx, a refuge against the failures of Marxism. However, a new truth came into view, one of significant importance. The transformation of the world, whose goal is to "change life," has two aspects. This movement cannot be conceived, or projected, or realized simply and unilaterally. Revolution and subversion are complementary: revolution acts on the political level, and subversion acts to destroy the political. Marx paved the way for revolution, Nietzsche for subversion. Revolution as such risks creating nothing other than new sociopolitical forms; subversion will abolish them by taking advantage of the political weaknesses of the revolution. For Marx, one would follow the other, just as the appropriation of nature by "human nature" would have to accompany the technological and scientific control of nature. Subsequent events concealed the illusion of a unilateral process and the complexity of becoming. New contradictions arose between revolution and subversion just as they had between domination and appropriation.

Was Nietzscheanism opposed to Marxism in an adversarial manner, though? This false claim (stubbornly maintained by Lukács) echoes an equally false claim—deceitful, distorted—that of a Nietzscheanism that is essentially and intentionally fascist and, therefore, reactionary. This is a form of absolute falsehood, primarily because Nietzscheanism does not exist. Nietzsche never advanced a philosophical and, therefore, systematic interpretation of the world. For a time, the most important period of his life for his theoretical work, he believed that interpretations of the world, values, could not be demonstrated. This he referred to as "perspectivism." Every evaluation defines an affirmation, that is, a point of view, a comparison, which is then legitimized, justified, "founded" (a term that is more Heideggerian than Nietzschean, but that is derived from Nietzsche's philosophical beliefs). Perspectivism and relativism go hand in hand. How do values arise? What are their origins? This is one of the many problems found in what can still be referred to as "philosophy," but that, according to Nietzsche, can also be termed "philology." For Nietzsche, values, affirmations, comparisons result from an inaugural act, a decision of the will to power. When Nietzsche thereby recognized the birthplaces of values (others would call them ideologies), he freed himself of philosophy itself and its sense of seriousness, of weightiness. He laughs, he dances. The dreary science, which so leadenly asserts itself, is counteracted by the gay science. This too is an act of understanding but one that overcomes naively and ponderously affirmative acts because it recognizes them for what they are. It no longer repeats the illusions that will engender morality, logic, and metaphysics. It differs by the recognition of their repetition. The danger of nihilism, however, will grow. How can one remain in this position, which is no longer tenable?

Either the philosopher who has recognized total relativity holds fast to that position, amusing himself greatly as a new skeptic or cynic; or he invents a value, a transcendental, a philosophy and ancient values, and whatever it was that gave birth to them (the will to power). By becoming Zarathustra, Nietzsche made a choice. He had but a single perspective, and he made it a truth beyond truth, a meaning beyond meaning. The Superman passed the test of relativism and nihilism. The superhuman, creative will, freed of the will to power, overcomes (transcends) it.

Zarathustra does not proscribe pleasure or sensuality. On the contrary, he seeks to achieve the innocence of sensuality, health, and pleasure. He rejects a pale and peaceful happiness but dissuades us from chasing after sensuality the way we might seek physical health.

> Do I counsel you to slay your senses? I counsel the innocence of the senses.[7]

> And how nicely the bitch, sensuality, knows how to beg for a piece of spirit when denied a piece of meat.... Your eyes are too cruel and you search lustfully for sufferers. Is it not merely your lust that has disgusted itself and now calls itself pity?[8]

> Behind your thoughts and feelings, my brother, there stands a mighty ruler, an unknown sage—whose name is self [*heist Selbst*]. In your body he dwells; he is your body.[9]

> The creative body created the spirit as a hand for its will.[10]

> "Lust is sin," says one group that preaches death; "let us step aside and beget children."[11]

Thus spoke Zarathustra. Subversion is poetic or it is nothing. "Only where the state ends, there begins the human being who is not superfluous: there begins the song of necessity, the unique and inimitable tune. Where the state *ends*—look there, my brothers! Do you not see it, the rainbow and the bridges of the Superhuman?"[12] Zarathustra does not reject the gay science; he carries it away with him for other ends.

What then is the gay science? We should recall Aristippus for whom pleasure excluded pain. To which Plato remarked that most pleasures are mixed with pain and that this mixture presented a practical problem for pleasure, which fell within the domain of philosophy. Pleasures are false like thoughts, impure like them, to the extent that they are no longer pleasures. How can we avoid sliding down this slope, which leads to pain just as it does to ugliness? For Schopenhauer pain alone was true, essential, fundamental; pain was briefly, very briefly, suspended in pleasure.

Nietzsche's analysis took issue with Aristippus and Schopenhauer. It extends that of Plato but radically modifies his position. What Nietzsche so bitterly rejects is the notion of satisfaction.[13] There is no pure and absolute pleasure any more than there is absolute pain (the word itself can be revivified in a way that transfigures it).[14] Life offers only compromises and ambiguities, an anxiety mixed with pleasure. The gay science avoids such traps. Many pleasures are traps, as are many pains. The memory of humiliation includes disturbing delights that tighten the sites of oppression around the oppressed. Repetition (half fictive, half real) of the painful event, through memory or reflection, strangely differs from the event, leading us back to it with a kind of morose gratification. Resentment sets particularly subtle traps for us; it disguises itself, wears masks, both to preserve its obscure enjoyment and to take revenge. After the liberation and even during the subsequent celebration, the effects of resentment can be felt, contaminating the victory.

There is no pleasure without movement, without activity, and, therefore, without effort. But only a superficial analysis, according to Nietzsche, treats effort as disagreeable. When there is effort, there is will. Inherent in the act, it bears within itself not only difficulty and exertion, but its own mobilization toward a goal. Effort, whether physical or mental, labor or free expenditure, contains its reason and its joy within itself. It seeks its recompense, but this is not external to it. Effort will overcome resistance, an opposite force, another effort. Its joy, its enjoyment, coincides with its victory, with the attainment of what it seeks. Struggle, even violent action, bears within itself the principle of its pleasure. For Nietzsche, there is no opposition between a "pleasure principle" and a "reality principle," because the "real" (as long as we do not conflate it with the platitude of the realist) cannot be dissociated from action, struggle, or the expenditure of creative energy.

Ambiguity dominates the affects just as it does thought and awareness. There is nothing that does not have two (or more) aspects, two sides, two (or more) values. There are no separable essences, no distinct activities, other than that of separating, of distinguishing analytically subsequent to an act or a decision. Ambiguity contains, that is, dissimulates and reveals, a profound contradiction—between pleasure and pain, between the affirmation that serves and the affirmation that saps vitality, between talk about appearances and veridical truth, between the mirror and what it reflects. Ambiguities, ambivalences, equivocations, blends, mixtures, mimicry, uncertain identifications, unfamiliarity, deceitful normality, and revealing anomalies, these words, these terms, these concepts, these metaphors describe the carnal situation of "being human" and express a little of its truth.

Satisfaction alone never produces pleasure; it is the fact that the will advances and masters whatever it finds in its way. The deepest phenomenon, which is concealed within sensation and knowledge just as it is in pleasure, is the action of a force. "Man does not seek pleasure and does not avoid displeasure. . . . Pleasure and displeasure are mere consequences, mere epiphenomena."[15] What does the living being want, down to the tiniest part of every organism? An increase in its capacity for action.

"Displeasure thus does not merely not have to result in a diminution of our feeling of power, but in the average case it actually stimulates this feeling of power—the obstacle is the stimulus of this will to power."[16] Pleasure and pain refer—although poorly, simplemindedly—to appreciations, judgments, the "yes" and the "no" of vitality, not those of logic. While pain may be something other than pleasure, it is not its opposite. "There are even cases in which a kind of pleasure is conditioned by a certain *rhythmic sequence* of little unpleasurable stimuli. . . . This is the case . . . in the act of coitus: here we see displeasure at work as an ingredient of pleasure."[17] "Every form of pleasure and displeasure seeks a complex result. . . . Pleasure or displeasure follow from the striving after [an increase of power]; driven by that will it seeks resistance, it needs something that opposes it."[18]

For the first time, an analyst describes desire and pleasure, a poet who insists on every aspect of a highly complex process: tendency and tension, excitation and obstacles, rhythms, profound ambiguity, an explosion of energy, the breaking through and crossing of a kind of threshold.

What we learn from the philosophers is, in retrospect, uniquely disappointing. With naïveté or subtlety, they reject pleasure, enjoyment, sensuality, and physical joy and promulgate spirituality. When they do exalt pleasure, they turn it into an entity that is, now and always, metaphysical.

By contrasting it with pain, hermetically, they make it incomprehensible, impracticable. Yet, when they examine real pleasures and the joy effectively attained, they denounce impurity; they seek the paths of the absolute: absolute joy, absolute pleasure, absolute pain. They abandon the relative to those who lack wisdom or knowledge: the humble, the poor, the mad (who do not need to know this—they do what they can, for better or worse, but never reach the status of philosophical object, or only up to a certain point, and then only recently).

It required the arrival of subversive thought for pleasure and enjoyment to resume their rightful place and for their actual, concrete conditions to be explored and recognized. Philosophy wished itself to be austere and the philosopher an ascetic of knowledge, an enemy of the body, an eminent bearer of the signs of the nonbody. When philosophy denies itself by overcoming itself, its truth appears. This is the truth of materialism as opposed to idealism, to spiritualism, although this formulation has a derisive, moralizing, still philosophical side. Antienjoyment versus enjoyment, the nonbody versus the body, this is the "true" formulation.

Philosophy cannot be subversive. Supporting as it does the association between knowledge and power, it remains inherently political; even when it criticizes the political moment, it incorporates and supports it. Therefore, it can play a political role and even support a political revolution, which is a limiting factor. Subversion attacks philosophy just as it does the State, as such. Its reasons and resources are found in poetry, music, the gay science, and the appeal to youth, the capacity for the transformation of the world found in art.

Thus, the critical analysis provided by philosophy confirms that of monumentality. There is indeed an analogical relationship between these two aspects, one theoretical, the other practical, of the so-called historical and social process. Like the monument, another expression of power, the philosopher rejects enjoyment, and subversion, in the name of enjoyment, rejects philosophy.

Is there no way out of this impasse, then? Our analysis confirms that the way out is blocked. The utopia of enjoyment is simply one among many utopias: perfection, happiness, beauty, purity. Nietzsche, the subversive, offers a fundamental reorientation: a new determination, nature as indeterminate. For the man who emerges, for better or worse, together with his awareness, above and outside nature, it is a source of possibilities;

viewed in isolation, in itself, it is chaos and confusion, but it enables awareness and thought to introduce order by emphasizing certain aspects of this confused and chaotic existence. In nature we find labor (there are a vast number of species that work, especially among the insect populations) and nonlabor (pillage or calm secretion of the indispensible), violence and nonviolence, destruction and creation, love and hate. There are other things as well, which fall short of or overshoot such oppositions, which are the result of human thought and human judgment.

Nature is a confusion of moments that human activities seek to separate, even if this requires identifying their interconnections and recreating them. Pleasure and fecundity (fecundation), for example, which are intimately associated in nature and which "mankind" has tried for millennia to separate. This would be part of the appropriation of nature, but it cannot be achieved without risk, including the risk of the death of pleasure and the risk of sterility during the course of a pursuit that would allow nature to escape.

This nature, which is understood as incomprehensible, which is determined to be indeterminate but determinable for and by us, does not separate pleasure from pain. But we must be cautious about words and their meanings. For does this imply that, for an animal, pleasure is indistinguishable from pain? No, no living being, except for a few perverted humans, enjoys suffering. This ambiguity and its analysis signify that for the living being, there can be no pure state; only the conscious and knowing being (and it is precisely this that constitutes knowledge-as-act) separates and plans to experience separately what it has divided—even, as we saw above, if he must, through some secondary operation, subsequently recombine these disjunct elements: their conjunction postpones confusion.

This analysis provides us with an important insight, a pathway through a series of obstacles. Wasn't the role of art—among other things—to orient lived experience toward joy by releasing it from confusion; to integrate suffering itself into joy, or at least its contemplation with joy? And by suffering we must also understand the fear of death, the ephemeral, appearance. The work of art was seen as selective when compared to natural confusion, integrative compared to some intended enjoyment. To the extent that architecture can possess a so-called aesthetic effectiveness, should it not be required to orient lived experience and lead it, through some form of intelligent intervention, toward plenitude? This is not to say that architecture can "produce" enjoyment the way we produce an object, or that architectural effects can supplant other "aesthetic" effects (placed between quotes because the anticipated effectiveness has nothing in common with aestheticism). Nor is it a function of architecture to signify enjoyment and illusion, an ambition that cannot but fail.

Can architecture accommodate certain conditions of enjoyment and pleasure—rhythms, obstacles, tensions—that desire overcomes? No doubt. No doubt—if you manage to speak of something other than words, if you succeed in convincing yourself of the nearly absolute error of statements assumed to be eminently reasonable.

For Heidegger, the poet speaks of dwelling. The representation of dwelling as an occupation of space collapses before the words of the poet; he doesn't describe the conditions of dwelling, for poetry speaks to the man who responds to language by listening to what it says, by recognizing the sovereignty of language. "Language beckons us, at first and then again at the end, toward a thing's nature."[19] Such poetry makes the being of dwelling because poetry and dwelling deploy their being as a way of taking stock, which gives man the measure suitable to his being. "Measure gauges the very nature of man,"[20] and he deploys his being as a dweller, as a mortal. For the heavens, man erects his dwelling, by building, whose being is found in measure. He has the power to bring earth and heaven to him in things, divine and mortal. This power "placed the farm on the wind-sheltered mountain slope looking south, among the meadows close to the spring. . . . It did not forget the altar corner behind the community table; it made room in the chamber for the hallowed places of childbed and the 'tree of the dead.'"[21]

This poetical-metaphysical description of a country house completely ignores enjoyment. It adds nothing, changes nothing. Philosophical rhetoric distorts or sidesteps the essential, as if the goal and meaning of "man" were merely the fulfillment of a destiny promulgated by the invisible, the occult.

Are we going to climb up from these abysses, reinvigorated and regenerated, having shed our skin, "more ticklish and malicious, with a more delicate taste for joy, with a more tender tongue for all good things, with merrier senses, joyful with a more dangerous second innocence, more childlike, and at the same time a hundred times subtler than one had ever been before"?[22]

6

ANTHROPOLOGY

Anthropology was able to free itself of the curse laid on it by evil fairies at the time of its birth. Today, it has rid itself of a form of intellectual asceticism embodied (or, rather, disembodied) in the work of Claude Lévi-Strauss. The amateur intellectualism of analysis reduced ontological realities to nomenclatures, to words and abstract relationships among concepts. The mental absorbed the social and with it the historical (time) into an abstract space of forms and structures.

This scientificity covered a series of illicit operations, carefully dissimulated within the envelope of structuralism. First, beneath the appearance of recognizing the specificity of the realities under consideration—so-called archaic societies—it submitted their differences to the categories of the Occidental Logos. The destructive activity of European reason—theoretically negative, practically devouring whatever resisted it—was revivified and now justified; intellectual reductivism completed the reduction begun by other means, claiming to compensate for earlier disasters. Second, anthropology sidestepped modernity. It appeared to indirectly approach the study of the contemporary world, but in actuality, it deflected critical lucidity by circumventing objective realities. By discovering "primitive" categories (family, exchange) in the contemporary world, it succeeded in erasing capitalism, the bourgeoisie, imperialism.

Its ideological clumsiness is such that countless ingenuous souls, believing themselves to be part of an avant-garde, took this attitude as a sign of boldness, others as a sign of subversion. But in actuality, it was no more than an enormous circle, the most vicious of all: we conceive of others as a function of the self, and we conceive of the self in terms of others, holding to a conception of the self that is reduced to the absolute minimum.

The attack against structuralism, a reactionary ideology in the service of a neocapitalist technocracy, was initially conducted on a general, theoretical, and methodological front. This ideology retained a degree of strength and appeal, which had been established on what was thought to be solid ground—anthropology. Today, dislodged from the epistemological center it assumed it had strengthened, this ideology is threatened on its own terrain.

Robert Jaulin discovered a connection between (a) logical relations of inclusion and exclusion, (b) spatial relations of interiority and exteriority, and (c) affective relations of belonging or not-belonging to the same group. The relation of the self to the self and to other selves is inclusive, reflexive, spatially and affectively interiorizing. The relation to groups of others is exclusive, exteriorizing, and tends toward indifference and hostility.

This overview doesn't explain anything, however. It only enables us to address the study of populations (the Bari and Sara people, for example) in order to identify effective differences.[1] The fundamental social unit is defined by the connection (the intersection) between the people of the Self and the people of the Other. A society, a civilization experiences an everydayness.[2] However, this everydayness does not consist of a vocabulary but of acts and usages that govern space and places of residence, productive efforts and the pleasures of consumption, skill and social behavior, the joys and sorrows of love, marriage, and procreation.

In this way space enters the thought that describes and analyzes societies unlike our own. And this confirms its formation as a social space in societies described by history and the other social sciences, not only ethnology and anthropology. Relationships remained without support, for knowledge. The relations described and analyzed by Jaulin involve groups that are effectively excluded by their inclusion and are distinguished and differentiated from one another in a determinate space. Social units correspond, although loosely, to residences (collective homes, quarters) in such a way that the society can be described in terms of its structures of production or marriage without inconsistency (although the connections are by no means mechanical because there are always choices, preferences, areas of uncertainty).

As a result, the knot of relations is not attached to contemporary vocabulary, to the terminology of relations. Nomenclature doesn't have the privileged role given to it by linguistic dogmatism, for which relations and words coincide, as if words pointed to things. The proper name, left out by formalist linguistics, is a term, a knot of relations, that designates the relations between a person and those who call him by that name (Charles, Robert, Henry). This leads outside formalism to the search for those in question and their interrelations. These interrelations include residences and the distribution or attribution of space, consumption, and production, primarily of food.[3]

With spaces and names, sexuality reenters anthropology, not in terms of the sexuality of orgasm alone or reproduction (which no description could ignore), but concrete sexuality, the kind that requires a place and a partner, opportunity and preference, in short, to parody advertising rhetoric, a "personalized" sexuality, which accepts (or rejects) commitment and marriage. The space of a house (the surrounding grounds, a garden, a path, fields, trees) signifies femininity, mother or wife. With marriage, the young man leaves the maternal space for that of his wife; he leaves his mother. The child's first space is the mother's womb; the second, the mother and her space, so that, among the three terms—woman, house, earth—a proximity is established that is simultaneously perceptible and symbolic. A wife, then, is another woman, another house, another land. The wife is a mother modified by the departure from the space of the house, the womb of the house. This creates the link between marriage, sexuality, and spatial and social organization. "The space associated with the wife—the house, her territory—will be, like that associated with the mother, bound to her class," which is to say, to the classification that defines the "world of the marriage" in the social unit.[4] In other words, in a society bound to the earth by production and consumption (food), the *sexual* relationship culminating (sometimes) in marriage involves two persons, each of whom is bound to a house, a land, and relatives. The site itself of the marriage is associated with a reciprocal transition from kinship to marriage, from one group of relatives to a related group through consanguinal or collateral relations. The person, bearing a proper name, is not an abstract individuality, outside space, someone who is involved in social relationships and embodies them materially. It is not enough to simply introduce some vague localization of social relationships. The partitioning of space is as fundamental and structural as that of time. As for nomenclature (a naming system), it is not based on filiation alone but on spatial operations. The terms "affinity" and "consanguinity" have a spatial connotation; a distance in space, as in sexual evaluation generally, separates those who can marry (or have an affair) from those who cannot. The prohibition consists in this distancing itself; the defense consists in the fact that, for thought and gesture, there are so many intermediaries that the infringement (the transgression) cannot be conceived or imagined. This twofold distance—real and abstract, spatial and mental—separates the people assimilated here, relatives and others, those whom an act can include in the first group and those who are forever excluded.

Space acts socially as a support for relations in general (production/consumption in a society where people live off the products of the soil) and, in particular, sexual relations. These may be prohibited because of proximity, vicinage, or immediacy; possible through mediation; impossible because of distance or the absence of relations.

This has several consequences. Space does not represent a place (or a group of places) marked by indifference, a site that either falls short of affective relations, together with natural space, or one that lies outside it, such as the abstract space of reflection, mathematics, and philosophy. Social space is impregnated with affectivity, sexuality, desire, and repulsion. The affections are not content to enhance objects seen in isolation, to become invested and crystallize on "beings." Relationships are impregnated and, consequently, so is their support—space. Affective colorations are not applied to space like a coat of paint, however. Space *is* terrifying or affirming, loved or feared, preferred or rejected. Affective distances are not separated by mental, social, or spatial distances. They are not arranged in terms of geometric or spatial structures (circles radiating out from a subjective center, quadrangular or other shapes) or as arbitrary projections endowing things with significations, here and there, as a result of accident or chance. A relative and approximate correspondence, but one sufficiently precise to orient gestures and acts, is established between these levels and aspects: logic, everyday life, sentiments.

Examples can be found in the tents of the Turkmens, described by ethnologists such as Jean Cuisenier, Guy Tarade, and Olivier Marc, and the dwellings of the seminomadic peoples who live in yurts, animal-skin tents that are still found in the suburbs of Ulan Bator (Outer Mongolia) and in Anatolia (Turkey), and among Uzbek, Kazakh, and Kirghiz herders in the Soviet republics. The Topak Ev, a large circular tent, should not be confused with the Kara-çadir. The latter, which is black and made of goat skin, is used to shelter men—chiefs and warriors. The Topak Ev, by contrast, made of light-colored felt, is used to house the women of the tribe, who also construct the dwelling.

The women's yurt, a closed world, round, reproduces the entire cosmos. The shamans teach that the sky is a dome made of stretched, sewn skins. And the yurt (Topak Ev) is itself a microcosm: the circular roof represents the sky. There is a hole in the center of the roof to let smoke out and allow the favorable influx from the sky to enter the home, where the woman resides—wife, mother, supreme good, burden, and joy. The house is a womb, the site of a twofold birth: a physical birth and a social birth, following which the male child will go live with the men, until he finds a wife and a new female house.

Everything has a meaning: the sewing of the skins, the fringes that terminate the edges of the skins or embellish the seams. Fringes and seams are the vehicles of magical interventions, celestial influxes. Ethnologists suggest that the fringes symbolize the wounds of womanhood, the blood of deflowering or a mythical childbirth, for they are sometimes arranged around lunar circles. Woven with care, the fringes bring about joy and enjoyment for the woman who maintains the yurt. The yurt is oriented toward the east; the woman, night and day, always faces west. Her oldest son has the best place, to the right of his mother and, therefore, facing east, the source of joy and clarity.

This is where the woman remains; she has her own domain, which encloses her completely (even though the yurt can be disassembled and transported easily). The yurt is the woman's place, while active, commercial, and military life takes place outside, beneath the awnings or upturned flaps of the Kara-çadir, the male tent. The woman maintains her household, utensils, and clothing in the Topak Ev; it is here that she prepares meals, receives her friends, takes care of the children, sleeps. The married man has nothing of his own; he only sees his wife at night, in the unlit yurt. For the young girl, her mother's tent is an inviolable fortress, where, whenever she is so inclined, she invites a fiancé, "secretly." A young girl will spend her adolescence preparing a yurt. She makes the felt, knots the rugs, embroiders curtains, weaves the strips of cloth, and braids the fringes. The husband will provide the skins and erect the tent.

This microcosm protects and encloses the women. A source of wealth and well-being, a recipient of life's benefits, the wife never leaves it. The tent simulates the cosmos and functions as a prison of femininity. The yurt, in a way that is both symbolic and concrete (practical), plays a generative role. It is here that social life is produced and reproduced, unchanging, immutable. It partially embodies the connection between worlds: that of the mother (and father) and that of the wife, that of men and the cosmos. The husband (symbolically) abducts the wife and transports her to his territory, but he must provide her—assisted by her own efforts and those of her father, who furnishes wool and silk—with a home that is as beautiful as possible, depending on the rank and wealth of the family, a home he will enter only when invited.

This list summarizes the space of the yurt and is based on the work of Olivier Marc:[5]

Topak Ev	Kara-çadir
mobile (nomadic)	stable (tendency toward sedentariness)
round (cupola)	angular and, often, triangular
felt, sheep's wool, silk	tendency to use durable construction materials (bricks)
fecundity	solidity
comfort	tendency to asceticism
happiness	

The plurality of symbols (the organization of daily life, affectivity, sensuality, even eroticism) cannot be separated from practice and, in this way, meaning is generated. The male and female principles, without being isolated, are distinct and combine spatially. Symbolism is attached both to the materials employed and to the spatial forms and structure of social space. It is even a component of construction methods (techniques of fabrication, use of materials). Love and passion in the landscape of the yurts have their tragic moment as well: when the fiancé carries off his bride-to-be from the parental home and rides with her on horseback to the space where he will be born anew, this time as a warrior-shepherd during his third birth, through the woman he has deflowered, through his mother-and-spouse. But the space of the yurt normalizes the drama of love.

There is nothing indifferent about this space. But although everything has a meaning and becomes part of a total meaning, nothing can be reduced to a sign—to the abstraction of a sign-thing. Although we cannot draw a utopian model, a proposal, a primitivist utopia from such a profoundly *enhanced* space, we can learn something.

What about the space of enjoyment? Sensuality, viewed independently, can be inscribed in a place: disreputable neighborhoods, whorehouses, bordellos. A localized and, therefore, functionalized sensuality, with a price tag attached, devoid of gratuitousness and grace, destroys itself. The space of enjoyment cannot provide a ready-made, consumable form of enjoyment. And consequently, neither can it provide the utopia of a "productivity" of enjoyment. Do enjoyment, joy, sensuality consist in the eradication of space and time? Would a space impregnated with affectivity tend toward hyperspace (the other, the beloved, being and death, sensuality abandoning the "real" for annihilation)?

This tragic vision of enjoyment disdains social space. The superhuman moment avails itself fully of its position. In it, everything that social space has separated from nature is reunited in the supreme, absolute, and final moment. But nothing can be said of this tragic moment. What can we build upon such an unreliable foundation, on this dream? Nothing, not even a utopia.

The Mongol yurt offers the image of a social space that is "normal" and yet made for the development of the human being. But this development is limited for both the woman (who is a prisoner) and the man (who is thrust into an outside existence with his flock and seeks stability as compensation, far more than the woman, who transports her microcosm with her).

A simple, but distant, example, all of which takes place within the scope of history: in the immediacy and reciprocal presence of the cosmos, of spontaneous life, in the already precise organization of time and daily life.

7

HISTORY

We can learn a great deal from history. Unfortunately, the general history that might contain an answer to the question exists only in cursory form. There are good histories of architecture, where we can learn of the inventions of the great masters—Palladio, Ledoux, Eiffel, Perret. However, the relationship between the architectural work and the economic, social, and political context is sometimes obscured by the history of technical innovation, the materials and techniques of construction. A theoretical development and critique are both still lacking. Respect and admiration for the architect, a mediator between gods and men, have paralyzed theoretical research by making it superfluous. But what is an architectural, or an aesthetic, or a critical theory of architecture? What purpose do they serve? Histories of architecture often amount to no more than collections of anecdotes and technical recipes.

There are good historical studies of the city, of urban reality, of urbanism. Rarely do they reach the level of critical analysis, for lack of a theoretical principle or political criterion. The historian establishes facts. He cannot, for example, ignore the growing importance of cities in the West after the late Middle Ages. Although there was an urban revolution at the time of the communal movements (thirteenth century), followed by a radical modification of the relationship between town and country in the fourteenth century, a qualitative change that had considerable consequences, such facts, although of historical importance, are invisible to the majority of historians for lack of the appropriate conceptual instruments. In other words, the historical concrete, social practice and social relations, qualitative elements of the process, fall outside their awareness, which follows a simplified temporal model (historical time). In describing the history of the city, its growth, its enormity, the history of a particular city is usually juxtaposed with the history of the development of the countryside in general. The relationship between town and country, with its specific dialectic, is rarely addressed. Another aspect that escapes so-called realist historians is that of utopia. They forget that every urban reality, every monumentality, every project bears within it a utopia: the often outsize hope of controlling time, of enduring, of becoming eternal, of imposing a manner of living (that of a dominant group) on all of society. As with philosophy and politics, creative activity in the urban field possesses this naive and grandiose appeal. It always invests projects with an enthusiastic passion that believes it can engage the future by creating it. It trumpets large urban projects, sites and places whose initial purpose has often been forgotten. (Who remembers the origins of the Place des Vosges in Paris? The site was originally used for the games of aristocratic youth, a place where the traditional nobility, the honorary nobility, and the *grande bourgeoisie* could meet, during a period when the elite customarily met in the Marais. The Place des Vosges bears the mark of a political project and a dream: harmony among the factions of the governing class, between royalty, youth, and love, a harmony that spread throughout the capital beneath the scepter of a despotic but relatively enlightened monarch at the beginning of the seventeenth century. The projects and dreams have vanished; the site remains, beautiful and seductive.)

Architecture, the monument, the city once had a meaning, primarily when seen from the perspective of a "higher order of things," as Nietzsche remarked, for this order supplied meaning and value. But also, and especially, from the perspective of the longevity of that order, ensuring that it was both persuasive and limiting, and, therefore, from the perspective of a future order as well: a possible centered on the present and the past.

Every city believes itself to be the city of the gods or its god, or the one God. The demoniacal city, the Babylon of the Apocalypse, was seen as the opposite of the City of God, its counterpart. This atmosphere, this meaning, appeared to be inexhaustible, infinite, enveloping the world like a magic veil. Beauty was part of the whole, but subservient. No one saw it, no one wanted it in the form of aesthetic beauty: its effect was felt to be superfluous. Beauty tempered the horror of internal struggles, foreign wars, famines, epidemics. It did not obscure man and was hardly able to promise happiness—except possibly in Venice.

The city and the urban, therefore, have been surrounded by various dimensions: past-present-future, realized-actual-possible, outdated-obsolescent-impossible (because any realization cuts off certain possibilities, such as the end of the city or its capitulation to an enemy, either internal or external). Utopia, inherent in preparing for the future, surrounded the urban. This led to the presence in the city of places—squares, monuments, roads—whose presence was total, whose knowledge was absolute, places that carried a range of meanings: palaces, temples, tombs. Ideological utopias have merely elaborated such diffuse utopias, which are inherent in the urban as such.

At a higher and much broader level, spatial planning, territorial development, the strategy of space do not yet have a history. Although very old, such practices have only recently attempted to form themselves into a science, into a discrete field.

What is lacking then is a *history of space*. How is it that religious and political space (which I have referred to as "absolute space") becomes wrapped in the networks of *relative space*, initially commercial (from the onset of commercial exchange to the use of global markets), then capitalist (the accumulation of capital followed by the global expansion of capitalism during its imperialist period)? We have only fragmentary knowledge of this metastasized process, the poorly assembled elements of a colossal puzzle, whose practice predates and overwhelms theory.

The history of space assumes the introduction of a number of concepts and their refinement through use, initially, those of *domination* (dominant-dominated space) and *appropriation*.

The concept of "mastery," for a long time considered necessary and sufficient (mastery of the forces of nature through technology, mastery of technology itself), has revealed its inadequacies. How can we master the process by which practice and the technologies of industrially advanced societies master nature? Technology and technical expertise have assumed the appearance of autonomous forces, acting independently, bringing with them activities and actions implemented for reasons of technical expertise in itself. An active group of technocrats has taken over this possibility. Moreover, mastery of the forces of nature—through knowledge, through technology—has revealed the destructive capacities of nature.

"Mastery" meant "domination," a concept with a more aggressive connotation. For Hegel, and even for Marx, this logical equivalence seemed obvious, inundating reason with clarity: to master an initially blind and spontaneous, and, therefore, natural, process and dominate it through knowledge and action. The two terms of the relation between practice and theory are really one, the base or foundation of rational "positivity." However, this conceptual and theoretical unity revealed a duality. Knowledge has a negative and destructive side. Absolute positivity is one of the illusions of abstract rationality. In contrast to the mastery-through-domination that destroys blind and spontaneous processes by adding knowledge, there appears mastery-through-appropriation. Appropriation implies and presupposes a form of mastery that does not destroy the natural process through the brutal intervention of know-how and technology. This is the concrete positivity that has traversed and overcome the moment of two-sided negation: practical with respect to the destruction of nature, theoretical with respect to critical knowledge and the critique of knowledge.

Scientific thought and public opinion barely rise to this level of analysis. They do so through their confused questioning of the environment, pollution, ecology, technology. A slow and confusing evolution. By making use of ecology and its kernel of scientific expertise, the theory of ecosystems, we can avoid the distinctions proposed here between domination and appropriation. The space of an ecosystem gives rise to feedback, homeostasis. When equilibrium is established, or reestablished, is domination still present? No doubt, but by whom, by what form of conscious intervention? And when a disturbance modifies this equilibrium, what has occurred? The student of ecosystems responds that these are automatic phenomena, sweeping away at one stroke the field of sociopolitical phenomena.

To implement the concept of a dominant-dominated space it was sufficient to describe and analyze a military space: a Roman camp, a medieval castle, a classical fortress. Such description held considerable interest given the many masterpieces of military architecture (especially those in Spain). Built on a carefully selected site, the military structure develops and, thereby, holds and protects a space frequently considerable in size. Of course, the site depends on geographical factors as well as on tactical and retaliatory capabilities: height, intersecting roads, the confluence of rivers, defiles. Site development often reaches a point of extreme complexity: fortifications, ramparts, ditches, underground passages, redoubts, and so on. Construction is based on specifically military criteria such as visibility, approaches, defense and attack, maneuverability of the various elements. Logistical criteria are subject to a contradiction that makes them subordinate. The greater the protection the location provides, the greater its isolation, the less ability there is to intervene to protect the surrounding space, to respond to attacks. Ultimately, we are presented with an isolated and inaccessible site that no longer plays a tactical and strategic role as a fortress, much as an exposed site would. It is important, however, to consider that the past does not determine military space, that is to say, the memory of accomplished actions. Nor does the present, the resources employed. The future is the determining factor: possible actions, aggressive activities, counteroffensives. The area around the developed military site is monitored (by visual and other means), controlled (politically, militarily), and always susceptible to violent intervention. In this case, the term "surroundings" assumes a concrete and precise meaning.

Analytically, such a location defines a *center*, a centrality determined by a given mode of production (feudal, for example, or capitalist) and by a given type of society within the mode of production (colonial, imperial, etc.). This center of power exercises spatial control, and its political action is a function of interests in the society of which it is a part: general interests for maintaining that society, particular interests of the hegemonic class or a given faction, private interests of a given group or political leader, king, general, and so on. The fortress is established and strongly supports its interests by focusing on longevity. It tends to suppress its opponents through violence of one form or another—threats or executions. With a finger on the trigger, the arrow poised to take flight, the fortress is always active; it is not desirable that violence should be unleashed on behalf of power.

Theoretically, a dominant-dominated space is conceived in terms of power and violence. Political power possesses powerful means of constraint. The best procedure, if one is to avoid wearing them out, is to not have to make use of them. Once unleashed, violence results in disorder and crisis. Threats alone are inadequate. The cannons must be aimed, the bombs must be suspended over our heads. Defensive strategy, which is the best kind of strategy, becomes offensive—always a risky proposition. The fortress is a stratagem of domination. The terms "dominating-dominated" refer, descriptively, analytically, theoretically, to the situation of a space. In the modern world, this stratagem extends to armories, police networks, the electronic control of space. The military site has a direct and indirect political function. It influences and defines a space. The military site, therefore, harbors the measure of social things, the center. A political space is composed of centers of strength and areas of weakness. A center of strength radiates governing political ideas outward; it organizes space politically.

Historically, Rome was the great fortress of the empire. Once it lost that capability, the empire fell. Imperial space was provided by the *urbs*, by roads, by the military camps distributed at strategic locations. The Spanish colonization of South America provides an admirable example of a dominating-dominated space. The needs of colonization and the relationship between Spain and its colonies determined the general configuration of that space: the ports, the connections between the ports and the metropolis, the transportation of assets (gold and silver, primarily). The territory of those colonized cities, their architecture, was determined by colonization as was the relationship between the cities and the countryside, between the cities and the metropolis.

In the modern world, the colonization driven by capitalism and its needs, initially established in distant lands, has returned, by an extraordinary backlash, to the great cities. This led, "invisibly," to the great reversals that were fated to occur. The dominating-dominated space that has been established can only be conceived by analogy to a semicolonial space: growing military and police surveillance, concentrations of servile populations, workers parked in encampments from which they head out to a daily job or some mediocre entertainment, outsized warehouses for buying and selling. An admirable example of the boomerang effect. The term "feedback" serves as an ironic embellishment, lending it a scientific patina that in no way alters the situation.

The dominating space is consecrated by violence or religious and political terror. It assumes, even in historical periods, the characteristics of an absolute space that predates history. Dedicated to death, it is decorated, or rather furnished, with tombs and funerary monuments devoted to gods, kings, and heroes of past wars. Invisibly or perceptibly, these "centers of strength" dedicate themselves to death—present, past, and future. Everywhere and always we find manifest the great hope of being able to endure, survive, maintain the conditions of existence. To the extent that a military architecture and military monuments exist—not just militarily equipped structures—they are the expression of that hope, one intended to impress the population. Consider the ostentation of the Invalides in Paris, an architectural masterpiece. Or the Japanese fortress. Power is boastful. It doesn't oppress, it protects. But protects against what? Why, against other oppressors, of course. It has no qualms about revealing itself, or decorating itself, or using seduction rather than threats. Such a hope might have a name: utopia, but an abstract utopia.

This analysis, however, does not fully address the modern context. The dominating-dominated space does not correspond to the needs of political strategy alone, to monuments and "centers of strength." After the First World War, scientific and technical experts began working in concert. Autonomous technology works through a form of State power that is itself autonomous, which is to say that it stands above society. It should be obvious that the autonomization of technology is not impersonal; well-defined individuals are the basis of that autonomy. They are known as technocrats. They cooperate with politicians inside the structures of the State, but like the military each has its own interests.

A slab of concrete, an immense field of corn, a colossal highway with its associated structures are as much a part of a dominating-dominated space as a military site. A highway is not restricted to cutting through lands and landscape as a means of transportation; it slices, separates, and destroys sites, without regard for its effect on the "environment," which it alters.

Yet the mastery of space does not always have this mortal character. Sometimes it generates a social life and tends toward appropriation. Nothing is more beautiful, among works of art, than a terraced landscape. Cyclopean laborers, peasants, sculpt mountains. And this becomes a problem for aesthetics, for how and why is it that people who have never thought of beauty can accomplish such beautiful works? The same can be said of many ports. What is more beautiful than the seaport prior to colonization: jetties, wharves, docks, enlivened by the coming and going of boats, have shown that domination (mastery) and appropriation have been able to work together. Spurred on by an audacious group of thalassocrats, a site for storing and exchanging goods, a meeting place for merchants, has assumed the appearance of the utmost refinement: Venice.

Appropriation can be defined by contrast with domination and simultaneously by opposition to ownership and its consequences. The appropriated space does not belong to a political power, to an institution as such. No power has shaped it based on the needs of its continued existence. It is not, therefore, a space devoted to death, either directly (tombs, for example) or indirectly (palaces, not excluding the palaces of knowledge and wisdom). An active group has constructed such a space: thalassocrats, a religious order, immigrants. Use value has priority over exchange value.

Descriptively, a cloister, appropriated for a life of contemplation, in a monastery, is assembled from cells (although these are "private" this has nothing to do with private property) with areas for prayer and various activities (a library, fields). In itself, the cloister provides a place for contemplatives to meet, to walk around, to pray. Its use, subject to the rules of the order and a schedule, has nothing to do with the exchange of goods and the abstract communication of signs.

Analytically, the enclosed space, through its connection with other spaces in the monastic community, is exposed to the possibilities of prayer and even of dreams: the sky, the divine, nature (always present within the cloister and represented by its columns and capitals). Theoretically, the cloister and the monastery incorporate in a space the world (and thus the utopia) of contemplative life as defined by a religion. The signified, mystical euphoria, and the signifier, the entire space, do not have an obvious relationship. The signifier leaves the signified indeterminate, in such a way that each of us can discover it for himself. Whenever art and artists want to signify something—the divine, for example—whenever they want to impose a meaning and a signified content, they succumb to the platitudes of so-called religious art. But what artist worthy of the name ignores the virtue of indirect expression? To yoke a signifier to a signified is an illusion and an error. In the cloisters, an unused excess of signs and symbols—capitals, architectural forms themselves—participates in the flight of the imaginary toward a transcendent reality. The cloister contains a finite infinitude: the unlimitedness of the imaginary, the symbolic, and the dream, exposed by a carefully defined collection of perceptible objects. Desire, returned to earth, is directed toward the divine.

What is a space of joy (for there is a contemplative joy, quite distinct from sensory-sensual pleasure)? Space alerts or awakens; it allows thought or imagination to depart without necessarily providing them with topics (contents, signifieds). This space of joy is not necessarily joyful. Quite the contrary, a joy that it allows or evokes may overwhelm it, just as music that makes us happy may not be joyful. A fragment of Beethoven gives joy through a form of anxiety metamorphosed by the music. This was how Dutch architect Constant Nieuwenhuys's "ambient structures" of 1953 worked, although, in his case, hesitatingly, as the experience was initially limited to space and color relationships.

Nonetheless, appropriated spaces, including certain spaces of joy, can be distinguished from spaces of fear, although they will never become the space of enjoyment. On the contrary, the use of sensoriality, which leads to a threshold beyond which the sensorial becomes the sensual, leaves needs and desires unfulfilled, and this results in the leap to transcendence—contemplation, the disappointing joy of an absolute that flees before us. The spatial work and architectural effect serve as intermediaries between the sensory and the metaphysical perceived and conceived by hypothesis as an object of contemplation. But they have failed to mediate between the sensory, the sensual, and the organization, by this means, of enjoyment or the active perception of space. Groups and organizations capable of appropriating a space for themselves did not generally have enjoyment as their goal and primary interest. At the threshold separating the sensory from the sensual, the architectural effect ceases; instead of orienting lived experience and perception toward the sensual, it allows a mass of "spiritual" possibilities, symbols, dreams, theological-philosophical abstractions, magical gestures, and rituals to spring forth.

The latent contradiction between domination and appropriation has exploded in the modern world. Technological and political domination is fundamentally directed at the product. Appropriation is a work (in the sense of a work of art) or it is nothing. Increasingly, dominating-dominated space is built up from individual components: private property extending to all of space; geometric and visual abstraction; a latent or acknowledged violence; exchange value, inseparable from private property; a homogeneity that, through its control, promotes the breakup and pulverization of space, the destruction of natural space.

Appropriation is defined by radically opposite and, therefore, incompatible components: the priority of use and use value over exchange and exchange value; a community that works space for its own use; collective management of the produced space; nature transformed in such a way that it can be regenerated.

Between domination and appropriation there is an activity, a mediating concept: *détournement*.[1] An initially spontaneous, almost uncertain, practice that soon becomes deliberate, détournement was born with modern art. By 1910, painters, freed from academicism, stuck bits of paper, dishes, porcelain, or glass to their canvases, a miscellany of objects and materials. Soon, musicians began mixing themes borrowed from popular song or other musical works into their compositions, themes detached from their content and diverted from their original meaning. (Stravinsky often employed this procedure.) With Eisenstein in the cinema and Brecht in theater, this approach became common practice and was accompanied by similar procedures and techniques: collage, montage, assemblage. It was inevitable that détournement, having become commonplace, would emerge as a distinct concept, which it did slowly but surely. This theoretical emergence was accompanied by a critique of originality, of origin, of the metaphysics of beginnings. The widespread scope of a practice originally thought to have been local had to be acknowledged. Theory soon recognized that every philosophy diverts—or circumvents—problems, topics, and concepts from earlier philosophies.

This throws a new light on the history of philosophy as well as the history of art. Marx diverted Hegelian dialectic for his own (revolutionary) use; he sidestepped the problem of the rationality of the future, of its orientation, that of historical time. The concept was thereby compounded by contrasting but complementary operations: to circumvent or to divert. Obstacles, insoluble problems—or those that appear to be—exhausted concepts, can be circumvented. Thought turns around, then abandons them. Other topics, problems, concepts are revealed through a series of operations on their context and serve as matter and material for other constructions. The concepts of "deconstruction" and "construction," of "découpage" and "assemblage" (somewhat less qualified) round out the notions of "circumvention" and "détournement."

We could say that the harmony introduced in the eighteenth century with its new understanding of music repurposed the musical use of intervals through counterpoint and an art based solely on melody and rhythm.

A family moves into a house already inhabited by another family and alters the space, appropriating it for its own use. An organization or an established institution takes possession of a building constructed for another organization; they appropriate it. Conquerors have appropriated older spaces, assuming they did not destroy what they occupied, just as revolutions and successive generations have done.

The history of space and architectural effects would assign considerable importance to these repurposings. Each has its own history, and détournement comprises a multitude of historical episodes. A remarkable example is the basilica, a Roman edifice used for secular encounters, primarily by merchants, that was repurposed by early Christianity for its own use.

The Marais quarter, in the center of Paris, a work of the seventeenth-century aristocracy, was precipitously and ruthlessly appropriated by the industrial and merchant bourgeoisie after the French (democratic-bourgeois) revolution. Monuments became buildings; luxurious private residences and palaces were transformed into workshops, stores, and apartments. The quarter, tied to the production of goods, became working class and dynamic, and lost its beauty; the gardens disappeared almost completely. In the same historic center of Paris, we find Les Halles, newly accessible after having been abandoned by the food and flower markets; appropriated by the youth of Paris, it has become a ludic space.

The moment of détournement has considerable historical and theoretical interest. In effect, the ancient terms and structures remain, but their function has changed; it is initially superimposed on an earlier function (or functions) that gradually disappears, ultimately giving way to a new use. This is followed by a confusion of language and activities that slips into the old frameworks, then reworks them, which the innovator can take advantage of. Psychological and psychoanalytical terms (substitution, transference, displacement) describe similar phenomena but are inadequate for analyzing the transformations of space. A "subject" who appropriates an earlier social morphology cannot be defined because it is reshaped during the process and is itself altered in turn. Christianity becomes aware of itself when it becomes established in the architectural, social, and political space of the Roman Empire.

Historians are mostly silent about the moment of détournement. As a transition, it seems to hold little interest for them as their attention jumps from an initial period (for example, the Roman basilica) to its termination and the beginning of the new period (Roman and Gothic art). In this way, they leap over centuries during which considerable innovation takes place.

Détournement is not yet creation. It prepares the way for it, appropriation moves forward. After Christianity appropriated Roman space, it invented its own space; it created the Roman church and Gothic cathedrals, established its own symbolism. Christian architecture abandoned earlier forms and became analogical, as churches assumed the shape of the cross. At the moment of détournement, new aspirations appear, transposing the earlier form whenever it reveals its limitations in the face of new practices and languages. At a given moment, détournement exhausts itself, and the form that has been used collapses, either because something new has been created or because the decline overwhelms its creative capacity (which appears to be the case for Les Halles today). The variations on the form, the new combinations and their elements, no longer satisfy demand. This is (generally) followed by production, the utopian moment. It is a reactive utopia, however, for the new occupants of the old space imagine that they can adjust to it, adapt it or adapt themselves, introducing modifications that appear extraordinary to them and that later are shown to be negligible. At the same time, they project transformations, and one day utopia is embodied in an innovative spatial practice.

Détournement assumes that space (the edifice, monument, or building) possesses a certain degree of plasticity. A hardened and signified functionality prevents détournement by fixing space, by restricting it in the form of a sign-thing. The functionality of Les Halles, constructed in the nineteenth century, was not rigidly inscribed in space because the structure consisted of a simple umbrella. And this led to its availability.

As a transitional, functional, and paradoxical moment, détournement is as distinguished from conservation as it is from creative production. During an interim moment, it marks the period when domination ceases, when dominated space becomes vacant and lends itself to other forms of domination or a more refined appropriation. When détournement is too successful, it becomes stabilized and, as a result, the possibility of new production implies a kind of failure of détournement. Although necessary, it is no longer sufficient once the requirement for novelty appears through the confrontation of practices and languages. An illustration of the historical process could be represented as follows:

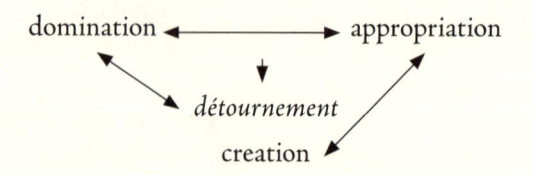

domination ⟷ appropriation
détournement
creation

The history of space leads to the dissociation of work and leisure, a dissociation characteristic (like so many others) of modernity. It begins with the disruption of the historical city. History leads to this historical moment itself, when economic factors cause historical processes as such to disappear. History leads up to the moment when other methods of analysis—sociological, psychological—take the place of historical analysis. The city appears to contain within it its principle of growth and development. A flexible form, integrated into a much larger whole, the nation, a system endowed with internal unity, it seemed destined to preserve that internal unity, and a certain autonomy. The history of the city, and of each city, reveals a marvelous unity in which forms, functions, and structures are associated. However, market pressure, especially the global market, tended, in the second half of the nineteenth century, to dissolve it within intersecting networks of circulation. Although dispersed along the periphery and in suburbs, its center is strengthened. This results in the paradox (dialectic) seen elsewhere: urbanization, the expansion of the city, the degradation of space. It is no longer urban or rural but is composed of a formless mixture of those two characteristics: ruralization of the city and urbanization of the countryside.

Functions are separated. The separation is inevitable, even indispensible, but it cannot be maintained once it becomes effective. As workers travel further from their homes and the places that allow them to support their social existence, that existence becomes increasingly untenable. The vital question of urban transport can only be considered theoretically as a symptom. Once the everyday has been separated from the non-everyday, work from leisure (entertainments, festivals, vacations), the disparities must be reassembled. That a space endowed with a specific purpose, or vocation, and constructed according to earlier needs can be turned into a space of enjoyment goes without saying: a warehouse may become a theater or a dancehall. This does not mean that the space of enjoyment is useless, however; the problem only becomes more acute.

Leisure activities often take place in empty spaces: fields of snow, beaches. To introduce an empty space into preexisting circuits and networks (commercial, financial, industrial) considerable effort must often be expended, resulting in the domination of the preexisting space: roads and highways, sewer and water systems, buildings, office blocks. This often leads to the destruction of the abruptly dominated space.

In the best-case scenario, the appropriation of an older space—town, village, local or regional architecture—allows it to subsist symbiotically with the modified (dominated) space. Leisure spaces are composed of natural spaces, dominated spaces, appropriated spaces and structures. To a certain extent, leisure activities need "qualified" spaces. To engage in such activities, we leave a space without quality, the quantitative space of production and consumption, in order to consume space and its qualitative properties: light, sun, the oceans, water, snow. We leave a space dominated by exchange to seek enjoyment in a space appropriated by and for our own use.

Leisure spaces provide a mixture for analysis. This border zone between labor (predominant) and nonlabor (virtual, indicated from afar by the arrows of automation), like all transitional zones, is characterized by its own conflicts, which exasperate the latent contradictions and the affected zones. Leisure spaces exhibit a formless but carefully determined mixture of détournement, of latent appropriation; through technical expertise a return to the immediate is revealed: nature, spontaneity. Use is strongly contrasted with exchange, even though their conflict is dissimulated beneath myths, abstract utopias, and ideologies: "Discover the countryside! Enjoy nature! Take a break from the daily grind!" A form of bodily culture is adumbrated, although awkwardly, and appropriated. This is where the body is revealed, where it reveals itself, bares itself, recognizes its importance. Use value comes to life in the face of exchange value.

Critical analysis can only treat the architecture of leisure as a simulation of enjoyment within a framework that prohibits it, namely the control of those spaces by economic and political forces. However, some features can be found in which an unfulfilled possibility appears: the priorities of use, of nature, of the immediate, of the body. The utopia of enjoyment tends toward the concrete.

Leisure spaces are contradictory, and the contradictions of space can be easily observed there. Use in its pure state is promised, but we enter circuits of exchange. Nature is promised only to recede from view or disappear entirely. We promise immediacy but provide merely illusion. We advertise bodily joy, but the body receives no more than a patina of enjoyment—a tan—and a spectacle: our somewhat denuded flesh, primed for a hypothetical pleasure. A parody of eroticism.

But specialization in the field of organized leisure can only go so far, for soon production forces the situatedness of pleasure to fall into line.

It's not clear whether those affected experience this failure or not. They experience a mix of satisfaction, joyful discovery—especially the memory of vacations—frustration, disappointment, a mix as difficult to analyze as the space that engenders it. Critical analysis shows the derisiveness of success and the regrettable side of failure. In leisure spaces, a promising "environment" is present. A rhetoric of space, overloaded with signs, corresponds to the rhetoric of advertising language, the brochures produced by travel agencies and airlines. Architectural discourse fertilizes advertising rhetoric, and vice versa. Every element is used, from nature itself to the most ingenious forms of sophistication (discotheques, nightclubs, bars, casinos, art exhibitions). The result is a parody of the festival, a caricature of enjoyment: the utopia of free days devoted to celebration and enjoyment within a pressurized space-time subject to the demands of profit and a return on investment.

8

PSYCHOLOGY AND PSYCHOANALYSIS

The psychology of pleasure and pain has done little to alter the claims of philosophy. Yet psychologists, psychiatrists, and psychoanalysts have helped accentuate the lived experience of pleasure and pain, enjoyment and suffering, noting their irreducibility to representations, to knowledge, to speech about (pleasure, pain, etc.). Knowledge, philosophy, and the sciences struggle to recover the irrecoverable and reduce the irreducible. What is assumed to be essential, or claimed to be by knowledge, is turned against the existential in an attempt to abolish it. This has nothing to do with the philosophical ideology of existentialism. The discovery of the specificity of lived experience could not have disturbed the structure of philosophical and scientific knowledge (only loosely connected to power) if there had not also occurred a crisis in philosophy, a crisis of knowledge, and a crisis of intellectualizing morality and asceticism, distinct from a crisis of power. (Crisis does not imply disappearance. Crisis also results in the frustration of whatever it threatens—morality, asceticism, the ascetic culture of deprivation, political power.)

Can we conclude that research in these fields has restored the body by victoriously contrasting the signs of the body to the signs of the non-body? No, because their research imperfectly occupies a contested terrain. It is surrounded by ambiguity. (Moreover, they discovered ambiguity, concept and reality.) On the one hand, this research is part of knowledge, wants to be knowledge, uses or claims to use operational concepts and effective techniques. On the other hand, it is surrounded by uncertainty, by lived experience: the affects, what is or what is not—pleasure and pain, enjoyment and suffering—although this formidable dilemma does not obey any logic, although there does not exist, barring some unforeseen discovery, any encoding or decoding of affectivity, as irreducible to information as it is to knowledge and abstraction. Knowledge struggles to reduce: uncertainty to certainty, ambiguity to the determinate, silence to speech, spontaneity to deliberation, the concrete to the abstract, pleasure to thought, and pain to the absence of thought.

This twentieth-century research has been disseminated and democratized, thereby making effective what Nietzsche, a critic of philosophy and political power, had torn from silence by writing "with his blood." That same research has dissimulated part of what the poet had discovered, especially the connection between emotion and space.[1] For the poet wished to use the body as a guide, convince us that the subject is a fiction. In this way, space, a substrate of energy, force, and its expenditure, and, therefore, of "physical" activity, occupies the place of the older, so-called psychic faculties—will, thought, reflection, desire. Psychology and even psychoanalysis have continued to study "subjects," "egos," subjective "topics," situated in a mental rather than a social space. So-called social psychology hardly ventured any further than "subjectivist" or "behavioral" psychology. It is not enough to claim that the "field of behavior" has a social and cultural "environment," that it is not given to the individual in the physical sense but is "acculturated" so the relationship of the human being (mental and social) to space can be extended. The shift from the physical to the cultural simply obscures the process.[2]

Nothing is more terrible than the flight of pleasure, joy, enjoyment in the face of pursuit. Yet in the West, where it is perceived as a curse, pleasure flees before discourse, both oral and written. The discourse of technology, like that of knowledge, attempts to grasp the flower of living flesh with steel forceps, with surgical tools. What could be more painful, said Eluard, than to not obtain pleasure with what you love, from what you love? Psychological and psychoanalytical discourse put on gloves in their attempt to trap pleasure and joy. They continue to escape, however, evading whatever traps are set for them. To accumulate the means of enjoyment (happiness, joy, pleasure) and know that it escapes us, to produce everything except what cannot be produced but occurs or arises—like grace, gratuitously—is an affliction that has ravaged the West. The critical analysis of space reveals this devastation, identifies it clearly. The annexation of a territory, no matter how busy and populous, by knowledge cannot take place without harm.

The principal error of these attempts is their inability to orient themselves correctly in relation to the everyday. They insert themselves between or within the quotidian, thereby unconsciously reflecting the cares of people who wish to rise above a hazardous existence subject to fortune and misfortune to a secure everydayness that they can accept and adapt to. That pleasure and desire might arise during a fortunate moment for which there is no recipe terrifies most people, who prefer security to uncertainty. Security is expensive, however, and in exchange we are forced to endure any number of tiresome satisfactions in our everyday life. Satisfaction is found in other products: the everyday and satisfaction go hand in hand. That the satisfaction of various needs, that the satisfaction of all needs, might go hand in hand with a kind of general malaise is lost to our practical understanding. The vast majority of people on the planet, those living in "underdeveloped" countries, who are unable to fulfill their everyday needs, dream only of rising to that level. They are not tempted by poetic transgressions or political infractions. The disciplines that address psychological "subjects" treat people who have experienced the everyday and who experience dissatisfaction on the model of those who struggle to achieve a guaranteed existence: not just bread but meat, not only wine but gas for the car. And as a result, we have the easy success of cures of adaptation and readaptation to the "real," in other words, the everyday.

How can we fail to note the importance of the death instinct, or death drive, in psychoanalytic thought. This negative life force comes into being as an explanatory principle. Initially, the ambiguity was resolved, according to Freud and his followers, in the interplay of opposing forces, Eros and Thanatos, the pleasure principle and the reality principle (later, the performance principle), the life drive and the death drive. This dialectic was soon changed into a mechanism in which the death drive predominated. Life transpired against a background of death; the living being (the body) was no longer the field on which rival forces confronted one another. Living existence was seen as a disturbance in relation to death, an error in relation to nothingness. Erotic drives were perceived as detours along the way to desire and a return to the inorganic, in other words, death. Freud stated this expressly in *Beyond the Pleasure Principle*.[3]

A growing sense of terror, with less and less relief, and greater suffering; a disturbance of the initial and final equilibrium of the inorganic—

this is the trajectory of the living being. And this can be generalized to society and history. The conscious struggle for existence possesses the characteristics of a curse: Ananke. Historical necessity is defined by the accentuation of the repressive character of paternal action, embodied in law. The death instinct is manifest in the division of labor just as it is in morality and economic organization, rooted as they are in the notion of yield and the performance principle. Freedom is concentrated in the imaginary, a mode of activity "freed from the demands of reality" (Marcuse).

A pleasure ego and a reality ego confront one another, but the struggle is unequal and the former always wins out. The pleasure ego, pleasant enough but useless, seductive (Narcissus, Orpheus) but false and, consequently, repressed, arises from consciousness, and with it the utopia of art, and the return of the repressed in dreams. All art presents an image of freedom, which is to say, "man" as a free subject, the negative image of alienation. With the appearance of reality, this image is represented as an apparently superannuated reality. Art gives rise to the repressed and represses it once more, but more thoroughly this time around and, therefore, forever. This is the death of pleasure. Death and the death instinct are triumphant, in spite of the lucidity and brilliance of art. They triumph over art because they become an integral part of art. If we acknowledge that the ultimate immediacy, death, reproduces the initial immediacy, the relation to the mother, do we then not strike a mortal blow against vitality on the planet Earth? And as surely as if we had launched our entire inventory of nuclear weapons. In doing so, we deny history and render it useless by allowing the archaic to return and none of our myths to disappear.

"Every man seeks to die in the world, wishes to die of the world and for its sake. In this perspective, dying means setting forth to meet the freedom which frees me from being, that decisive separation which permits me to escape from being by pitting action, labor, and struggle against it—and thus permits me to move beyond myself toward the world of others."[4]

And why not? Among the developments and comparisons, why not this one? Some promote work, others rest, others struggle or love; they turn them into absolutes. Death lends itself to such stratagems. But what prevents us from promoting space? To promote death is astonishing. It is a form of nihilism, which Nietzsche wished to overcome in *The Gay*

Science and through his concept of the Superhuman. Nietzsche believed we should say "yes" to life while avoiding the appropriation of death. One tried to "give a purer sense to the words of the tribe" without noticing that death triumphed over those strange voices.[5]

Of course, the triumph of death can be understood and explained by the system, by neocapitalism and political power. Our only way out is through death. Death's call, desperate, magical, and religious, can be understood as a desperate appeal for the death of the system. Yet this is how the system is finalized and becomes totalized. Those who wish to denounce it, and believe they are doing so, turn into priests of fatalization, whose solemn closure they intone. This radical pessimism betrays Nietzsche's tragic optimism as much as Marx's rational optimism.

Neither capitalism and the bourgeoisie nor the Judeo-Christian religious tradition are adequate to explain this malaise. Through language, through the facilitation of pathways co-opted or deflected by the drives, psychoanalytic knowledge manipulates forces that it cannot control. It seeks appropriation and fails. Having pointed out the irreducibility of pleasure, it struggles to reduce it, initially by condemning privation and frustration and identifying a symptom: the symbolic or real construction. In seeking causes and reasons, psychoanalysis changed the symptom into an explanatory diagram. We forget that Western man on the road to absolute labor and abstract space first castrated animals then himself.

This knowledge, however, was willing to appear as part of the modern episteme, to be recognized as absolute knowledge, effective within the current context. But it cannot escape the consequences of this attitude. In spite of the verbal precautions, the refinement of its techniques, the *conceived*, given pride of place and viewed as central, destroys *real life*—even after having identified and revealed its fragility. The error consists in the fact that Freudian research ignores Nietzschean subversion, ignores the insurrection by which enjoyment in the broad sense becomes the meaning, and the only meaning, of life, of art, of utopia. In the end, pleasure along with its conditions, its causes and reasons, was cast into the clutter of the unconscious, where it was destroyed. This was a way of acknowledging its impotence, of throwing our hands up to the sky in the face of the surrounding chaos.

To hope that "affective investments" provide their authors with a "surplus value" of enjoyment is merely a pious wish and naive transposition of capitalist economy as long as we fail to recognize the extent to which this process is normal for the body, beginning with its initial immediacy (at least during growth and as it tends toward full maturity). Consequently, the problem is not to provide this normal tendency with a theoretical structure but to embed it in a space that provides it with support. The only response to the powers that decree the death of pleasure along with the death of God, after the death of man, is permanent insurrection.

It is unlikely that such single-minded pursuit experienced throughout the entire Western world has nothing to teach us about space. Analytic research teaches us that the individual is most generally found at the intersection of two roads: he can either return inward, toward a cocoon, the original space (the womb, home), or cut the umbilical cord and set out for open space with all its attendant risks. There is nothing in common between this and the well-known choice between vice and virtue. The choice—and, therefore, the margin of freedom—has drastic consequences for the individual. Perhaps such a choice is made at every moment, with every step taken in space.

Studies inspired by psychic analysis have shown us that the principal character in the patriarchal constellation has always been, together with the father, the mother's brother and the eldest son. Formerly, in the center of space—made virile as a result—there ruled a male character. Those analyses enable us to predict that in the future—perhaps starting today—that central character will be the daughter. The woman's place is changing. It is no longer one that simultaneously brings the Mother into being and reproaches her for being the Mother. The Daughter wants to live.

Analysis has also identified different types of sexuality: homosexuality, bisexuality, transsexuality, which, far from excluding one another, are assumed. This sexuality is defined as an attempt, a project, for a sexualized individual to experience itself as the other sex. Once transsexuality is understood, its value becomes clear. Yes, it involves forms of transvestism, of "inverted" tendencies, but all art assumes the existence of transsexuality and makes it a part of lived experience. To the extent that Mozart's music in *Cosi fan Tutte* makes me, a man, experience the emotions of the two young women (which in this magical opera cloaks all sorts of distortions, disguises, masks, and masquerades), I achieve a momentary transsexuality; to a certain extent I experience my desire as that of the other sex. Like so many others, it is a ploy: identification will fix on another "subject" the uncertain subject enchanted by his uncertainty. And his enjoyment will be lost.

Against the background of psychic identity (lost or found in an ever-changing game, that of Shakespearean theater), four sexes confront one another: m–m, m–f, f–f, f–m. Why does space not incorporate this complexity, providing, of course, that it does not make it permanent. To the very limited extent that physical locations were marked by sex (based on a coarse representation in which hollows are female and points are male), only a summary opposition was adumbrated. Why not diversify those marks? In this way only differences would be multiplied and then maximized through some kind of "optimal" position. The libidinal vocabulary does not prescribe the possibles; it simply introduces all sorts of possibilities.

Psychology and psychoanalysis have emphasized ambiguity. Although not as relevant as Nietzsche in this regard, the addition of descriptive content is of the greatest interest. Every situation is ambiguous. The anxiety of ambiguity leads to the simultaneous formation of enjoyment and the need for a solution (a resolution). The source, and resource, of affectivity is ambiguity. So intolerable, so unbearable that everyone escapes it only to return, ambiguity—not death—generously provides the background, the "frame" that is, in fact, nothing like a frame. Providing we can resolve it, ambiguity opens every door. Let us assume, with some degree of generosity, that the word "unconscious" refers to a formless "basic" existence. However, I do not agree that the term, which claims to be scientific, refers to another existence, analogous not to the increasingly opaque translucidity of the deep waters just below the surface but to a terrestrial layer beneath those waters. The analogy is misleading because the metaphor is overblown. Below consciousness, as above it, there is the body (my body).

The concept of ambiguity has something specific and difficult about it, which is that its conceptual presentation tends to dissolve this "object" that is not an object. Ambiguity cannot resist investigation of the mode of the thing, of objectality. If I think about my ambiguity, I dissipate it. The moment I begin to examine it coincides with the moment it ceases to be; but I do not examine it: I reflect my reflection, my reflexive act. This is the meaning of the expression "self-awareness." Reflection and the use of the concept, therefore, assume a considerable number of precautions. Ambiguity, by hypothesis or definition, can be read in at least two different ways in our somewhat pedantic modern language. In classical language, it is interpreted, and the majority of interpretations are part of the concept. The same was true of the concepts of "lived experience" and "pleasure." The argument that observation and reflection modify the object, an argument used and abused in relation to the most solid objects, here assumes a differential value. But as soon as we begin to grasp such powerful and fragile modes of existence, as soon as we claim to manipulate them, we risk destroying them.

Ambiguity cannot be reconstituted. What can we determine from an analysis that separates the components? Ambiguity. Yet by taking the product of that analysis to be an ingredient, death results. Ambiguity cannot be reconstituted by mixing life and death, Eros and Thanatos, immediacy and mediation, pleasure and suffering (or the "real"). The body and the life of the body are ambiguity, from which is detached, at every moment, a decision, an intentional gesture, a willed act. Ambiguity cannot be identified with indifference, however, even though this negative concept allows us to get closer to it than the simple rearward projection of differences. Immediacy is appropriate, but a lost and rediscovered immediacy is already something different. That concept and conceived as such tend to dissipate any fundamental ambiguity like a puff of smoke is a dramatic situation that cannot fail to have consequences. Among others, the space represented and socially realized cannot sustain ambiguity, which it brutalizes and summarily dissipates.

Angles, definite spatial forms, cannot support ambiguity. Space reorders sensations and sentiments within chaos, intentional (built) space more strongly than spontaneous (physical) space. Like abstraction, like political power, space would have the power to reduce all fantasies except for the imaginary, which binds the infant physically with its mother, and which subsequently appears not only in the reduction of pleasure but in every "real" pleasure. Could this be the knot of the enigma, the secret of the incompatibility between pleasure and social organization, between architecture and enjoyment?

Yet haven't painters always re-created sensory-sensual ambiguity so that, through line, expressive, relatively specific forms would appear? The ambiguity of color and line enabled them subsequently to emerge separately, before being recombined in an alliance unlike their initial fusion.

The simultaneous emergence of form and color, of sensoriality and sensuality, of what speaks to the senses and what is addressed to the understanding, may characterize great painting. Likewise, music arises from an "indifference" to repetition and difference, within which repetitiveness and differentiality are contrasted: theme and variation, rhythm and its variants, harmony and diversification.

If painting and music offer a return to indifference and ambiguity so that so-called aesthetic works—which do not dissipate but integrate their moment (time and place)—can arise before our eyes and ears, why can't architecture achieve similar results with space? In truth, the architectural effect always risks obeying the law of power, which cannot allow disturbance or disorder. And yet, the spaces analyzed earlier—the space of contemplation, the space of dream—are able to control ambiguity, to orient it toward certain and uncertain enjoyment.

The arabesque, with its exceptional linearity, is equally ambiguous. Sometimes the line is assertive, emphatic; it assumes an autonomous force without becoming preoccupied with surfaces; and the work tends toward graphism. But sometimes, on the contrary, it succeeds in linearly connecting things that are objectively foreign to one another.[6] It decorates surfaces and separates while uniting them; demarcation takes precedence over the mark, and line enhances colored surfaces. Sometimes the influence of the arabesque is like a "simplistic result" and sometimes like a "line of force," the movement of color and form.[7]

What could be clearer or more evident, apparently, than the brilliant surface of a mirror? Reflection, contemplation are derived from the mirror in such a way that it has come to symbolize thought and awareness: a reflective surface in which the transparent image of opaque things takes shape, in which the opacity of its depth is metamorphosed. But the mirror's ambiguity is immediately on display. Nothing is more unlike the thing than its image, its other in the mirror. Mirages and images, transitional objects (but from whom to what?), mirrors are doubled. The *reflective glass [glace]*, cruel falsity—"cold water by weariness frozen in your frame"[8]—differs from the *mirror [miroir]*, strictly speaking, which is friendly, favorable, a human symbol of desire and the encounter of the self with the self, a mirror of truth.

Narcissus sees his image in the spring's still waters, and narcissism is immediately split in two. Either Narcissus lets himself slip into the water and perish from the encounter, lost in his own reflection and his own image; or he finds himself, in the marvelous immediacy of the self encountering the self, filled with desire. The miracle is accomplished by the spring's waters, source of vitality. Narcissus overcomes the opposition between subject and object, natural and artificial, immediacy and mediation; in place of autoeroticism, the world opens itself to him in its Dionysian embrace. In love, the mirror of the other (or the other as mirror) reveals more than an image. Space, finite and infinite, nullified and exposed, is the beloved Being.

A transitional, or transactional, object, ambiguity and symbol of ambiguity, does the mirror define, as psychoanalysts after Freud believed, the fundamental relation with reality? If by mirror, we are referring to a localized object, a precise reflection, I would have to say no; that object in which the image is bound very precisely can only play a transitory role. Do we really believe that the infant becomes conscious of itself, of its body, of its unity, in the mirror of its mother? I have already answered this argument and the objections concerning that object. The best mirror, the most faithful, the most favorable, is a tree, a plant, a hill, a space. All of space serves as a mirror, and if space betrays us, who or what will take its place? When those who clumsily manipulate speech ask that things be presented on a human scale, isn't it the mirror of space they are asking for?

That, in order for pleasure to arise, it might be necessary to abolish the relationships among powers, and fantasies of force, so that an absolute immediacy (a distant analog of the initial relationship with the mother) can be restored, and that this should take place in the immediacy of mirror space through the sudden proximity of the self to the self through the other, would justify the line of questioning undertaken here. Mirror space does not comprise only transitional or functional objects; it reflects vitality.

Enjoyment, which includes pleasure, escapes anxiety through imagery and symbolism. The life that presents the divine offering cannot be planned or arranged. It is bound up with encounters, accidents, fantasies. It takes place during the unfolding of imaginary scenarios. Outside space and time, the lightning flash of profoundly pure pleasure abolishes the distance between two intersecting desires, an eternal instant.

Yet there are objections. Suffering too provides an opportunity for imaginary scenarios, for architectural constructions built to provoke anxiety and fantasies of anguish. The garden of Erec (erected? ereken?) reversed the pathway of the cross, a vast, tragic fabrication constructed in spaces in which a multitude of components played a part, a cruel landscape of stones and scrub. The affective investment exposes a political investment: the difficult climb, the steps to Calvary, the painted statues, scenes from the Passion and lines from the Gospels, mottos, extreme fatigue, and at the summit, death and salvation, declared, proclaimed by a luminous chapel, symbol of the church triumphant (a written description found among the stations of the cross on the road to Gata, between Alicante and Valencia). The infinite distance between departure, suffering, and the end, death and redemption, excludes immediacy, the physical proximity of the self to the self, and of the other to the self. Would the reversal of the garden of agony and the pathway of suffering give rise to a scene of enjoyment, realized across an entire landscape, where architecture (in the narrow sense: construction) would be no more than an element? In place of the blood evoked and, sometimes, flowing from the hands and feet of pilgrims, there would be fresh, flowing water and abundant vegetation. Nothing that "signified" sensuality, but fully signifying immediacy.

The places of enjoyment, therefore, would not have pleasure or sensuality as their function (their signified). The functional space of the offer—the discotheque, the bordello, the promenade where the sexes flirt—does not escape the death of pleasure. It executes it. The hell of the places of love, as paradise is sometimes called. The tireless pursuit of dead pleasure is hell. The place of sensuality need not be sensual. It does not replace passion. Is there a space in the places enchanted by passion? Erased in a moment, this space only reappears in memory, colored by the love that found it. What is paradise without love? A rather ordinary place. There can be no love, or passion, or desire in paradise, which is far too perfect. And yet, places perpetuate a desire they did not bring into being; appropriated space cannot give rise to what it assumes it does. Places have no way of giving beings what can only come from themselves, the vitality known as desire. These are not sensual spaces but spaces of disdained love, aphrodisiacal places like the gardens of Armida, Calypso's grotto, Morgan's castle—heartbroken sorceresses because forsaken. I prefer the invincible tower of air in which Merlin the magician was kept under a spell by Viviane his beloved, who would visit him and bring him happiness.

Psychology and Psychoanalysis

The site of enjoyment, if it exists, perpetuates what hostile space can kill, erode, exterminate. It assumes the presence of bodies, makes them available by shedding, like heavy clothing, psychic obstacles from the past, from the memory of other places.

Proust provides a wonderful description of such availability, as modern psychologists recognized with the appearance of *In Search of Lost Time*:

> My walks that morning were all the more delightful because I used to take them after long hours spent over a book. When I was tired of reading, after a whole morning in the house, I would throw my plaid across my shoulders and set out; my body, which in a long spell of enforced immobility had stored up an accumulation of vital energy, was now obliged, like a spinning-top wound and let go, to spend this in every direction.... The wind pulled out sideways the wild grass that grew in the wall, and the chicken's downy feathers, both of which things let themselves float upon the wind's breath to their full extent, with the unresisting submissiveness of light and lifeless matter. The tiled roof cast upon the pond, whose reflections were now clear again in the sunlight, a square of pink marble, the like of which I had never observed before. And seeing upon the water, where it reflected the wall, a pallid smile responding to the smiling sky, I cried aloud in my enthusiasm, brandishing my furled umbrella: "Damn, damn, damn, damn!"[9]

In nature, which is to say, in the body, it is difficult to differentiate the sensory from the sensual. "Immediacy" refers, in fact, to that ambiguous state where initial sensations and perceptions still delight us—the mother's heat and warmth, the space of the womb and its vicinity, the house, if there is one. Analysis destroys this immediacy, space as well, charged with mediations, means (instruments), the intermediary (transitional objects, carriers of messages sent by other objects, directing their intentions toward them).

Sensoriality can be analyzed, but an analysis that, as the one here, claims to be utopian can only continue by developing an effective (practical) analysis. Neither colors nor senses can be determined according to natural laws alone. The initial (immediate) continuum is divided into distinct elements, and those discrete units are given names: the range of sounds and colors together with the names that designate each approximately isolatable unit are derived from social practice. They change with languages and societies. We speak of "culture," but the word adds nothing to our understanding of the initial continuum, undifferentiated and insufficient, or to the study of the analysis conducted through the use of words and techniques relative to the continuum. The theory and history and music, theories of painting, have revealed the prodigious complexity of the classification of senses and colors.

There is nothing simple about the sensory, and nothing elementary about aesthetics, in the simple and strong sense of understanding perceptible data in order to play with and on them. To believe that we are playing with colors by painting a wall demonstrates considerable aesthetic naïveté. A color is an emotion and a judgment, and a choice (a "value").

Once language and manual practice have made a selection (a range), materials and equipment are ready for combination. In this context, the combinatorial logic of elements and units provides the rules, implicit or explicit, for the production of results. However, this logic has its limits. That the continuum can be divided and reassembled in a thousand different ways (and possibly an indefinite number of ways) assigns limits to that logic. It is valid only within a predetermined framework. The invention of a new division, the introduction of new elements, changes the combinatorics. As noted above, it functions by the détournement of the existent, then by introduction and invention (creation) after the moment of détournement-evasion. The same is as true for colors and sounds and their use as it is for being and nature, susceptible to an indefinite number of interpretations and perspectives. The immediacy of the continuum confers upon it a quality and properties: it becomes the spatial support of mediations, interpretations, perspectives.

The sensory field comprises (a) visual sensations, which are themselves three-dimensional (luminous, chromatic, graduated, in other words, determined by the intensity of the lighting, by color and shade, by saturation); (b) auditory sensations, whose complexity does not need to be demonstrated (intensity, level, timbre) so that they alone determine a differential field, that of music; (c) olfactory sensations; (d) gustatory sensations (poorly discernible from olfactory given the ambiguity of the physical); (e) mechanical sensations (touch and pressure, penetration); (f) thermal sensations; (g) kinesthetic sensations (position, resistance and security, opposing or auxiliary forces); (h) static sensations (weight, translation, rotation); and finally, (i) the affects (tickling or caressing, pinching, accompanied by sensory pleasure and pain).

The sensory affects connect the domain of the perceptible senses to the domain of the "sensual" senses. How can we dissociate the two domains? And yet they are separated by a threshold, for, having identified them, art rewrote them in the form of aesthetics. Sensory excitation, or even exaltation, may remain below the threshold of sensuality. Overexcited sensuality can even assume an intellectual appeal that eludes sensuality; it strongly supports aesthetic cerebrality, as shown by almost all of modern art, whose emphasis is on the sensory rather than the sensual, and this includes literature and architecture. Words, lacking in isolatable significations—discrete units—support the perfect asceticism of the intellect. As do spatial forms, angles, straight lines, curves.

An art based on aesthetics, that is, on the sensory-sensual as a whole, reconnects with the unity of what the analytic practice of society has separated. It restores immediacy, freed of any initial confusion, through their mediation in and of space. Immediacy is not situated at the level of sensation. There is no sensation without mediation or activity, and, therefore, no sensation as such, no sensation without appreciation with its implicit judgment. Pure sensation has never existed. Immediacy is found within the bounds of the sensory, within the indiscernible ambiguity of the sensory and the sensual. It is also found beyond it, in the unity of the sensual and the sensory of a space.

But restoring immediacy by placing it on a par with aesthetic sophistication does not imply a return to nature. It would not mean trying to rediscover what had been lost along the way. And here, psychoanalysis provides an important argument: immediacy cannot be completely lost. Disdained, overlooked, sidelined, it persists in the body, in physical ambiguity, from which forms are detached, and where enjoyment is born.

On the level of immediacy, how can pleasure be distinguished from enjoyment? They are separated, but only much later. Pleasure supports mediation; it involves mediation, carries it along with it, which is why it is able to endure, for it possesses subtleties and gradations. Enjoyment, however, is merely a flash, a form of energy that is expended, wasted, destroying itself in the process.

Taste (organic and aesthetic) provides pleasure. Enjoyment requires immediacy, whether conserved or restored. There can be no pleasure without enjoyment, no enjoyment without pleasure. Maintaining this separation results in a paradox, something unsustainable. It is, therefore, space (or a space) that maintains the connection between pleasure and enjoyment: by preparing pleasure, by calibrating it, by enabling it to surround enjoyment, even if enjoyment, in the narrow and absolute sense, has no space. Enjoyment, in the broad sense, gathers pleasure and enjoyment, in the narrow sense, in a space by restoring immediacy (the body).

9

SEMANTICS AND SEMIOLOGY

To begin this chapter, I assume the following statements or propositions to be self-evident. If the reader feels there is something arbitrary about these claims, I encourage him to investigate other sources, whose identity and content I leave it to him to discover.[1]

   a. Language, speech, and discourse occupy a mental time-space and designate a social space, providing it with orientations and situations, by means (mediation) of various representations, primarily through the use of proper names, place names, and so on.
   b. Mental space, the space of thought and language, of reflection and representation, is bound by social space. Beyond the horizon of social space is found the world, the horizon of horizons, the one I will discover if I go as far as I can go along the road of my perceptions.
   c. Discourse that is not directed toward a space is reflected back on itself, becomes self-contradictory, or agrees so closely with itself that it becomes logology, a vicious circle, tautologically coherent. Having lost any reference to "the other," discourse has no reference outside itself. The objective social significations of reference disappear and meaning is lost—along with enjoyment. This does not imply a term-by-term, point-by-point correspondence between social space and mental space, any more than it does between objects and unspoken words (relations).
   d. I propose a moratorium on logology.

Semantics and semiotics (or, if you prefer, linguistics and semiology) study meanings and significations. In principle, semantics, closely associated with linguistics, studies verbal signs, speech and language, discourse.

Semiotics (semiology) studies nonverbal signs—we are all familiar with the simplest forms: highway signs. Having said this, however, we find that the competence of these two fields of research presents certain problems. In principle, architecture is based on semiotics, just as music or heraldry. But what about graphic designs, hieroglyphs, ideograms, writing systems? What about the voice and speech?

There is a strong tendency to equate semiology with semantics, which is considered to be rigorous and which examines formal sign systems, languages. This focus subordinates nonverbal signs (including architecture and monuments) to verbal signs and, therefore, subordinates them to private signs and significations. The opposite focus subordinates the science of signifiers to semiology, which is broader and capable of appealing to whatever escapes the narrow rigor of verbal systems: the unconscious, depth, impulses, and so on. Within the context of this research, what happens to symbols that are endowed with imperceptible meanings: fire, light, streams, trees? Should they be categorized as belonging to nonverbal systems? As archetypes do they escape all formalization? This is an extremely difficult problem to address, for it involves poetry as much as architecture.

I tend to think that there is a radical difference between symbols and signs, as there is between signification and meaning. The reduction of the symbol to the sign goes hand in hand with the reduction of meaning to signification. Monumental works, like works of art, like philosophy, are charged with symbols; they are symbolic because they have meaning, which is to say, values. That a multitude of objects have significations and could even be said to be sign-objects is obvious in the modern world. That meaning has disappeared to the benefit of a superabundance of significations is a less evident truth than that a space as such, rather than the objects occupying it, may have meaning, may continue to have signification. There were—and still are—spaces rich with meaning and beauty (a landscape being one example). There are signifying spaces: a subsidized housing project, for example. There are nonsignifying and, therefore, neutral spaces (an intersection) whose signification may have become obscured (a bank).

I have already shown that a system of signs (and not just words or symbols but sign-things, signifying objects reduced to their actual signification) tends to be formed into a closed system. It should be obvious, then, that architecture does not fall outside this system because the system of signs comes into being with the social system and tends to coincide with it.

By reducing the "real" to this abstract minimum we approach nothingness. The list of reductive powers extends from language and merchandise to money (sign-objects marked for and by exchange), religion, morality, knowledge, and power (knowledge because it elevates the sign to intelligibility; power because it negates the "real" that might resist the State). In short, everything tends toward reductivism. Everything, that is, except the irreducible. Everything prohibits it, except the unspeakable. The irreducible is pleasure and enjoyment combined, undifferentiated, physically given, indestructible, with bodies and their relationships. Space is not the least of these reductive powers. Abstract space, the space of signs, signs in space, and signs of space. Should writing, then, be categorized among these reductive powers, as a space and system of signs? And by this, I am referring to writing in general. As for the writer, he has decided that his only relationship shall be with the self, his words, his language, his speech, his knowledge. All the more reason that his writing will have the opportunity to behave reductively, which does not prevent it from making desperate appeals to the "other," to love, enjoyment, grace, power.

The role of the language sciences, semantics and semiotics (already doubled), is strangely ambiguous. On the one hand, these sciences are forced to turn systems of signification, verbal or nonverbal (objectal), into scientific models. They seek to demonstrate that the "real" can only be known in terms of such a model; consequently, they try to demonstrate the closure of this real, defined by a form—language and its system. They go so far as to reduce language itself to information and formal communication, to a coherent ensemble of operations pertaining to messages, encoding and decoding. The diversity of such codes defines the multiple aspects of the "real," and this "real" is determined according to a handful of operative concepts: information and redundancy, entropy, reading-writing.

On the other hand, some followers claim to have a secret that will free them from the system they promote. Certainly, they are right to want to free themselves. But how would they do this, by what means? They want to situate a within and without of the sign, break the combinations whose necessity they have established, provoke a rupture, trace essential or substantial differences. While they struggle to demonstrate the closure of discourse, they also announce the liberation of the signifier through the destruction of syntax, by a change in the production of signs and significations. Will they succeed? Logology has supplanted egology, the complacent and affirmative description of the "subject." Couldn't it return by a roundabout way? But in that case, the writer assumes he is the subject of a discursive revolution.

Should they accept the system, allow themselves to be locked inside the prison house of signs? They say no and claim that signifying practice will revolutionize language. It will prevent them from being drawn into the initial and final identity put forth by metaphysics, by idealism, by a religious and humanist tradition that has been repudiated. Textual practice alone, with its own laws of expression, would suffice; without reference to anything external, it would have the ability to produce and reproduce signs without conforming to established models. This includes knowledge and discourse about current knowledge, the law and the ability to designate a kind of transcendence of the within, an infrastructure domain, a pre-predicative region accessible to it. In this way, a break would be possible *from within*, a fault, a fissure in the form of an edge, a trace in the form of an inscribed difference. The practice of writing, literature, would traverse the system and release something radically *other*, which would transform that practice and the system along with it. A perfect liberation that would leave room for the wildest, most spontaneous, unspeakable kind of enjoyment or future liberty, for absolute and resolute novelty. *Nonmeaning* would allow us to modify the system of signs as if knowledge, as if discourse were seeking to get to the bottom of things, to an ontology (Heideggerian or Freudian).

The same people who tie the knot of logic around language find themselves the not-so-enchanted prisoners of this glass tower (unlike Merlin in his tower of air, who experienced happiness). They are obsessed with leaving, from the top or the bottom makes no difference, with discovering a fault (an edge), with mapping a difference and finding a reference for discourse other than the self. They don't wish to return to the old values, to lost meanings, to the metaphysics of the original, or to the origins of metaphysics. They hope to explode the system from within by acting to destroy its articulations, by working, through writing, on the signifier,[2] although each attempt at departure or flight results in the creation of signs around which the system is reconstituted, writing absorbing whatever seeks to deny it.[3] The self-criticism that sees itself as a form of adversarial critical theory merely succeeds in revivifying the system by bringing it to fruition. It does so by enabling significations to circulate in an apparently closed space, treating them as a kind of vital fluid.

The death of the old faith in language, a death that followed the death of values (God and "man") brought about the imperialism of the science of language, a totalitarian dictatorship of discourse that captured anyone who attempted to escape it. The attempts detailed above constitute the interior life of the system, without which it too would die, frozen, fixed, turning dizzyingly around itself, a tourniquet, a vicious circle, tautology: logology. Perhaps they "unconsciously" desire another space; that the most systematic among them assume they're the lords of the system is hardly surprising.

Systematic minds with their reciprocal criticisms and self-criticisms (integrating and integrated, co-opting and co-opted) continue to surprise us. They lag behind a dogmatism, are never contemporaneous with themselves. It wasn't so long ago that there were those who felt, who were confident that they were justified in their belief in Christianity, were embedded in Christian morality, surrounded by religious institutions, the church, the commandments, the law, theology, and metaphysics. Then they realized that God was already dead, just when both young and old believed themselves to be its prisoners. This was followed by the secularization of theological-metaphysical truth, existentialism being one example. Twenty-five or thirty years ago, existentialists claimed to be locked inside. Inside what? Why, freedom, of course. A story is told of a young existentialist who, slightly drunk, was found walking around the outskirts of the Luxembourg Gardens in Paris. Just outside the park gates, he grabbed hold of the bars and cried "Let me out! I'm locked in!"

During that same period, economists railed at those who wished to free themselves of economic laws, economic determinants, the system of coherent growth. Systems can be no more than pseudosystems and closures fictions. Whether it's called capitalism or neocapitalism, the capitalist mode of production has never succeeded in becoming coherent, in establishing itself as a totality. It has only pretended to do so, simulating cohesion and a coherent politics. It never overcame the contradictions that arose in historical time, much less those of space. Coherence, cohesion, and logic are not always strategies, sometimes they are simply ideologies. What are we to make of the "system of signs"? Like semiology and the other sciences of language, it replaced history and political economy as dogmatisms inherent in the mind of those who preferred exactitude to subtlety. The system? Merely a series of faults upon faults, fissures upon fissures, failures, deficiencies, collapse. It has been shattered by the irreducible, which leads to subversion, as well as by more or less political forms of revolutionary struggle, violence as well as radical critique. Reductive powers are added, contradict one another, counteract one another, separate.

I want to push my argument as far as it will go. Doesn't everything in contemporary architecture behave as if architectural discourse determined the tactics and strategy of construction through the efficient kindness of developers, advertisers, influential officials, and the tacit (or solicited) consent of "users"? Formerly, symbols and meanings escaped language, the nonverbal did not lead to the verbal, supporting rather than deriving from it. The architectural effect arose from this influence of objects on subjects, inhabitants. Today, it's as if architectural discourse, a signifier stuffed with significations (including the "furnished habitat," lifestyle, etc.) had displaced, replaced, or supplanted the architectural effect of former ages. As in other cases, construction aligned itself with discourse, with verbal signs and discontinuity. Architecture has been reduced to construction, which has been reduced to communication, and space to the commutativity of its elements, exchangeable and interchangeable.

And yet, are there any truly closed systems? Does closure, which is to say, completion, exist other than in the knowledge of those who perfect the system by defining it, and in so doing, mastering, dominating, even appropriating it? The irreducible, as we have seen, is not a zone of knowledge that is inaccessible to ordinary knowledge but can be penetrated through the refinement of our tools or by some circuitous route. It's not a zone of consciousness that is "normally" inaccessible and yet reached through the help of supplementary knowledge. The irreducible is the evidence of *lived experience*, of real life: pleasure and violence rather than discourse about desire or verbal violence. There is no inaccessible depth within discourse, language about language, consciousness about consciousness, the speech that comes before speech, abyss.

There is no first, hidden system within discourse, for the production of discourse, which would be reproduced in the manifest system. There is no determinable nonmeaning based on signifiers and significations, because it determines them. Nor is there pre-predicative thought. With such models, philosophy has shown itself to be near collapse, as demonstrated by the Heideggerian system, which no longer wishes to be a system but remains one all the same. And within discourse there are affects, affectivity. Language, along with thought, like work, like knowledge, is outside it. They distinguish themselves, they separate, from the affective zone, undifferentiated from them but never indifferent or definable by indifference. In this region of affects, pleasure and enjoyment are no longer distinguished, even if they must subsequently part ways. From this zone in which it was born, from which it escapes, the project targets a space. If language and specific activities—work, knowledge—escape it, they no longer have the right to deny their birth, place, and time. If they cease to deny affectivity, if they fail to clear a way forward while illuminating the path, they will be lost in the absurd.

Within, in the existential residue, an irreducible affectivity immediately manifests itself. Beyond lies the *known*, which has recognized lived experience, in other—and better—words, the gay science and the prospect of a space of enjoyment, once logology is overcome. In this space, pleasure and enjoyment meet once again. Or could do so. Yes, this is a utopia, but a concrete utopia. Immediacy is the body in its space. Lived experience has become a work that has no need to express itself in discourse nor to claim it is unspeakable.

Should we work on writing, on signifiers? Should we attribute to literature a redemptive power? Transcend social practice with textual practice? No. What is articulated is not outside the body because the body is composed of members, of segments. And yet, in carnal and physical experience, the units are not separable. The domain of discrete units cannot be distinct from lived experience. Their difference stimulates thought, and consequently, thought does not have the right to deny such difference by setting itself up as a criterion.

Semantics and semiotics hold a respectable but limited place in our general understanding, and in our understanding of space in particular. A proper name, whether first name or family name, is not defined as a term in a nomenclature, an item in a vocabulary whose inventory could be concluded with a bit of [effort]. It maintains relations, is part of a network. What is true of personal names is also true of place names. The unity of the place named doesn't isolate it but, on the contrary, identifies it in the network of roads, paths, movements, dangers, and favorable circumstances.

Semantics and semiotics have emphasized the concepts of message and code, thereby risking an emphasis on communication and the reduction of understanding to information. Proper names, however, are overencoded. An indefinite number of codes, encodings and decodings, information and messages, is attached to them. With respect to this village or this mountain that lies before my eyes, I could identify the site, the climate, the vegetation, the physical composition, the wildlife, the inhabitants, and so on. The number of maps and topologies I could prepare is unlimited, for each network of relations is itself connected to other networks. The knot has a proper name. Examination of the proper name shows no trace of the unfortunately well-known opposition between "nature" and "culture." What it denotes and connotes is simultaneously completely nature and completely culture. Mightn't it be that whatever is associated with a proper name is what provides joy or enjoyment, that retains or unleashes violence?

As noted earlier, this necessary appropriation of space is not sufficient. The naming of places can be traced to the most distant prehistory. Its earliest manifestations can be found in the origins of organized society: hunting, gathering, fishing, herding. If someone were to compare this practical deciphering of space, which begins with place names and the mapping of paths, to forms of writing, we would be forced to acknowledge that it is a very special form of writing, one that considerably predates the specific limitations of the written line.

It could be said that modernity has achieved the zero degree of architecture (by transposing a concept that is highly relevant to literary criticism).[4] Although this is true, it doesn't add much to the critical analysis of abstract space and the disappearance of architectural effect as an effect of meaning. The platitude, the horizontality of writing that focuses on denotations and signifieds, corresponds quite well to functionalism in construction, and the building to the degree zero of monumentality. Writing styles that predate modernity have some relationship with monumental meaning. But the actively reductive nature of the building, of the function of the signified, of the space that contains sign-things, risks becoming obscured by the literary analogy.

The application to architectural space of a semiological concept, the zero degree, does not imply that we could use other concepts, such as "reading-writing." It's true that a monument and an architectural space can be read. But that they can be defined as texts is something else entirely. Neither the concept of reading nor that of writing are appropriate for space, nor is the concept of a code, mainly because practice (social and spatial) is not part of those concepts.

I'll return to the argument given earlier. Those who unthinkingly apply such concepts to space (built or not built, but architectural, like a garden or the countryside around a town) assume that that space contains a message. The message can be decoded. Because it is addressed to people, it can be read. It can be compared to writing. It is based on several more or less common codes, the code of knowledge, the code of historicity, the code of symbolic interpretation (religious, political).

But this theorization reverses practice. In fact, the transmitter is a human being (individual or group, family, inhabitants of a unit, neighborhood, village). Humans continually transmit messages that are not only addressed to the intellect but carry emotions, passions, feelings, and, thus, a welter of surprises and redundancies, arising from multiple codes and overflowing codifications (for example, the code of politeness and its infractions). They emit a bundle of undifferentiated flows that are nearly tantamount to physical ambiguity. As noted earlier, those individuals, those groups, the places where they interact, have proper names. Architectural space refracts their message in the definite form of injunctions, prescriptions, prescribed acts (rather than signs, words, or inscriptions). It sorts through the flows, intensifies those selected, transforms them into rules, assigned gestures. This is a space of practice and a spatial practice. Space decodes people's impulses, if we choose to employ that term; it is not people who decode space.

The countless relations that are established among proper names (persons, places) are characterized by being overencoded. Whenever we move or act, we choose the code that is appropriate at that given moment, based on our intentions and actions. Developed space imposes certain choices; it responds to the radar of every "subject" discerned, who ceaselessly explores the possibilities, availabilities, and incompatibilities (forbidden) of that space.

This notion of overencoding determines and, therefore, limits the application of semiological concepts to space and architecture. Overencoding results from the indefiniteness or indetermination that is attached to defined (finite) operations of encoding and decoding. It is situated on the same level as proper names in the sense that they are used as supports for the appropriation of space.

It is here that art and the artist are found and, therefore, the architect as well in the sense that he is distinct from the engineer, or the developer in the modern world. He has at his disposal a number (undetermined) of codes that can be made use of. They include sensory codes as well as codes for the social relations embodied in the structure. The structure itself is not, however, the objective realization of one or more codes. Polyvalence (more complex than ambivalence) is much more appropriate to the architectural work than the realization of a so-called architectural code. Relationships with users are not coded, however. They escape codification—through scarcity or through excess. But would the art (which helps define but does not exhaust the concept) associated with the structure be that of enjoyment?

Roland Barthes states, with wonderful concision, "The text of pleasure is not necessarily the text that recounts pleasures, the text of bliss is never the text that recounts the kind of bliss afforded literally by an ejaculation."[5] What applies to texts can also be applied to spaces and their texture, mutatis mutandis. In this case, the well-known relation between signifier and signified plays only an indirect role, if it plays any role at all.

For millennia figures of femininity signified fecundity. The Greek statue freed itself of this meaning. Did it then come to signify pleasure? Yes and no. A statue of Aphrodite no longer signifies maternity; neither its belly nor its breasts assert the physiological and social function of reproduction. Nor does the goddess of love "produce" sensuality. The finest statues possess a degree of modesty, surprise, almost evasion. They are available for enjoyment but express this only indirectly. What this signifier signifies is uncertain—uncertain and, therefore, free.

The pseudorevolutionary project to produce language or new signifieds through the release of signifiers, through the destruction of syntax, seems destined for failure. That such a move might inspire literary works is not impossible; that the meaning of those works would be failure appears inevitable. What must change is the paradigm. Paradigmatically, such an approach, based on viewing things in oppositional terms, which has received considerable emphasis, is absolutely inadequate. Take "open/closed" for example. The door has a meaning: it is a "desirable fissure"

(Claudel), "doors open on the sands, doors open on exile" ("Exile" by Saint-John Perse), "cosmos of the gaping cavern" (Bachelard).[6] But the paradigm is quickly exhausted.

To play on the paradigmatic opposition between signs of the body and signs of the nonbody, between absence, abstention, abstinence, on the one hand, and joy and enjoyment, on the other, between real life and the meaning of life, and thus to emphasize one rather than the other, the one that until now has received value and meaning, that is the nature of the project. The project is one of space rather than discourse (writing or speaking). It is contained neither in a cloud nor in a code. It does not even exclude anamorphic progress—even beyond the use of undecodable symbols: water, the tree, fire, and so on—an anamorphic space, peopled with objects, escaping codes and encoded combinations, a created world in contrast to worlds of vision and intellect, to mannerism as well as conventionalism. The innovator of this point of view stated that art simply reproduces the visible, which it makes visible. Klee advanced, somewhat more boldly than the surrealists, toward a space of metamorphoses—beyond the borders of discourse and metaphor—that may yet be seen as a space of enjoyment.

10

ECONOMICS

The meaning of the term "economics" has changed several times in modern scientific terminology. After encompassing the concept of household organization (the meaning of the Greek for "economy"), it came to refer to economic abstinence. In the human sciences, this meaning has recently become broader and more obscure, shedding any contact with politics. Consequently, we need to distinguish the economic in the narrow and strong sense, political economy, from the word in the broad sense. Freud and other psychoanalysts speak of psychic economy, the operation of the conscious-unconscious mind as a whole, which allowed drives to be discharged and recharged, to be expended and a path to be cleared toward their expenditure. Generally speaking, economy refers to the use of resources, regardless of their origin or nature, and the renewal of reserves, the organization of circuits of distribution, and their disappearance through use. In this sense, based on its archaic meaning, we could possibly speak of an economy of enjoyment. Before examining the scope of this signification, let's turn to classical political economy through the critical analysis found in Marx.

In analyzing capital and capitalism, Marx begins by distinguishing the use value of a given object, a consumable good, a product of social labor, from its exchange value. This distinction, which Marx borrowed from earlier economists, the great English writers Adam Smith and David Ricardo, has often been rejected because only partly understood. How can the mode of social existence of an object while it circulates as merchandise be distinguished from its mode of existence when someone uses it? Do things like sugar and coffee exist differently when they are before me, on my table, or when they're on a shelf at the grocer's or stored in a warehouse? While it circulates as merchandise, calculated in terms of money, the product is removed from use and leads an existence that is both abstract (reserved, hidden, appearing in different registers, and stored in enclosed environments) and concrete (the private wealth of an intermediary, a distributor, etc.). Exchange value has only an indirect relationship with the materiality of the thing. What will influence its value and price is the amount of social labor necessary for production and transport, and creditworthy demand, which can also be evaluated in terms of money.

During use, the materiality of the thing (sugar, coffee, fabric) resumes its place. Usage possesses an immediacy—direct contact, that of a need that awaits its moment, with the thing—whereas exchange takes place through various modalities (intermediaries). In the materiality of a thing, there is a relationship with nature, although that nature (wool and fabric, wheat and bread) may have been transformed by labor. By and through use, a fragment of nature has been simultaneously set aside, reserved, and modified, shifted, often made unrecognizable (even more so as ancient custom requires that those who have worked on a thing obliterate all traces of labor from it).

The first unrecognized consequence of this analysis is that nature is the source of use value, the resource of use. This is not a nature that has been interpreted philosophically, considered in ideological terms, morally elevated (or devalued). It is practical nature. It is both a source and a resource of use because it supplies the first model and because usage implies an immediate relationship between the product and the being of nature, notwithstanding its modification by social activity: the body (my body). To make use of an object means to eat it, drink it, wear it, and so on. A second unnoticed consequence is that use value defines social wealth, while exchange value—the sequestration of use, the substitution of money and, therefore, capital for the diversity of things—enriches intermediaries. Socially, it is an illusory wealth. At some point we could imagine a society in possession of an enormous quantity of gold, of stored goods, and various useless products, and dying of hunger and thirst in the midst of this so-called wealth.

Whenever Marx considered this paradoxical possibility, which he used to refute mercantilism, he thought especially of Spain after the second half of the sixteenth century, ruined by the gold it had stolen from the Americas and causing the ruin of Western Europe (through the subsequent increase in prices). He may also have been thinking of England as he knew it: forced to purchase goods above their use value yet having access to enormous exchange reserves. A paradoxical and disturbing situation.

Today, I can easily imagine a country that produces quantities of sophisticated objects but lacks potable water or breathable air or wool or silk or wood or stone, lacks any source of energy and is forced to make use of whatever energy is available to produce water (though in smaller quantities and of lesser quality than formerly obtained from its rivers), air, and light industrially. What was once abundant, having now become scarce, all of nature would have to be reproduced just as it was being exhausted or destroyed. The absurdity of the simple reproduction of a nature destroyed by man is no less irrational than the world Bertrand Russell describes in the Meadows report.[1] Likewise, a head of state, a prince, a king, or an emir could die of hunger or thirst alongside a warehouse filled with gold if, by some miracle, the pathways of exchange, which give gold its power and allow those who have it to control the world, begin to shut down.

Nonetheless, in the modern world, these terms are antinomically (but still virtually) separated: on the one hand use, concrete wealth, enjoyment, and on the other hand abstract wealth and frustration. Enjoyment by means of abstract wealth takes on the appearance of an abstract utopia itself. Although enjoyment through concrete wealth remains utopian, its nature shifts rapidly toward the concrete (practice).

The distinction between exchange value and use value takes place for Marx on a formal level that approximates pure logic. This initial difference reappears throughout his theoretical development, revisited and enriched, for example, when he shows that the capitalist makes use of the worker's labor force, which he has purchased on the labor market. In the enterprise, in order to set the machinery in motion, in order to make use of raw materials and facilities, the capitalist productively consumes both living labor (the labor force) and the inventory of raw materials and tooling. A more familiar concept is derived from the comparison of productive with unproductive consumption. Their unity creates the mode of production and enables it to continue (to reproduce itself). Dialectically, productive consumption also consumes—in particular, it consumes the labor force—while unproductive consumption, by destroying such an enormous mass of objects, maintains the production (and reproduction) of social relations, so-called productive relations.

The most profound level of contradiction is found in the modern world's relation to space. On the one hand, space is given over to consumption, broken up for exchange (buying and selling, exchange implying interchangeable objects). On the other hand, natural space is transformed, modified, developed by technology and new forms of knowledge. The use value of space endures in the face of exchange value because space has value only in relation to a site, a center, or a schedule. The use of space has a number of specific features. Diversity for one. The driver of a car or truck makes use of the road; the hiker makes use of a field or wood or mountain; the athlete makes use of a stadium; the dweller makes use of a building, a house, an apartment, a lodging. What's more, the use of space is unlike other uses in that it cannot be destroyed. Whereas consumption devours everything in its path, clearing the way for other objects, the consumption of space, through use, is very slow. In this sense, space can be compared to luxury goods or art. However, this prevents "users" from knowing that they have access to use value on a practical level. And as users they learn of it only indirectly—without any additional expense but at their own expense—through the discomfort of transport in the area, distance from a center, and so on.

The economic and technical treatment of nature tends to destroy, whereas the treatment of space tends to reduce (to the exchangeable, filled with signs alone). The unity of these two aspects is found in the radical negation whose continuation allows the regime to persist, to reproduce itself: negation of use, of enjoyment, of nature (leaving aside various other aspects: malaise, nihilism, feminism, the death of this or that, etc.). This generalized negativism is concealed by positivism, realism, practicalism, and pragmatism, as well as by a paternal concern for "needs" large and small.

How can the destructive and reductive capability I have described be curtailed? Only a space of enjoyment, which is to say one where use (as opposed to exchange) prevails, responds to this highly relevant question. Only an economy of enjoyment that replaces an exchange economy can end that which kills reality in the name of realism (in truth, cynicism).

This may be utopian, but how else can we describe a project that superimposes subversion on revolution and assumes that all that exists will be completely overturned: all forms of power, political or other, whether systems or not?

However, every time you make use of an object, every time you obtain enjoyment (and not merely satisfaction), every time you find a place genuinely pleasing and enchanting, every time you rediscover, with its native generosity, not exempt from cruelty, some part of the natural world, you enter this utopia. You may say that this doesn't happen very often and that, after all, you're content with your satisfactions and don't feel that commerce and money sully things, that everyday life is moving along quite nicely and that I've assumed a point of view that is sublimated, artistic or aesthetic, outside daily life, your own. But wait a minute! Your disdain for the aesthetics I have tried to contrast with abstract aesthetics is a bit too strong. Are you certain that the succession of your satisfactions and the experience of daily life, as I have described, will allow you to survive if you cannot refresh yourself in a short bath of enjoyment from time to time? There are people who roll from satisfaction to satisfaction; but they soon lose sight of needs themselves, they lose their appetite for things, for anything at all. They grow old prematurely, without maturing. They are marked by the sign of death. It happens that some very proper people, politicians, thinkers, the rich and powerful, carry this mark. I'm not preaching morality or religion. I'm not referring to the mark of sin but the mark of absence: the absence of enjoyment.

This is not a construct of fear, of sublimation. No, nothing is closer than this utopia. It is as close as can possibly be to the living body, for it experiences it without interference. Otherwise, it dies, and this death in no way resembles spiritual or material (physical) death. What is true of the utopia of enjoyment is true for the utopia of nonwork. Nonwork sounds absurd and, yet, automation is a fact, it is underway, it's knocking at the door, a part of the total transformation of the world.

Before leaving economy in the customary sense—accumulation, growth, investment—to envisage an economy of enjoyment, it would be useful to point out some of the contradictions normally manifested (they appear, are discovered, then become known) in this field.

There seems to be an undeniable contradiction between indefinite growth (known as exponential growth ever since the appearance of the reports published by the Club of Rome) and the limits of growth (Meadows group at MIT).

These texts have provided a pretext for an ideological overflow that should not come as a surprise. Fog fills the void. On the one hand, the partisans of growth (which is to say, the majority of politicians speaking on behalf of the interests of the nation-state, on behalf of a dominating class, a fraction of a hegemonic class, a technocratic caste, and so on) have not adhered strongly to models that have fallen into disuse but have maintained the pursuit of growth without regard for the resulting contradictions concerning space, the disappearance of resources, or their distribution (gasoline, for example). They do not see that the assumption of infinite growth, turned into a supreme political truth, has taken on the sinister appearance of political utopia, the most abstract, the deadliest of all. The other clan has declaimed the end of growth, called for zero growth, stated that growth must be replaced with a stagnant equilibrium based on a return to nature and the primacy of the ecological (a natural space). The once exciting ideology of growth is no more than a handsome mask on the face of death, misfortune, and uncertainty.

These rival ideologies overlook analysis and theory. Ours shows how, against the interference of politics and economics, questions can be raised. Resources cannot suddenly disappear, but political factors can lead to the sudden scarcity of some resources. The contradiction between infinite growth and finite resources nonetheless persists. Yet the analysis of productive forces reveals a decisive alteration. These forces have made a qualitative leap. Over and above their growth, an internal difference among these productive forces has begun to appear. Technology and knowledge are making their way toward the production of space.

Growth without development tends to interrupt its exponential curve when joined with development (qualitative). From that point on, growth begins to look like a strategy rather than an economic necessity.

The production of space, yes, but what space? This question, the true question, the right question, the proper expression of the problem, comes to the fore, slowly but surely, in the full light of day. What space? The space that destroys nature, which envisions it without precaution, or the space that addresses all of nature, not merely its resources, but space as a whole, without, however, isolating it in its pure state by restricting nature to reserves and parks?

The struggle can be brought to the enemy's camp in the form of the economics it assumes it has mastered. The calculation of the social cost of destruction (not only usable resources but nature itself, its water, its forests, its pastures) has only just begun. Our familiarity is limited to certain domains, associated with highly visible projects: maps of automobile accidents, the costs of production of a soldier or student, and so on. Several measures proposed by the Meadows report can be used, without necessarily accepting "global equilibrium."

Naturally, nothing prevents us from contemplating the application to space of a soft technology (multiplication of the network of trails and footpaths, in addition to other means of circulation, including walking, bicycling, or traveling in air-cushion vehicles [!] in specific areas, solar heating, etc.). But these approximations, trials, and hesitant advancements do not resolve the essential question: space.

Some on the left claim—and not only in France—that the struggle for space is of no interest to the working class or the masses; that it concerns only an "elite," intellectuals, middle-class aesthetes, who make use of this activity to retain their privileges as recently minted luminaries.

These aftereffects of radical leftism overlook subversion in order to emphasize revolution, which tends toward ideology. Revolution will take place in the factories and only in the workplace. It will be determined by the intervention of classes, initially in the area of economics and then through the politicization of the economic struggle. Class subjectivism marks this theorization, once known as "workerism." It is preserved in certain milieus that believe themselves advanced, or evolved, and is winning over others who think they are part of an avant-garde.

The only objective criterion of the class struggle involves surplus value, which is to say, the objective and driver of the strategic activities of the hegemonic class. The production of surplus value, whether it be partial or perpetual or global, defines class struggle. When partial and temporary, it is economic, demand-oriented; when global, it becomes political—and it does so objectively, not through the intervention of a political group, or parties, or militants.

But the defense of space at a given point results in the formation of surplus value in a sector of capitalism that is gaining in importance (real-estate speculation, construction, urbanization, and land-use planning, in short, the production of space). When generalized, the defense of space—which would not exclude offensive approaches, the development of projects and plans that differ from official plans—would threaten the formation of surplus value in itself.

An economy of enjoyment couldn't be limited to producing the objects we like (who? where?), to investing such objects with feelings and affects, or disposing of them in space so that they might circulate. Some American psychologists have termed this phenomenon "cathexis," referring to a magnification of objects that may modify the decor but does nothing to alter their context.

Such a project differs little from the most banal aestheticism. It supplants the manufacture of trinkets, of art objects. What receives the strongest affective cathexis? Kitsch. Objects on which the drives can fixate, and which we would enjoy, would provide no more than an object-like mechanism, a manipulation of affects through the intermediary of things.

The economy of enjoyment assumes a profound transformation: with use restored to its proper place, space would be constituted on new foundations. This assumes the existence of a space of enjoyment that is unlike any abstract space: the space of growth, which uses bulldozers to raze anything that might resist, passively or actively. In this space, the status of objects can be determined only by their relation to the body and the body's status: to rhythms, to carnal situations.

Demanded, reclaimed by the so-called humanities, this renewed economy was wrong to formulate itself in terms of a given specialized science: psychology or psychoanalysis, primarily, but sociology, history, and ecology as well. The reclamation was localized in a mental, psychic, cultural, and aesthetic space, rather than being directed toward social and, therefore, spatial practice. Yet discourse has the ability to survive in mental space and circulates freely within such a space. As for social space, intervention is much more difficult.

11

ARCHITECTURE

Until now we have surveyed, or explored, architecture in the form of an oneiric landscape. At times it even gave way to larger questions about space, ambiguity, and so on. We need now to take a closer look at architecture and architectural discourse. In doing so, if this analysis uncovers a principle (or principles) of classification for architectural works that is related to enjoyment and the virtual space of enjoyment, the time spent on such a pursuit will not have been in vain. With that end in mind, I turn now to an examination of several architectural works and texts, in roughly chronological order.

Rome. The West has received a great deal from Rome: several languages, its meticulous approach to juridical matters, the law of private property. It is not certain, however, that we have taken from the Romans what was best about them. Pagan Rome has been carefully filtered by Christian Rome, even though the filters have sometimes functioned poorly. In the sixteenth century, for example, they ceased to function completely, a phenomenon not in line with Christian tradition.

Among the Romans, until their long decline, we find a powerful sense of civic involvement that connected individuals to the city. The most important pleasures were experienced within a social framework; in other words, private and public were not yet separated, and the public did not yet have the unpleasant, almost ridiculous, character it has assumed in our society, where the social and socialization are generally met with disapproval.

Who invented the bathroom? When did its use begin to spread? With the bourgeoisie. In the Christian West, the lengthy decline of public baths prepared the way for its adoption. The recent use of private or public pools has only partly corrected this mistake on the part of the West, something Islam has avoided.

Take, for example, the Baths of Diocletian in Rome. This enormous space, covering nearly fifty-seven acres, was a small city in the City of Cities, and surrounded by a vast park. Intended to cultivate the body as well as the mind, the Roman baths are one of the most original architectural creations that history has known. A succession of rooms followed one another along an axis, which served as both hallway and vestibule and which led to a gigantic open-air pool more than half an acre in size. This was followed by a vaulted hall, also surrounded by pools. Around the large pool were palaestrae, gyms, and massage rooms, together with a variety of sporting or domestic paraphernalia for the patrons (client, visitor, consumer—none of the words are suitable). Once they had warmed their muscles, the patrons crossed a series of rooms, the heat increasing as one progressed, to ultimately reach the caldarium. Even today, the buildings themselves appear to be characterized by a degree of luxury next to which our own cultural institutions and stadiums appear to descend from barbarians and puritans, more ascetic than they are subpar. What can we say about the interior? The pool was a marble lake surrounded by colonnades, covered with mosaics in which the statues were reflected. The rooms contained flowing fountains, colonnades, niches decorated with statuary; paintings and mosaics adorned the surfaces of the walls, which were covered with stucco and precious materials (onyx, porphyry, marble, ivory). The baths contained, in addition to the gymnasiums and palaestrae, a number of rooms devoted to physical development, promenades, works of art that turned those rooms into museums, and spaces for permanent exhibitions. There was also a park where visitors could meet and talk, and a public library. No one was excluded from partaking in this luxury (women were admitted on certain days) from the slave to the emperor himself, who had made the baths his personal project and who was not averse to making use of the sumptuous palace he had offered to the people of Rome.

The baths were a space of enjoyment, yes, perhaps the most successful of architectural spaces. There is one reservation, however. While there is nothing sensual about them, they were, in a sense, the place where the body as well as the mind prepared itself for sensuality. And the preparation for sensuality in such a context may already constitute a kind of sensuality. There was nothing erotic in this, of course, but the statues, the paintings, the beauty—didn't they themselves constitute the best preparation, the best way to approach eroticism? The baths remain for us an irreplaceable example of multifunctional architecture—polymorphous and polyvalent.

Gupta art. Here is an art that is devoted to eroticism and sensuality. At least apparently. The "erotic cathedrals" (Octavio Paz) of Khajuraho and Ajanta (the temple caves) were built under the Gupta emperors of the fourth to the sixth centuries.[1] These were collective works with contributions from poets, priests (who indicated which symbols to use), actresses and hetarae (for their familiarity with the human body and all its expressions), and sculptors (who were familiar with anatomy but avoided using it for its own sake, without reference to its meanings and symbols). Erotic scenes play an essential role here; they are symbols of happiness, eternity; they express a primal unity.

Architecture, therefore, has not refrained from displaying the details of female beauty animated by the act of love: the hair, the eyes, the breasts, the slender waist and generous hips, together with all the refinements of jewelry, makeup, mirrors, and diaphanous clothing. Every movement, every gesture expressed passion. The scenic movement of physical love connects it to the symbolism of fertility, to the metaphysical idea of the principle of the world, the fecund unity. The lotus, the tree and the tree goddess, the celestial musician, the Great Mother who is sometimes virgin, sometimes matron, sometimes the mistress of sensuality, sometimes goddess of love are part of the dizzying materialized symphony of enjoyment. The gods, or at least their sculpted images, obeyed a gestural code that corresponded with the cosmic (metaphysical) system: several heads signify omniscience, several arms omnipotence. The yogic position indicates transcendence and the standing position authority. The lotus in the hand of a god represents nature and the period of growth, the shell reflects organized space, and the drum skull belongs to the divinities of cruelty. Vishnu, king of the heavens, seated on the solar eagle Garuda, sleeping on the serpent of eternity Nirantar, is embodied in Rama, the hero, and in Krishna.[2] Is it not correct, then, to claim that we have here an example of an art (architecture) of sensuality?

If there had been, somewhere, a space of sensuality, it isn't here, in the erotic cathedrals, that we should be looking for it. Although the Gupta temples provide a space for representing sensuality, they are absolutely not a frame for it. Intended to elevate the soul through the joy experienced by bodies in contact, they paint that joy but never ask the faithful to engage in such acts in the temple itself, which would be the only way it could become a setting for such sensuality. In fact, these enormous, fantastic temples, often carved into the rock, for all their monumentality suggest neither pleasure nor sensuality. Can we even speak about architecture in this context? Covered by a profusion of stone figures, the Gupta temples often disappear beneath the sculptures that allow us to ignore their very form. But for all that, the temples are a hymn to the love of life in all its forms, to nature, to pleasure: animals, monsters, men and gods and plants all dance a sarabande of joy and love. Erotic, but never obscene, the sculptures help show us the path to love, but a divine love that could be achieved through carnal love. For the Hindus, love was a means of achieving the love of God, it was religion, rite, never gratuitous or profane, which is why I feel they were able to make it a form of art. Because eroticism was a form of prayer, the beings represented wear an expression of ecstasy, an ecstasy that was both physical and spiritual, divine. It was absolute love through the flesh, but an absolute love for God. It's possible that Gupta art, at a certain period, may have reflected a purely profane libertinage, but the temples are silent about this. Animals and humans are all beautiful, more or less stylized but with the same expression of amorous ecstasy on their faces and in the highly spiritualized line of the body, with the exception of the female breast, which is cosmic and round as a sphere. It is love in the broad sense, not merely erotic but a love of life in all its forms, including the love of art. Not only do these characters make love, and in the most varied positions, with the most diverse partners, and all with the same joy, but they dance, play music, and almost never work: the Gupta sculptures portray a culture of the total body. Here, space is limited by the body itself; the space of sensuality is formed directly from the body of the other. The culture of the body is so important in this context because it's the body that constitutes space: the temples are there merely to impart this truth.

Outside the city, architecture serves a different function than it does within. A Palladian residence is situated within the texture of rural space but, most importantly, it occupies that texture differently than an urban mansion. Especially if it were positioned as a visual object, stating from afar, by its facade, the rank and wealth of its owner and the pretensions of his lifestyle. To claim that Palladio built urban palaces in the countryside, detached from their texture and somewhat modified as a result, does not diminish his architectural genius, it merely situates it. Palladio holds a place in a long tradition; among the Romans, architecture was not only directed toward public structures, baths, arenas, theaters, but toward private residences as well (the villa of Lucullus exemplifies this typology).

This distinction between urban and rural architecture, taken as a principle of classification, does not get us very far, however. On the other hand, the architecture of the private residence is susceptible to two distinct modes of existence. Either it results from a plan imposed upon the architectural work, whether monument or building, in which case the architect obeys the urbanist and, through him, the influence of political authority and the lenders, who hold a controlling influence. The so-called urbanistic level (which generally covers influence from above) allows architecture no more than a slender margin of initiative. This is the case for political cities (capitals established to dominate a vast space) and is sometimes true of entire continents (Spanish America); but it's equally true of small towns drawn up according to a preexisting plan (Vitry-le-François, Richelieu, and so on, in France).

Or, architecture—successful architecture—plays a determining role. By expanding, by being perfected, it has exercised a decisive influence over a much broader area—the urban. But this can only occur in cities that have not been subject to a political order and have developed without a preexisting plan, spontaneously. This is true of a large number of Italian cities such as Padua. And it is this that makes them so beautiful and so agreeable. When the distant order—that of the State, that of determinant economic relations—is imposed upon the near order, beauty as well as enjoyment disappear. When the near order is able to come into existence and expand its influence, however, beauty and enjoyment remain possible. For, here, a degree of appropriation takes place (even in the presence of private property), whereas where the distant order prevails domination tends to abolish all forms of appropriation.

During the sixteenth century, the entire West turned from the primacy of the countryside to the city. Formerly, the countryside, agriculture, and landownership were predominant, but now, in the historical cities where organic and spontaneous growth remained a vital force, architecture influenced the overall reality of the city. In Padua, the houses are not built to present uniform facades to the gaze of passersby but to coordinate the succession of vaulted porticos that expand the street for pedestrians. This strictly architectural requirement results in a unity and diversity that is both pleasant and beautiful.

During this period, utopia was doubled. There existed a strictly urban utopia: the thinker conceived of a city in a distant order, political or cosmic. He imposed a plan on the city, often inspired by Plato (*The Critias*, the myth of Atlantis and the people of Atlantis in *The Republic*).[3] There was also a profound architectural utopia, whereby the thinker conceived of a monument or building and an "appropriated" style, and he gave that style and that appropriation to the entire city.

Is this why, during the Renaissance, abstract utopia and concrete utopia had already begun to separate? Abstract utopia was inspired by philosophical and cosmological considerations; it projected a representation of space into the urban core. Even when the image of the city claimed to be egalitarian, space was still one of domination (divine or terrestrial, cosmological or political), cosmic domination being transposed into domination by the ideas of utopian thinkers. To this category belong the utopian constructions of Thomas More and Tommaso Campanella, and Rabelais's Abbey of Thelema. The design of this utopian city is round because the sphere and the circle were still considered to be perfect, cosmic.

Concrete utopia has its point of departure in spatial practice, in the effective appropriation of a dominant space, an opportunity for a space of representation to take shape: that of pleasant habitations associated with definite but still multifunctional structures. We know that to this category belong projects by Filarete (Antonio di Pietro Averlino), Leon Battista Alberti, Leonardo da Vinci, and others. In Leonardo we find a form of purely aesthetic research and can speak of an attempt to define both a space and an architecture of enjoyment. However, because they were already based on a vague functionalism, there was nothing concrete about the majority of these architectural projects.

These considerations lead us to Claude-Nicolas Ledoux. As a concrete utopian, he designed the city as an architect. He defined it thus: "The emerging city, each of whose structures I wish to justify, might be inhabited by men whose reason and self-interest will have some hold over them."[4] And, as a revolutionary, he addressed the people directly: "People, a unity drawing respect from each of its component parts, you will not be forgotten in the construction of art: at an appropriate distance from the cities shall be constructed for you monuments that rival any palace!... There, in the entertainments that will be offered and the festivities you will be part of, you will be able to erase the memory of your pain." Ledoux describes the design of the structure intended for these recreations: "The upper story was covered in the center and overlooked the gardens; there, drinkers seated in cabarets placed on either side left considerable space for dancing." No gaming houses in the center of town, Ledoux asks only for "a building of small proportions, located in the center of a vast field where art might combine the benefits of a rural location, productive orchards, prairies; ... we ask for an empty lot that will be used for tennis, dance halls, chess, backgammon, cards; restaurants, cafés, orchestras ... a gaming house more necessary than a hospice." And the god of inspiration, taking inspiration from the architect, describes his Oikéma, the house of pleasure, this way: "The valley enclosing this structure is filled with seductive enchantments, a gentle breeze caresses the air.... The amorous wave shivers by the shore.... Oh, mobile fiber! You grow excited, the artery accelerates its movements and ruptures the thread that sustains the principle of life. Where am I? The flash of pleasure bursts forth and the empire of pleasure couples these charming grounds to the dawn of desire." Ledoux's philosophy and cosmology fed his architectural discourse, which was considerably different from his projects and their actual realization, which began with the Royal Saltworks at Arc-et-Senans. His plan was to build a workers' city, where salt water could be processed to extract salt. His philosophy is expressed eloquently, even grandiloquently: "Insensate atoms, be grateful to the universal Soul.... The creator spreads his bounty before you. The intellectual world for which he has been made offers you a graduated scale that receives the afflux of beings electrified by the celestial flame.... There stands the architect, surrounded by whirlwinds and clouds with whom he struggles for control of the heavens."[5] We are not far, here, from the Masonic tradition, with a cosmology that is similar to Platonism. But the design of the saltworks is quite concrete. There is a building for the director, others for the workers and the processing of salt, and a pleasure palace in the shape of a phallus, a kind of whorehouse for the workers' recreation.

Fourier. The criticism of the combinatorial logic of the passions, which was quickly entered into the record of questionable scientificity, shouldn't consign Fourier's discoveries to the depths of oblivion, and especially that of a concrete connection between social and affective life and space.

The edifice occupied by a Phalanx does not in any way resemble our constructions, whether of the city or country; and none of our buildings could be used to establish a large Harmony of 1,600 persons—not even a great palace like Versailles nor a great monastery like the Escorial. If, for the purposes of experiment, only an inconsiderable Harmony of 200 or 300 members... is organized, a monastery or a palace (Meudon) could, [although with some difficulty,] be used for it.

The lodgings, plantations, and stables of a Society conducted on the plan of [a] Series [of] groups, must differ vastly from our villages and country towns, which are intended for families having no social connection, and which act in a perverse manner; in place of that [chaos] of little houses which rival each other in filth and ungainliness in our little towns, a Phalanx constructs an edifice for itself which is as regular as the ground permits.[6]

How can we classify architectural works, determine types? How can we periodize architectural history based on those classifications? It's not obvious that accurate periodization would mean the exclusion of all other forms of classification. The multiplicity of classifications, here or elsewhere, is the primordial truth, which relativizes scientific authority.

Inside/outside, external/internal are highly pertinent relations. Coupled with the primacy of one of the terms and their possible synthesis, they can serve as useful criteria. Hegel cataloged them, with some slight modifications. At certain times and in certain places (historical eras, societies, cultures) one has taken precedence over the other. In the East, the exterior as a whole—the world—takes part in the concept of internal space. In the West, starting with the Greeks and Romans, the reverse tends to be true, at least from the point of view of overcoming their opposition. For Hegel, the predominance of the exterior provides architecture with its symbolic character. The edifice, marked by the world, subject to the image of the world, symbolizes it; its practical function is subordinate. The predominance of the internal, on the other hand, makes an edifice independent, subject solely to the laws of harmony, but not incompatible with a practical and social function, nor even with spirituality. This is what characterizes classical architecture.[7] Based on this classification, the erotic cathedrals of India would be classified as symbolic architecture, while the Baths of Diocletian or Caracalla would be considered classical. This would explain the surprising fact that India's erotic cathedrals, laden with sexual symbols, are in no way sensual while the Roman baths are more a space of enjoyment than a space filled with representations of enjoyment.

The proposed contrast is not entirely convincing, however. It is difficult to acknowledge that a Greek or Roman temple has no relation to external space, no symbolic character. The internal space of the Pantheon, for example, is its most important feature, yet the dome represents the cosmos, with the cupola corresponding to the sky.

Here, we need to distinguish between the symbolic and the analogical. Can they be clearly differentiated, however, when they are so often confused, when the symbol is taken to be the analogon (and vice versa), as in the case of the phallus? The symbolic object can differ in endless ways from what it symbolizes and, yet, correspond to it through an encoded magical and mystical connection. Thus, an upright stone symbolizes constancy, force, virility, propriety. It is a part of a whole, which that part reflects or designates. The analogical, on the other hand, reproduces, at least partially or apparently, the principle it claims to represent. It is based on clearly represented similarity. The symbol could be compared with metonymy and the analogy with metaphor. In light of this, the Roman Pantheon can be better understood as a form of analogical architecture than as a form of symbolic architecture.

In deepening this analysis, we discover that the symbolic generally has a relation to magic. An object taken as a symbol of an inaccessible reality (distant or transcendental) possesses the wide range of presuppositions associated with that reality. Through contact and immediacy, contiguity, contamination, and close participation, it communicates them. It purifies or sullies. It makes use of contiguity, syntagmatically. By contrast, the analogy assumes a representation; it functions by simulation, by mimeticism, by remote participation, by reference to a paradigm—which assumes a space, and mediation.

An example borrowed from folklore: there was a time when a barren woman in the south of France would try to heal her sterility either by going out at night and touching an upright stone, a menhir, or a bell clapper (magic by contact with a symbolic and sacred object associated with the cosmic principle of fecundity) or by clothing herself in the skin of a freshly slaughtered goat that had recently calved (magic by analogy).

The woman became pregnant by simulating, by participating, in spite of the death of the animal, in life, in fecundity. We can maintain that a Romanesque church or crypt, tomb, sarcophagus, or the relics contained in it play a central role that relies on the symbolic. The Gothic cathedral—luminous, rising toward the heavens—is analogical. The Romanesque church summarizes the world and its drama: sin and death—ordeals—salvation and redemption. The Gothic church recounts a different drama: the fallen soul suffers, then rises to ascend toward the light.

This would lead us to distinguish between a magical-religious architecture, symbolic in nature, operating within a sacred (absolute) space defined by the contiguity between sacred objects, and an analogical architecture, often narrative and historical, mimetically relating an event, such as a victory (a triumphal arch). The architectural effect would differ entirely depending on whether it was symbolic or analogic.

This distinction can be maintained and it enables the architect to use either the symbolic or the analogic based on distinct codes. However, they cannot be completely dissociated. The discourse of magical ambiguity cannot be duplicated. Only when the analogical is subject to a new paradigm (the body and the nonbody) does it have the right to enter the space of enjoyment on its own. The entry of the symbolic could only be subordinate.

12

CONCLUSIONS (INJUNCTIONS)

Let us retrace the path we have taken. Following an intentionally restrictive approach, a limited investigation focused on architecture expanded into space, the relation between space and nature, between the everyday and the noneveryday, between use and exchange. But the initial question remains. For it is at the architectural level that the space of enjoyment is projected, the space of use and reclaimed immediacy. At this level, social practice does, or does not, resolve its new problematic. Here, the irreducible becomes manifest, expands, imposes itself in turn. The result is that architectural transformation moves apace with other transformations—those of the everyday, of work (or nonwork).

The initial reductive act—dialectical reduction in contrast to reductivism—is justified by its implications. It has helped shift certain concepts, especially the concept of architecture (architectural effect). A null effect, "abolished shell whose resonance remains,"[1] the effect of meaning gives way to the effect of enjoyment. Passing through crisis, a vacuum, a zero degree, the building, the functional, the sign-object.

The other levels (urban space, global space) have not disappeared, nor have their problems been resolved. But they can be clarified through the exploration of concepts: the production of space can be clarified.

The initial suspensive act has taken on meaning during its trajectory. It does not consist in some abstract suspension, a methodological fiction; it is not based on reductivism either, but helps to illuminate it. It has enabled us to undo multiple reductive powers, to elucidate their mode of existence and action. Those powers combine their effects, and their combination is central to their logic and strategy, but it cannot become fully coherent through the elimination of conflicts. Within knowledge, criticism (critical knowledge and the critique of knowledge) disturbs the establishment of a fixed absolute, just as it does inside the State and inside the power structure.

Reductive powers cannot form a system in spite of the fact that they struggle to do so and, within abstract space, their latest instruments have shown how effective it can be. This instrumental space (maintained by technocrats) seeks to be a totalizing space retroactively with respect to the powers that would help to establish it over the course of historical time. If it hasn't succeeded, it's because of contradictions, old and new, the newest being specific to this space.

This initial act of suspension thus assumed a total meaning: antitotalitarian, antisystematic. It suspended whatever undermined it because what undermined it was incapable of complete coherence, of total cohesion, utopically sought by reductive powers.

The irreducible was manifest from the beginning and in this way lost its blind and spontaneous nature, which grew into a vital capacity, a principle for organizing space. The irreducible can be specified, can be named. It bears two inseparable names: enjoyment-violence. Repressed enjoyment, oppressed, refused, reduced, becomes violence. Violence demands enjoyment, becomes enjoyment (cruel, derisive, but powerful). As with the violence of power, the violence that responds to it is sometimes latent, sometimes manifest, and always "real."

The presence of the irreducible, in its expansion (theoretical and virtually practical), transforms knowledge. It frees it of its reductive nature, which binds knowledge to power. It gives to this conceptual development (expansion) an active character: accusatory—not merely critical—a subversive project of an other reality (not unreal or surreal but differently real). In this way, communication (community, communion) between enjoyment and violence is developed on the theoretical plane. Theoretical violence, implementation and accusation, prepares and virtually supplants practical violence while opening a path to enjoyment.

There is no thought without a project, no project without exploration—through the imagination—of a possible, a future. Therefore, there is no plan without utopia. Even the most realistic form of power has its utopia:

to endure. There is no social space without an unequally distributed stock of possibles. Not only is the real not separated from the possible but, in a sense, it is defined by it and, therefore, by a part of utopia. This utopian character has been made evident in the approach taken to space in all its manifestations: dwellings, towns, monuments. Therefore, it does not only belong to dreams, to imaginations of the future, but to all spatiality (even the most realist and utilitarian, such as military architecture). So-called utopian projects, fashionable during certain eras (the Renaissance, the eighteenth century) have merely plucked from the "real" those aspects that are most utopian. They have gathered them together, thereby accentuating their utopian character without producing it.

An opposition is continuously at work between abstract and concrete utopias. This enables us to distinguish utopists from utopians. The analytical difficulty arises from the fact that the abstract excels at assuming and giving the appearance of the concrete. In the sixteenth century, concrete utopia appeared to be an architectural utopia (formed on a practical basis) and abstract utopia manifested itself as an urban utopia (with a cosmological foundation). But the latter was surrounded with ideological justifications, primarily egalitarian, which gave it the appearance of the concrete, whereas architectural utopia appeared to be the dream of specialists. Today, however, abstract utopia relies on technocrats; they are the ones who want to build the perfect city. They concern themselves with the "real": needs, services, transport, the various subsystems of urban reality, and the urban itself as a system. They want to arrange the pieces of a puzzle to create an ideal. Contrast this with concrete utopia, which is negative. It takes as a strategic hypothesis the negation of the everyday, of work, of the exchange economy. It also denies the State and the primacy of the political. It begins with enjoyment and seeks to conceive of a new space, which can only be based on an architectural project.

From where does the concrete character of this negative utopia arise? It comes from considering the total body. Analytical and critical thought (including the critique and self-critique of knowledge) restores the notion of the total body. It refutes the parodies of the total body found in so-called physical culture (gymnastics, sports) or leisure space (tanning as an ideology). It rejects—without necessarily fetishizing an elsewhere, another society, another civilization—the relation of the body to space and to its own space in the West, according to the Western Logos: rigidity, discontinuities, harsh angles, affected attitudes. Critical thought shows how these attitudes are inflicted on the body from childhood, beginning with primary education, above all to instill a sense of social discipline, work discipline, and so on. Critical thought reveals the disintegration of this relation.

Architecture has established "enveloping spaces" to impose and preserve this relation. But revealing it, together with all the associated reductive effects, is not the same as formulating a hedonist philosophy (similar to philosophical hedonism). An entirely different project is involved, one of turning the world upside down and establishing a base that is unlike earlier bases, a foundation unlike earlier foundations. What is being determined, what is at work is a question of direction. But not a direction for "research," rather, a way of orienting life that seeks to change it, practically, socially, poetically. For the body is the source of poetry: poiesis.

At the center of the theory and the possible new practice lies the total body, simultaneously reality and value, in its prodigious and unrevealed complexity. The total body soon reveals its ambiguity, its twofold composition as a body occupying a space and a body producing a space. In other words, a natural body (material, employing its articulated members) and a social body (using abstract forms, primarily language, for its destructive and creative activity). Analysis has discovered other ambiguities and dualities associated with the body, one of which is particularly important, namely, an energetic process (the accumulation and expenditure of energy) and an infrastructural process (receiving and storing information).

A pedagogy of the body would account for these complexities rather than reducing them the way current academic disciplines do. This would be an important part of the revolution of the body that is being prepared in various, more or less subversive, ways. This formation of the body, which would quite consciously connect the conceived to the lived (and conversely), assumes a form of qualitative knowledge still in a state of germination and promise. Rhythmanalysis, for example.

The environment. This pseudoconcept has revealed several contradictions of the modern world related to society and space itself. It is, however, based on a misunderstanding and a fundamental illusion. What is important is what is environed, the body, and not the environment, which risks becoming merely a metaphor (the transposition that would set it aside). An architect who wants to decipher environments or the reader of environing spaces would lose all contact with the conditions of his practice, the production of space, becoming a functionary, a specialist, an expert, at the service of others.

The body, the environment, if we insist on using the term, possesses a bipartite structure. It always comprises the near and the far order, that is, enveloped and enveloping spaces: objects in space occupy a place, which always remains exactly localized. Those objects, relatively close to materiality *(materia prima)* and nature are often stable: a tree, isolated or in a wood, a stone along the roadway or on a mountain, the bed of a river over which water flows.

Enveloping spaces indicate connections and relations among sites; they subordinate them to networks in which the centers of strength with which they are associated bear proper names. These ensembles are both practical and physical; they possess a logistics (a village, a grouping of rooftops, paths leading in and out, electrical cables, and so on).

The environment extends between two poles: matter and abstraction, not nature and culture. Between these two poles countless spaces are interspersed. Each has its own code, but the ensemble itself is not encoded. On either side, at either end, near each pole we find delirium, the nature-object (a gorge, a rock, a river, lightning) or a formal and abstract object, the surreal and the unreal. All degrees, all intermediaries are located in this interval. All the "surroundings." An infinity. The minimal difference in maximal difference and, therefore, an analog spatial texture remote from a verbal text: between a cry and logic. Multiple, countless "niches." Only one thing can be entirely excluded: the enclosed space, like a black box that conceals its workings.

To take the total body and place it at the center implies the introduction of a new paradigm; juxtaposing the signs of the body with the signs of the nonbody is merely a first approximation. To propose a paradigm means proposing something other than an empty form, a syntactic variation within existing encodings; it means [overcoming] infinite difference.

Spirit/matter, ideal/real, reason/unreason, man/nature, nature/culture—such outmoded contrasts are incapable of establishing a new paradigm; they should be replaced by body and nonbody, which implies enjoyment and suffering, or by appropriated and dominated. And these should be considered together.

In this way the conditions of enjoyment can be concretely realized. It follows that architecture will involve a space that is more or less the analog of the total body. Specifically, this means that the architect does not use the body as a model (it cannot be modeled because it is unexplored totality, partly known and partly unknown). He does not seek either to symbolize it or to signify it. Architecture and architectural effect and the production of space do not have enjoyment as their goal—realized mainly by signifying it through symbols—they allow it, lead to it, prepare it. Again, it would be erroneous to hold that enjoyment is the result of architectural effect.

The architect will value the multifunctional and the transfunctional rather than the merely functional. He will cease to fetishize (separately) form, function, and structure as the signifieds of space. In place of the formal, or rather formalist, idea of perfection, the architect will substitute that of incomplete perfection (which is pursued, which is sought in practice) or, preferably, that of perfect incompletion, which discovers a *moment* in life (expectation, presentiment, nostalgia) and provides it with an expression, while making of this moment a principle for the "construction of ambiance" (the work of Constant Nieuwenhuys, for example). It is not through form but content that the architect (similar to the designer in the design process) can influence social practice.

The analog of the total body—the appropriated body, use—these determinants imply the following for architecture and the architect:

a. The possible use of a multiplicity of codes and encodings (the visual being only one of them, or the sensory, or communication in space) without privileging any of them, based on the principle that there is no encoded architectural or spatial effect. Anything that can be inventoried and attached to a referent can be coded and decoded. Materials and equipment are merely one encoding among many others. The same is true of drawings (plans, cross-sections, facades). There is no encoding of the possible, but the architectural "real"—constructed, and appropriated, space—cannot be known without a reservoir of possibles.

Earlier, I was able to define (although not exhaustively) art through over-encoding. In choosing among the largest possible number of codes, a specific number cannot be determined. The greater the architect's familiarity with codes, the greater his ability to choose and manipulate them.

b. This means that the architect does not act on signifieds in general, or a particular signified for that matter, but on signifiers (multiple, open, enjoyment being one signified among others), without, however, "transforming" those signifiers. His concerns and preoccupations lie on either side of such signifiers and signifieds, outside the relation between signifier and signified. His power, limited but real, is important in that he can select the referent (nature, sensoriality, materials). He can even opt for a moral code.

c. This does not mean that the architect considers himself in terms of a sensation-based aesthetics, that is, as an artist. The production of space overcomes older categories separating art from technology, the knowledge of sensation and sensuality. The architect is a producer of space.

d. This means that he acknowledges multiple rhythms and elements (water, earth, fire, air). Whether or not there is a code for these elements remains to be seen. The use of water, for example, needs to be carefully studied, especially given the difference between the East (where water circulates inside inhabited space and is an essential part of its appropriation) and the West (where the dwelling dominates the water, whether river, pond, or lake). The same applies to air, fire, and earth.

e. If someone succeeds in détournement, in turning something from its intended use, he gets closer to creation. But such redirection is not invention.

The space of enjoyment cannot consist of a building, an assembly of rooms, places determined by their functions. It cannot consist of a village, a small town, which have been repurposed to a certain extent. Rather, it will be the countryside or a landscape, a genuine space, one of moments, encounters, friendships, festivals, rest, quiet, joy, exaltation, love, sensuality, as well as understanding, enigma, the unknown, and the known, struggle, play.

Places and instants of moments. Gods like those of antiquity. No signs!

An art of space? A space of art or the arts? Such questions are poorly formulated. To successfully manage the transition from the sensory to the sensual would be a first approach, preferable to those borrowed from art or its history.

Conclusions (Injunctions)

The importance of this threshold, which had become an abyss, has been pointed out throughout this book. The sensory, its intensification, its "exploitation" have all been successfully attempted by art, including architecture (spontaneous or learned). But with the appearance of the threshold, the break, the caesura, everything stopped, and something else appeared: in place of the unreal, the imaginary, the appropriated illusion, was the harsh reality of domination; in place of contemplation and the dream, the harsh law of profit.

To treat all of space as a work that no longer stands in opposition to the product and, therefore, as an activity both productive and creative that subjugates the opposition between work and product would be a better approximation of the central problem. The work is unique, the product repetitive and, therefore, cumulative (repeatable and resulting from separate and cumulative activities).

Works have become background decoration for production and consumable products. But we cannot assume that we can turn every fragment of space, every town, every room into a unique work. We cannot exclude the employment of materials and equipment that have been inventoried, codified, subjected to technical operations. That the repetitive, the product, no longer subjugates the work is the goal. In this way, we make the transition from a reactive to a concrete utopia.

All the problems of art can be newly presented as a function of space.

It can be assumed that, today, all the works of all societies, past and present, can be gathered together. For the entire past? Initially through language and knowledge—history, aesthetics, criticism. This assumes that a colossal operation such as this will be successfully conducted, even if it means moving in reverse. Works occupy space and become words. Words and concepts must now return to space, the space populated with works that have appropriated it.

NOTES

Translator's Note

1. Jacques Lacan, *Écrits*, trans. Bruce Fink (New York: W. W. Norton, 2006), 761. Fink discusses several key Lacanian concepts in his endnotes.
2. "The right to the use and enjoyment of another's property and its profits." See *Merriam-Webster's Dictionary of Law* (Springfield, Mass.: Merriam-Webster, 1996), 519.
3. *Trésor de la langue française*, http://atilf.atilf.fr/. See the entry for *jouir*: "Éprouver de la joie, du plaisir, un état de bien-être physique et moral procuré par quelque chose."
4. "No one can doubt that what we are dealing with here [the translation of a text] is interpretation, and not simply reproduction. A new light falls on the text from the other language and for the reader of it. The requirement that a translation be faithful cannot remove the fundamental gulf between the two languages." Hans-Georg Gadamer, *Truth and Method*, 2nd rev. ed., trans. rev. by Joel Weinsheimer and Donald G. Marshall (New York: Continuum, 1988), 386.
5. Tim B. Rogers, "Henri Lefebvre, Space and Folklore," *Ethnologies* 24, no. 1 (2002): 21–44, available at http://id.erudit.org/: "'the logic of space' (as we study it in the academy), with its apparent significance and coherence, actually conceals the violence inherent to abstraction."

Introduction

1. Jan Potocki, *The Manuscript Found in Saragossa* (London: Viking, 1995 [1847]). I would like to express my gratitude to Mario Gaviria for making the manuscript available to me, his permission to publish it, and our many conversations since 2008. I would also like to thank Nicole Beaurain for her support for this project, our conversations, and access to her photographic archive. My research on Lefebvre's manuscript was supported by a range of institutions. It was initiated at the Swiss Federal Institute of Technology in Zurich (ETH), Faculty of Architecture, Institute of History and Theory of Architecture, continued at the Canadian

Center of Architecture (CCA) in Montreal, and finished at the Manchester Architecture Research Centre (MARC), University of Manchester. Most of this research was carried out by me as the 2011–13 A. W. Mellon Postdoctoral Fellow at the Center for Advanced Study in the Visual Arts (CASVA), National Gallery of Art in Washington, D.C.; CASVA also supported me by covering the costs of the permissions for the publication of the illustrations. Draft versions of this introduction were presented at the aforementioned institutions as well as at Harvard University, Yale University, and University of Paris–Nanterre, and I am grateful to the participants of these lectures and seminars for their feedback. At various stages of my work on this introduction, it was read by Nicholas Adams, Neil Brenner, Thierry De Duve, Caroline Maniaque-Benton, Ákos Moravánszky, Therese O'Malley, and Christian Schmid, whom I would like to thank for their comments. Special thanks goes to Robert Bononno for our exchanges during his work on the translation. I am grateful to Pieter Martin of the University of Minnesota Press for his incessant support of the project, and to Deborah Oosterhouse for the copyediting of the book.

2. Henri Lefebvre, "The Right to the City" [1968], in *Henri Lefebvre: Writings on Cities*, selected, trans., and intro. Eleonore Kofman and Elizabeth Lebas (Oxford: Blackwell, 1996), 63–182; Henri Lefebvre, *The Urban Revolution*, trans. Robert Bononno (Minneapolis: University of Minnesota Press, 2003 [1970]); Henri Lefebvre, *Du rural à l'urbain* (Paris: Anthropos, 1970); Henri Lefebvre, *Espace et politique: Le droit à la ville II* (Paris: Anthropos, 1972); Henri Lefebvre, *La pensée marxiste et la ville* (Paris: Casterman, 1972); Henri Lefebvre, *The Production of Space*, trans. Donald Nicholson-Smith (Oxford: Blackwell, 1991 [1974]); Henri Lefebvre, *De l'État* (Paris: Union générale d'éditions), 4 vols: vol. 1, *L'État dans le monde moderne* (1976); vol. 2, *Théorie marxiste de l'État de Hegel à Mao* (1976); vol. 3, *Le mode de production étatique* (1977); vol. 4, *Les contradictions de l'État moderne: La dialectique et/de l'État* (1978). For complete bibliography of Lefebvre's texts on space and urbanization, see Łukasz Stanek, *Henri Lefebvre on Space: Architecture, Urban Research, and the Production of Theory* (Minneapolis: University of Minnesota Press, 2011).

3. Mario Gaviria, letter to Ernesto Udina, February 5, 1974, archive of Mario Gaviria, Saragossa. The Spanish translation of *Vers une architecture de la jouissance* by Ernesto Udina was delivered to Gaviria in 1974, but never published: Henri Lefebvre, "Hacia una arquitectura del placer," archive of Mario Gaviria, Saragossa.

4. The manuscript was typed by Nicole Beaurain on the basis of Lefebvre's handwritten notes.

5. Henri Lefebvre, *Vers une architecture de la jouissance*, archive of Mario Gaviria, Saragossa, Spain, 214; chap. 12 in this volume.

6. David Harvey, *Social Justice and the City* (Oxford: Basil Blackwell, 1988); David Harvey, *The Urbanization of Capital* (Oxford: Basil Blackwell, 1985);

Edward Soja, *Postmodern Geographies: The Reassertion of Space in Critical Social Theory* (London: Verso, 1989); Edward Soja, *Thirdspace: Journeys to Los Angeles and Other Real-and-Imagined Places* (Oxford: Blackwell, 1996); Rémi Hess, *Henri Lefebvre et l'aventure du siècle* (Paris: Métailié, 1988); Rob Shields, *Lefebvre, Love and Struggle: Spatial Dialectics* (London: Routledge, 1996); Stuart Elden, *Understanding Henri Lefebvre: Theory and the Possible* (London: Continuum, 2004); Christian Schmid, *Stadt, Raum und Gesellschaft: Henri Lefebvre und die Theorie der Produktion des Raumes* (Stuttgart: Steiner, 2005); Andy Merrifield, *Henri Lefebvre: A Critical Introduction* (London: Routledge, 2006); Neil Brenner and Stuart Elden, "Introduction. State, Space, World: Lefebvre and the Survival of Capitalism," in Henri Lefebvre, *State, Space, World: Selected Essays*, ed. Neil Brenner and Stuart Elden (Minneapolis: University of Minnesota Press, 2009), 1–48; Laurent Devisme, *Actualité de la pensée d'Henri Lefebvre à propos de l'urbain: La question de la centralité* (Tours: Maison des sciences de la ville, 1998); Chris Butler, *Henri Lefebvre: Spatial Politics, Everyday Life and the Right to the City* (New York: Routledge, 2012). For discussion and bibliography of Lefebvre's reception, see Stanek, *Henri Lefebvre on Space*.

7. Margaret Crawford, "Introduction," in *Everyday Urbanism*, ed. John Chase, Margaret Crawford, and John Kaliski (New York: Monacelli Press, 1999), 8–15; Mary McLeod, "Everyday and 'Other' Spaces," in *Gender Space Architecture: An Interdisciplinary Introduction*, ed. Jane Rendell, Barbara Penner, and Iain Borden (London: Spon, 2000), 182–202; Mary McLeod, "Henri Lefebvre's Critique of Everyday Life: An Introduction," in *Architecture of the Everyday*, ed. Steven Harris and Deborah Berke (New York: Princeton Architectural Press, 1997), 9–29; Iain Borden, *Skateboarding, Space and the City: Architecture and the Body* (Oxford: Berg, 2001); Iain Borden et al., eds., *Strangely Familiar: Narratives of Architecture in the City* (London: Routledge, 1996); Dell Upton, "Architecture in Everyday Life," *New Literary History* 33, no. 4 (2002): 707–23; Sarah Wigglesworth and Jeremy Till, "The Everyday and Architecture," *Architectural Design* 68, nos. 7/8 (1998): 7–9.

8. Eve Blau, *The Architecture of Red Vienna, 1919–1934* (Cambridge, Mass.: MIT Press, 1999); Nancy Stieber, "Space, Time, and Architectural History," in *Rethinking Architectural Historiography*, ed. Dana Arnold, Elvan Altan Ergut, and Belgin Turan Özkaya (London: Routledge, 2006), 171–82; Łukasz Stanek, "Simulation or Hospitality: Beyond the Crisis of Representation in Nowa Huta," in *Visual and Material Performances in the City*, ed. Lars Frers and Lars Meier (Aldershot, England: Ashgate, 2007), 135–53.

9. McLeod, "Everyday and 'Other' Spaces," 189.

10. Borden, *Skateboarding, Space and the City*, 1, 12.

11. Lefebvre, "Hacia una arquitectura del placer," 1; chap. 1 in this volume; Lefebvre, *Vers une architecture de la jouissance*, 32; chap. 2 in this volume.

12. Henri Lefebvre, *Critique of Everyday Life*, vol. 1, *Introduction*, trans. John Moore (New York: Verso, 2008 [1947]); Henri Lefebvre, *Critique of Everyday*

Life, vol. 2, *Foundations for a Sociology of the Everyday*, trans. John Moore (New York: Verso, 2002 [1961]); Henri Lefebvre, *Critique of Everyday Life*, vol. 3, *From Modernity to Modernism (Towards a Metaphilosophy of Daily Life)*, trans. Gregory Elliott (New York: Verso, 2006 [1981]); Antoine Haumont, Nicole Haumont, Henri Raymond, and Marie-Geneviève Raymond, *L'habitat pavillonnaire* (Paris: Centre de Recherche d'Urbanisme, 1966); Nicole Haumont, *Les pavillonnaires: Étude psycho-sociologique d'un mode d'habitat* (Paris: Centre de Recherche d'Urbanisme, 1966); Marie-Geneviève Raymond, *La politique pavillonnaire* (Paris: Centre de Recherche d'Urbanisme, 1966). For other works of the ISU and their discussion, see Stanek, *Henri Lefebvre on Space*.

13. For bibliography and discussion, see Stanek, *Henri Lefebvre on Space*, chap. 1.

14. Lefebvre, *Vers une architecture de la jouissance*, 36; chap. 2 in this volume.

15. Alain de Botton, *The Architecture of Happiness* (New York: Pantheon Books, 2006); Friedrich Nietzsche, *The Gay Science* (New York: Barnes & Noble, 2008 [1882]).

16. Lefebvre, *Production of Space*, 58.

17. Lefebvre, *Urban Revolution*, 160; for the development of arguments about the "second" or "secondary" circuit of capital, see David Harvey, "The Urban Process under Capitalism: A Framework for Analysis," *International Journal of Urban and Regional Research* 3, nos. 1–4 (March–December 1978): 101–31.

18. Lefebvre, *Production of Space*, 353, 385.

19. Telephone interview with Mario Gaviria, March 2012.

20. José Miguel Iribas, "Touristic Urbanism," in *Costa Iberica: Upbeat to the Leisure City*, ed. MVRDV (Barcelona: Actar, 1998), 108.

21. Jacques Rancière, *Proletarian Nights: The Workers' Dream in Nineteenth-Century France* (London: Verso, 2012 [1981]); Jacques Rancière, "Good Times or Pleasure at the Barriers," in *Voices of the People*, ed. Adrian Rifkin and Roger Thomas (New York: Routledge & Kegan Paul, 1988), 45–94.

22. Herbert Marcuse, "On Hedonism," in *Negations: Essays in Critical Theory* (London: Mayflybooks, 2009), 119–49.

23. Walter Benjamin, *The Arcades Project*, trans. Howard Eiland and Kevin McLaughlin (Cambridge, Mass.: Belknap Press, 1999); Christina Kiaer, "Rodchenko in Paris," *October* 75 (1996): 3–35; Werner Sombart, *Luxury and Capitalism*, trans. W. R. Dittmar (Ann Arbor: University of Michigan Press, 1967 [1913]).

24. David Crowley and Susan E. Reid, eds., *Pleasures in Socialism: Leisure and Luxury in the Eastern Bloc* (Evanston, Ill.: Northwestern University Press, 2010); Łukasz Stanek, ed., *Team 10 East: Revisionist Architecture in Real Existing Modernism* (Museum of Modern Art in Warsaw/distributed by University of Chicago Press, forthcoming in 2014).

25. Václav Havel, "The Power of the Powerless," in Vaclav Havel et al., *The Power of the Powerless: Citizens Against the State in Central-Eastern Europe* (Armonk, N.Y.: M. E. Sharpe, 1985), 38.

26. Paul Lafargue, *The Right to Be Lazy* (Chicago: C. H. Kerr, 1975 [1880]); Pierre Naville, *Le nouveau Leviathan*, vol. 1, *De l'aliénation à la jouissance: La genèse de la sociologie du travail chez Marx et Engels* (Paris: Anthropos, 1967), 489.

27. L'Internationale situationniste, *De la misère en milieu étudiant considérée sous ses aspects économique, politique, psychologique, sexuel et notamment intellectuel et de quelques moyens pour y remédier* (Paris: C. Bernard, 1967).

28. "V.L.R.: Peut-on être heureux à la Courneuve?," *Actuel* 7 (April 1971): 4–7.

29. "Henri Lefebvre," *Actuel* 26 (December 1972): 7–8; see also "Henri Lefebvre sur la guérilla urbaine," *Actuel* 7 (April 1971): 10–11; Henri Lefebvre, "La dictature de l'oeil et du phallus," *Actuel* 18 (March 1972): 48–53.

30. Jean-Francois Bizot, "Les villes brûleront," *Actuel* 18 (March 1972): 2–11; "Avant-Après," *Actuel* 12 (September 1971): 40–41; for a discussion of the journal *Actuel* in relationship to architecture in France, see Caroline Maniaque-Benton, *French Encounters with the American Counterculture, 1960–1980* (Burlington, Vt.: Ashgate, 2011).

31. The seminar took place at the Centro de Enseñanza e Investigación, Sociedad Anónima (CEISA); see Mario Gaviria, "La ampliación del barrio de la Concepción," *Arquitectura* 92 (1966): 1–41; Mario Gaviria, *Gran San Blas: Análisis socio-urbanístico de un barrio nuevo español* (Madrid: Revista Arquitectura, 1968). In his paper "Les nouveaux quartiers périphériques des grandes villes espagnoles" (*L'architecture d'aujourd'hui* 149 [1970]: 17–21) Gaviria announced the publication of the Fuencarral study, but this publication was not carried out and both existing copies of the study were lost (telephone interview with Mario Gaviria, August 2012). For a discussion, see Charlotte Vorms, "Les sciences sociales espagnoles et la ville contemporaine," in *Sortir du labyrinthe: Études d'histoire contemporaine de l'Espagne*, ed. Xavier Huetz de Lemps and Jean-Philippe Luis (Madrid: Casa de Velázquez, 2012), 457; Victoriano Sanz Gutiérrez, *El proyecto urbano en España: Génesis y desarrollo de un urbanismo de los arquitectos* (Sevilla: Universidad de Sevilla, 2006), 75.

32. Gaviria, "La ampliación del barrio de la Concepción," 28–32; Gaviria, "Les nouveaux quartiers périphériques," 20.

33. Henri Lefebvre, "Intervention au séminaire de sociologie de Madrid" [1968], in Lefebvre, *Du rural à l'urbain*, 235–40. Gaviria was instrumental for the Spanish translation of *The Right to the City* (1968) and of *Du rural à l'urbain* (1970); see Céline Vaz, "'Les Pyrénées séparent et relient la France et l'Espagne': Henri Lefebvre et la question urbaine espagnole à la fin du franquisme," *L'homme et la société* 185–86 (2012): 83–103. In the wake of 1968, Lefebvre gathered a large audience in Spain. The symposium in Burgos (September 1970) organized by José Vidal-Beneyto and Mario Gaviria, which focused on Lefebvre's ideas about the city, language, and everyday life, gathered more than 120 intellectuals, including several architects such as Ricardo Bofill, Juan Antonio Solans, Manuel de Solà-Morales, and Óscar Tusquets (see Eduardo G. Rico, "Henri Lefebvre: Symposio

en Burgos," *Triunfo* 433, September 19, 1970). Lefebvre's exchanges with Spanish architects included the collaboration with Bofill on the "City in Space" project (Stanek, *Henri Lefebvre on Space*, chap. 4) and his exchanges with the "Laboratory of Urbanism" at the architecture school of Barcelona (Vorms "Les sciences sociales espagnoles," 457; e-mail exchange with Manuel de Solà-Morales, November 2011). Other architects close to Lefebvre in Spain at that time included Fernando Roch and Ramón López de Lucio. Discussions with sociologists were another important conduit for Lefebvre's presence in Spain, including the 1974 international symposium of urban sociology in Barcelona, with Lefebvre's assistant and PhD student Jean Baudrillard and Manuel Castells, his colleague at Nanterre, present (Henri Lefebvre, "La production del espacio," *Papers: Revista de sociologia* 3 [1974]: 219–29). These exchanges resulted in papers circulating in academic networks, but also interviews and polemics in broadly accessible press ("15 preguntas a Lefebvre," *Triunfo* 341, December 14, 1968).

34. Gaviria, "Les nouveaux quartiers périphériques," 18; see Lefebvre, *Urban Revolution*, chap. 1.

35. Mario Gaviria, interview for "Profils perdus: Henri Lefebvre [2]," France Culture, March 10, 1994, Inathèque de France, Paris.

36. Gaviria, *Gran San Blas*, 2.

37. Mario Gaviria, "Prólogo," in Henri Lefebvre, *El derecho a la ciudad* (Barcelona: Península, 1969), 10.

38. Gaviria, "Les nouveaux quartiers périphériques," 20.

39. Henri Lefebvre, "Les nouveaux ensembles urbains (un cas concret: Lacq-Mourenx et les problèmes urbains de la nouvelle classe ouvrière)" [1960], in Lefebvre, *Du rural à l'urbain*, 122; Stanek, *Henri Lefebvre on Space*, chap. 2.

40. Interview with Mario Gaviria, Saragossa, September 2008; Iribas, "Touristic Urbanism." Gaviria contradicts the statements repeated on the Spanish Internet that "according to Henri Lefebvre Benidorm is the best city built since the Second World War"; see, e.g., http://www.hosbec.com.

41. Mario Gaviria, "Dos proyectos de investigación," in *Campo, urbe y espacio del ocio*, ed. Mario Gaviria (Madrid: Siglo Veintiuno de España Editores, 1971), 183–84; Mario Gaviria, "Urbanismo del ocio," in Gaviria, *Campo, urbe y espacio del ocio*, 141, 143.

42. For Lefebvre's comments about Dumazedier, see his "Besoins profonds, besoins nouveaux de la civilisation urbaine" [1967], in Lefebvre, *Du rural à l'urbain*, 199.

43. Joffre Dumazedier, *Vers une civilisation du loisir?* (Paris: Éditions du Seuil, 1962).

44. Joffre Dumazedier and Maurice Imbert, *Espace et loisir dans la société française d'hier et de demain* (Paris: Centre de recherche d'urbanisme, 1967).

45. See *L'architecture d'aujourd'hui* 147 (1969–70), 162 (1972), 175 (1974).

46. *L'architecture et les loisirs: Documents du congrès / XIème Congrès mondial*

de l'*Union internationale des architectes*, *Varna*, *September 1972* (Sofia: Section nationale bulgare de l'UIA, 1975); see also *L'UIA, 1948–1998* (Paris: Epure, 1998).

47. Joffre Dumazedier, "Logement et loisir en 1985," *Cahiers du Centre paritaire du logement*, December 1964/January 1965, 14–17; Jacques Lucan, *France, architecture 1965–1988* (Paris: Electa "Moniteur," 1989).

48. Dumazedier, "Logement et loisir en 1985."

49. Antoine Haumont and Henri Raymond, *Les équipements sportifs dans la région parisienne* (Paris: Institut de sociologie urbaine, 1968); Henri Raymond, *Espace urbain et équipements socio-culturels* (Paris: Copédith, 1976); A. Y. Solinas "Essai d'organisation touristique à Castel Sardo [Sardaigne], Italie" (master's thesis, Institut d'urbanisme de l'Université de Paris, 1967); Robert Cattiau, "Histoire générale des festivals et essai d'une phénoménologie des festivals français" (master's thesis, Institut d'urbanisme de l'Université de Paris, 1967); see also Agnès Villadary, *Fête et vie quotidienne* (Paris: Éditions ouvrières, 1968).

50. Lefebvre, *Production of Space*, 58; see also Stefan Kipfer and Kanishka Goonewardena, "Henri Lefebvre and 'Colonization': From Reinterpretation to Research," in the forthcoming volume edited by Ákos Moravánszky, Christian Schmid, and Łukasz Stanek (Aldershot, England: Ashgate).

51. "Adjudicación de los programas de la Fundación Juan March," *A. B. C.*, March 8, 1972, 51; Mario Gaviria, *España a go-go: Turismo chárter y neocolonialismo del espacio* (Madrid: Ediciones Turner, 1974); Mario Gaviria, *El Turismo de playa en España: Chequeo a 16 ciudades nuevas del ocio* (Madrid: Editorial Cuadernos para el Diálogo, 1975); see also Mario Gaviria, *El escándalo de la "Court Line" (Bancarrota del turismo español)* (Madrid: Editorial Cuadernos para el Diálogo, 1975); Mario Gaviria, "La producción neocolonialista del espacio," *Papers: Revista de sociología* 3 (1974): 201–17. See also the video "Entretien avec Mario Gaviria, par Łukasz Stanek, Zaragoza, 2 février 2013," on http://www.henrilefebvre.org.

52. Eugenia Afinoguénova and Jaume Martí-Olivella, "A Nation Under Tourist's Eyes: Tourism and Identity Discourses in Spain," in *Spain Is (Still) Different: Tourism and Discourse in Spanish Identity*, ed. Eugenia Afinoguénova and Jaume Martí-Olivella (Lanham, Md.: Lexington Books, 2008), xix.

53. Henri Lefebvre, introduction to *Libro negro sobre la autopista de la Costa Blanca*, ed. Mario Gaviria (Valencia: Editorial Cosmos, 1973), xiii–xiv.

54. Lefebvre, *Production of Space*, chaps. 4–6; Gaviria, "La producción neocolonialista del espacio," 202–4.

55. Henri Raymond, "Le littoral et l'usager: De la mer considérée comme monument historique. Interview de Henri Raymond, sociologue," *L'architecture d'aujourd'hui* 175 (1974): 28–30.

56. Lefebvre, *Production of Space*, 385.

57. Donella H. Meadows et al., *The Limits to Growth: A Report for the Club of Rome's Project on the Predicament of Mankind* (New York: Universe Books, 1972).

58. Pierre Guilbaud, Henri Lefebvre, and Serge Renaudie, "International Competition for the New Belgrade Urban Structure Improvement" [1981], in *Autogestion, or Henri Lefebvre in New Belgrade*, ed. Sabine Bitter and Helmut Weber (Berlin: Sternberg Press, 2009), 1.

59. Lefebvre, *Production of Space*, 58; Lefebvre, *Urban Revolution*, 97; see also Manuel Vázquez Montalbán, "La especulacion del paisaje," *Construcción, arquitectura, urbanismo* 1 (1970): 25, and Manuel Vázquez Montalbán, "Los ritos de la fiesta o los estuches transparentes," *Construcción, arquitectura, urbanismo* 4 (1970): 47–49.

60. Antonio García Tabuenca, Mario Gaviria, and Patxi Tuñón, *El espacio de la fiesta y la subversión: Análisis socioeconómico del Casco Viejo de Pamplona* (Donostia, Spain: Lur, 1979).

61. See Françoise Choay, *L'urbanisme, utopies et réalités: Une anthologie* (Paris: Éditions du Seuil, 1965).

62. Benjamin, *Arcades Project*; Susan Buck-Morss, *The Dialectics of Seeing: Walter Benjamin and the "Arcades Project"* (Cambridge, Mass.: MIT Press, 1989); see also Benjamin's comments about Ibiza written during his prolonged stay on this Balearic island in 1932 and 1933: Walter Benjamin "Spain, 1932," in *Selected Writings*, vol. 2, *1927–1934*, ed. Michael W. Jennings et al. (Cambridge, Mass.: Belknap Press, 1999), 638–52.

63. Lefebvre, *Production of Space*, 384; Lefebvre, *Vers une architecture de la jouissance*, 53–58; chap. 3 in this volume; Jean-Antheleme Brillat-Savarin, *Brillat-Savarin's Physiologie du goût: A Handbook of Gastronomy* (London: Nimmo & Bain, 1884 [1825]).

64. Henri Lefebvre, "Autour de deux dates 1937–1957," in *Paris–Paris 1937–1957* (Paris: Centre Georges Pompidou, 1981), 404; Lefebvre, *Vers une architecture de la jouissance*, 69–70; chap. 3 in this volume.

65. Jérôme-Pierre Gilland quoted in Rancière, *Proletarian Nights*, 3; Lefebvre, "Les nouveaux ensembles urbains."

66. Lefebvre, "Hacia una arquitectura del placer," 1; chap. 1 in this volume.

67. Lefebvre, "Les nouveaux ensembles urbains," 119.

68. Ibid.

69. Henri Lefebvre, "Utopie expérimentale: Pour un nouvel urbanisme" [1961], in Lefebvre, *Du rural à l'urbain*, 133. For the illustrations and discussions of these two projects, see Stanek, *Henri Lefebvre on Space*; see also Henri Lefebvre, "Bistrot-club: Noyau de vie sociale" [1962], in Lefebvre, *Du rural à l'urbain*, 141–43; Henri Lefebvre, "Propositions pour un nouvel urbanisme" [1967], in Lefebvre, *Du rural à l'urbain*, 183–95; Henri Lefebvre, "Thèses sur la ville, l'urbain et l'urbanisme," in "Spécial Mai 68," supplement to *AMC* 7 (1968): 3–7.

70. Lefebvre, *Production of Space*, 26.

71. See August Schmarsow, "The Essence of Architectural Creation," in *Empathy, Form and Space: Problems in German Aesthetics (1873–1893)*, ed. Harry

Mallgrave and Eleftherios Ikonomou (Santa Monica: Getty Center for the History of Art, 1994), 288–89.

72. See, for example, the catalog of the exhibition "50 Years of Bauhaus" prepared by the Württembergischer Kunstverein, *Bauhaus, 1919–1969: Musée national d'art moderne, Musée d'art modern de la ville de Paris, 2 avril–22 juin 1969* (Paris: Les Musées, 1969). In *The Urban Revolution* (193) Lefebvre refers to this exhibition shown in Paris among other cities, which, as a contemporary critic noted, distorted the view on Bauhaus by omitting its internationalism, its interdisciplinarity, its social program, and its political orientation (Jean-Pierre Cousin, "Quel Bauhaus? Apropos d'une exposition," *L'architecture d'aujourd'hui* 143 [1969]: lxvi).

73. Ákos Moravánszky, ed., *Architekturtheorie im 20. Jahrhundert: eine kritische Anthologie* (Vienna: Springer, 2003); Adrian Forty, *Words and Buildings: A Vocabulary of Modern Architecture* (New York: Thames & Hudson, 2000).

74. Stanek, *Henri Lefebvre on Space*, chap. 3.

75. Gail Day, *Dialectical Passions: Negation in Postwar Art Theory* (New York: Columbia University Press, 2011), 70–131.

76. Lefebvre, *Urban Revolution*, 99; Walter Gropius, *Apollon dans la démocratie* (Brussels: La Connaissance; Paris: Weber, 1969 [1968]), 159.

77. Bruno Zevi, *Architecture as Space: How to Look at Architecture* (New York: Horizon Press, 1974); Christian Norberg-Schulz, *Existence, Space, and Architecture* (London: Studio Vista, 1971).

78. Léonie Sturge-Moore, ed., *Architecture et sciences sociales: Séminaire annuel, 22–26 juin, 1972, Port Grimaud* (Paris: Centre de recherche sur l'habitat, 1972), 18; Lefebvre, *Production of Space*, 104.

79. Bernard Tschumi, "The Architectural Paradox," in *Architecture and Disjunction* (Cambridge, Mass.: MIT Press, 1996), 32.

80. Łukasz Stanek, "Architecture as Space, Again? Notes on the 'Spatial Turn,'" *Spéciale'Z (École Spéciale d'Architecture à Paris)* 4 (2012): 48–53.

81. See the comments by Pierre Riboulet during the debate "Architecture et politique," *L'architecture d'aujourd'hui* 144 (1969): 9–13; for the general context, see Jean-Louis Violeau, *Les architectes et mai 68* (Paris: Éditions Recherches, 2005).

82. Pierre Riboulet, "Éléments pour une critique de l'architecture," *Espaces et sociétés* 1 (1970): 37.

83. Manfredo Tafuri, *Theories and History of Architecture* (New York: Harper and Row, 1980), iii.

84. Lefebvre, *Vers une architecture de la jouissance*, 4; chap. 1 in this volume; see also Lefebvre, *Vers une architecture de la jouissance*, 206–8; chap. 11 in this volume; Henri Lefebvre, "Espace architectural, espace urbain," in *Architectures en France: Modernité/Postmodernité* (Paris: Centre Georges Pompidou, 1981), 40–46.

85. "L'urbanisme aujourd'hui: Mythes et réalités. Débat entre Henri Lefebvre, Jean Balladur et Michel Ecochard," *Cahiers du Centre d'études socialistes* 72–73 (1967): 7.

86. Lefebvre, "Hacia una arquitectura del placer," 1; chap. 1 in this volume; see also Lefebvre's preface to Haumont et al., L'habitat pavillonnaire, 23.

87. Lefebvre, preface to Haumont et al., L'habitat pavillonnaire.

88. This opposition comes back to Ernst Bloch, based on the Hegelian understanding of "abstract" as impoverished, one-sided, and isolated, and "concrete" as embedded in the world of related and interacting things; see Ernst Bloch, *The Principle of Hope* (Cambridge, Mass.: MIT Press, 1986 [1954–59]); Stanek, *Henri Lefebvre on Space*, chaps. 3 and 4.

89. Lefebvre, *Vers une architecture de la jouissance*, 217; chap. 12 in this volume.

90. Henri Lefebvre in "Fables pour le futur," France 2, June 19, 1970, Inathèque de France, Paris.

91. Lefebvre, *Vers une architecture de la jouissance*, 217; chap. 12 in this volume.

92. See *Paris Match*, nos. 951 and 952 (1967).

93. Lefebvre, *Vers une architecture de la jouissance*, 217; chap. 12 in this volume.

94. Lefebvre uses such expressions as "mettre en suspense par un acte de pensée" and "mettre en parenthèses"; see Lefebvre, *Vers une architecture de la jouissance*, 77, 4.

95. Lefebvre, *Vers une architecture de la jouissance*, 3; chap. 1 in this volume; cf. Lefebvre, *Vers une architecture de la jouissance*, 35–36; chap. 2 in this volume.

96. Lefebvre, *Vers une architecture de la jouissance*, 82; chap. 4 in this volume.

97. Léonie Sturge-Moore "Architecture et sciences sociales," 4; see Lefebvre, *Critique of Everyday Life*, vols 1–3.

98. Lefebvre, *Vers une architecture de la jouissance*, 36; chap. 2 in this volume.

99. On "counterprojects," see Lefebvre, *Production of Space*, 381–83.

100. These postulates were among the reasons leading to Lefebvre's expulsion from the PCF, a process that can be reconstructed on the basis of the PCF archives. First, Lefebvre's travel to Yugoslavia while disobeying the contrary recommendation of the Party (1956) resulted in his public denunciation by Maurice Thorez, the general secretary of the PCF (see note by Victor Michaut, December 12, 1956, dossier Commission Centrale de Contrôle Politique [CCCP], 261 J 6/9, Seine-Saint-Denis, Archives Départementales; "Réunion du Comité central du PCF, 14/15 février 1957, Ivry, intervention Maurice Thorez," audio recording, 1 AV/ 7024–7031, CD: 4AV/ 3714, Seine-Saint-Denis, Archives Départementales). Second, Lefebvre's anti-Stalinist publications of 1957–58 were condemned as "revisionist" and "ignoring the contributions of Lenin" and "some valuable passages" of Stalin (see Henri Lefebvre, "Marksizm i myśl francuska," *Twórczość* 4 [1957]: 9–32, translated as "Le marxisme et la pensée française," *Temps modernes* 137–38 [July–August 1957]: 104–37; Henri Lefebvre, *Problèmes actuels du marxisme* [Paris: Presses universitaires de France, 1958]; note of Jean Suret-Canale, dossier CCCP, 261 J 6/9, Seine-Saint-Denis, Archives Départementales). Finally, Lefebvre's participation in the Club de gauche and his attempts at establishing a new journal were seen as "fractional activity," and the CCCP recommended his

"public exclusion [from the Party] for one year," which was never suspended (see memoranda of the CCCP to the Secretariat of the Central Committee from April 4, 1958, and May 27, 1958, dossier CCCP, 261 J 6/9, Seine-Saint-Denis, Archives Départementales).

101. Henri Lefebvre, "Une vie pour penser et porter la lute de classes à la théorie," *La nouvelle critique* 125 (1979): 44–54; see also Henri Lefebvre, "Quo vadis?," *Révolutions* 236 (1984): 9–12; Henri Lefebvre, "Penser à contre-courant?," *Autogestions* 14 (1983): 99.

102. *Programme commun de gouvernement du Parti communiste français et du Parti socialiste (27 juin 1972)* (Paris: Éditions sociales, 1972); Henri Lefebvre, "La planification démocratique," *La nouvelle revue marxiste* 2 (1961): 71–93.

103. *Programme commun*, 65–66.

104. François d'Arcy and Yves Prats, "Les politiques du cadre de vie," in *Traité de science politique*, ed. Madeleine Grawitz and Jean Leca (Paris: Presses universitaires de France, 1985), 4:261–300; George Ross, *Workers and Communists in France: From Popular Front to Eurocommunism* (Berkeley: University of California Press, 1982), 241–42.

105. *Urbanisme monopoliste, urbanisme démocratique* (Paris: Centre d'études et de recherches marxistes, 1974), 365–66.

106. "Pour un urbanisme: Rapports, communications, débats. Texte intégral du colloque, Grenoble, 6–7 avril 1974," special issue, *La nouvelle critique* 78 bis (1974); François Ascher, Jean Giard, and Jean-Louis Cohen, *Demain, la ville? Urbanisme et politique* (Paris: Éditions sociales, 1975).

107. See Jean-Louis Cohen, "Grenoble 1974: Pour un urbanisme....," in *Organiser la ville hypermoderne: François Ascher, grand prix de l'urbanisme 2009*, ed. Ariella Masboungi and Olivia Barbet-Massin (Marseille: Parenthèses, 2009), 58–59.

108. Comments by Manuel Castells and François Hincker, in "Pour un urbanisme," 312, 310.

109. "Exposition d'urbanisme," Fonds Francis Cohen, 354 J 84–85, Seine-Saint-Denis, Archives Départementales.

110. Max Jäggi, Roger Müller, and Sil Schmid, *Das rote Bologna: Kommunisten demokratisieren eine Stadt im kapitalistischen Westen* (Zürich: Verlagsgenossenschaft, 1976).

111. Henri Lefebvre, "Spazio urbano e questioni di democrazia," *Parametro* 8, no. 61 (November 1977): 6.

112. Henri Lefebvre, "La Commune et la bureaucratie," in *Le centenaire de la Commune de Paris: Le socialisme français et l'Europe Centrale* (Warsaw: Wydawnictwo Uniwersytetu Warszawskiego, 1972), 53–54.

113. Manuel Castells, Francis Godard, and Vivian Balanowski, *Monopolville: Analyse des rapports entre l'entreprise, l'État et l'urbain à partir d'une enquête sur la croissance industrielle et urbaine de la région de Dunkerque* (Paris: École pratique des hautes études, 1974); for discussion, see Éric Le Breton, *Pour une critique de*

la ville: La sociologie urbaine française, 1950–1980 (Rennes, France: Presses Universitaires de Rennes, 2012).

114. Monique Coornaert, Claude Marlaut, Antoine Haumont, and Henri Lefebvre, *Le quartier et la ville* (Paris: Les Cahiers de l'IAURP, 1967), 44.

115. "Henri Lefebvre sur la guérilla urbaine," 11. Lefebvre moved to 24 rue Rambuteau with Nicole Beaurain in 1965; they moved to no. 30 at the same street in 1971. After the split with Nicole in 1975, Lefebvre lived in this apartment with Catherine Régulier until 1990 (e-mail exchange with Nicole Beaurain, March 2013; e-mail exchange with Thierry Paquot, May 2013); see also Mario Gaviria, radio interview for "Profils perdus," France Culture, March 10, 1994, Inathèque de France, Paris.

116. Marc Mann, "La rénovation du centre-ville d'Ivry," in "Pour un urbanisme," 209–12.

117. Jean-Louis Cohen, "Giscard l'architecture," *La nouvelle critique* 85 (1975): 60–63.

118. Jean Renaudie in the debate "L'architecture parle-t-elle politique?," *La nouvelle critique* 73 (1974): 71.

119. Jean Giard, "Rapport final," in "Pour un urbanisme," 316.

120. Paul Chemetov and the editors (Jean-Philippe Chimot, Jean-Louis Cohen) in the debate "L'architecture, parle-t-elle politique?," 65, 72.

121. Lefebvre, *Vers une architecture de la jouissance*, 222; chap. 12 in this volume.

122. Karl Marx, *German Ideology* (New York: International Publishers, 2004 [1846/1932]), 53.

123. Lefebvre, *Vers une architecture de la jouissance*, 41; chap. 2 in this volume.

124. Brian Newsome, *French Urban Planning 1940–1968* (New York: Peter Lang, 2009); René Lourau, *L'instituant contre l'institué* (Paris: Éditions Anthropos, 1969); René Lourau, *L'analyse institutionnelle* (Paris: Éditions de Minuit, 1970); René Lourau and Georges Lapassade, *Clefs pour la sociologie* (Paris: Seghers, 1971). For Lefebvre's comments on institutional analysis, see his *La survie du capitalisme: La reproduction des rapports de production* (Paris: Anthropos, 2002 [1973]), 51–52; and the postface by Rémi Hess, "La place d'Henri Lefebvre dans le collège invisible, d'une critique des superstructures à l'analyse institutionnelle," 197–214.

125. Félix Guattari, "Entretien (1)," in *L'intervention institutionnelle*, ed. Jacques Ardoino et al. (Paris: Payot, 1980), 123.

126. Georges Lapassade, "L'intervention dans les institutions d'éducation et de formation", in Ardoino et al., *L'intervention institutionnelle*, 186–87.

127. Pierre Joly, "Rénovation du Centre d'Ivry: La ville est à réinventer," *Oeil* 220 (1973): 52–59.

128. Renaudie in "L'architecture parle-t-elle politique?," 69.

129. Henri Lefebvre, "Constituez vous en avant-garde," *Archivari* 4 (1984), unpaginated. This review discussed the projects in Aubervilliers (René Gailhoustet, 1975–86), Givors (Jean Renaudie, 1976–82), and Saint-Martin d'Hères (Jean Renaudie, 1974–82).

130. Lefebvre, *Vers une architecture de la jouissance*, 4–6; chap. 1 in this volume.

131. Henri Raymond, "La qualité du logement," in "Pour un urbanisme," 109–13.

132. Lefebvre, "The Right to the City," 158–59.

133. Jean Aubert in Jean-Louis Violeau, "Utopie: In acts...," in *The Inflatable Moment: Pneumatics and Protest in '68*, ed. Marc Dessauce (New York: Princeton Architectural Press, 1999), 50.

134. Henri Lefebvre, *The Explosion: Marxism and the French Revolution*, trans. Alfred Ehrenfeld (New York: Monthly Review Press, 1969 [1968]), 104.

135. For discussion, see Stanek, *Henri Lefebvre on Space*, chap. 4.

136. Lefebvre, *Urban Revolution*, 131; Lefebvre, *Production of Space*, 167.

137. Lefebvre, *Urban Revolution*, 98–99.

138. For an introduction, see the dossier on CERFI in *Site Magazine* 2 (2002), 10–20.

139. "La ville-ordinateur," in "Les équipements du pouvoir: Généalogie du capital 1," *Recherches* 13 (1973): 18; "La ville-métaphore," in "Les équipements du pouvoir," 47–48.

140. "La ville-métaphore," 35ff.

141. See François Fourquet. "L'accumulation du pouvoir ou le désir d'État: CERFI, 1970–1981," *Recherches* 46 (1982).

142. Le Breton, *Pour une critique de la ville*, 143.

143. Ibid., 147.

144. Isabelle Billiard, "Editorial," *Parallèles* 1 (1976): 3; Anne Baldassari and Michel Joubert, "Architectures," *Parallèles* 1 (1976): 48; see also Liane Mozère, "Projet d'hôtel d'enfants," *Parallèles* 1 (1976): 69.

145. Michel Anselme, "Le petit Séminaire, chronique raisonnée d'une réhabilitation singulière," in *Droit de cité: À la rencontre des habitants des banlieues délaissées*, ed. Albert Mollet (Paris: L'Harmattan, 1987), 105–48. See also the account of CERFI's participatory research on the temporary use of a building in Sèvres, in *Recherches* 19 (September 1975).

146. Interview with Anne Querrien, Paris, July 2012.

147. Anselme, "Le petit Séminaire," 144–45.

148. Henri Lefebvre, "Éléments d'une théorie de l'objet," *Opus International* 10–11 (1969): 20.

149. "Trois milliards de pervers: Grande Encyclopédie des homosexualités," *Recherches* 12 (March 1973); "Les équipements du pouvoir"; Lion Murard and Patrick Zylberman, *Ville, habitat et intimité: L'exemple des cités minières au XIX siècle, naissance du petit travailleur infatigable* (Fontenay-sous-Bois, France: CERFI, 1976).

150. Henri Lefebvre, *Rhythmanalysis: Space, Time, and Everyday Life*, trans. Stuart Elden and Gerald Moore (London: Continuum, 2004 [1992]), 27; Lefebvre, *Vers une architecture de la jouissance*, 220; chap. 12 in this volume.

151. "Henri Lefebvre," 7.

152. Ibid., 8.

153. Lefebvre, *The Explosion*.
154. See Stanek, *Henri Lefebvre on Space*, chap. 4.
155. Lefebvre, *The Explosion*, 105.
156. Henri Lefebvre, interviewed in "Enquêtes sur les causes des manifestations," broadcast on Canal 1, May 11, 1968, Inathèque de France, Paris.
157. Karl Marx, *Capital: A Critique of Political Economy* (London: Lawrence and Wishart, 1974 [1887]), http://www.marxists.org. For bibliography and discussion, see Stanek, *Henri Lefebvre on Space*, chap. 2.
158. Lefebvre, *Production of Space*, 52, 167, 212, 380, 410; Henri Lefebvre, *La production de l'espace* (Paris: Anthropos, 2000 [1974]), 65, 194, 245, 438, 439, 442, 471.
159. Stephen Heath, "Translator's Note," in Roland Barthes, *Image-Music-Text* (New York: Hill and Wang, 1977), 9. A footnote about the difficulties of translating *jouissance* into English has long been a genre in itself. While in this introduction I am following the solution preferred by most translators of academic texts—leaving the word in French—in the following text by Lefebvre *jouissance* was translated as "enjoyment" in order to stay faithful to the general character of his book, which was written in an accessible language for the French reader. "Enjoyment" was preferred over several candidates, including "bliss," which was used in the translation of Roland Barthes's *The Pleasure of the Text*, trans. Richard Miller (New York: Hill and Wang, 1975 [1973]). However, "bliss" lacks an effective verbal form (in contrast to French *jouir*) and connotes religious and social contentment (Heath, "Translator's Note," 9). "Pleasure" would be the simplest choice, but it was particularly unhelpful, since Lefebvre himself changed the title from *Vers une architecture du plaisir*, suggested by Gaviria, to *Vers une architecture de la jouissance* (interview with Mario Gaviria, Saragossa, September 2008). Another reason was that in psychoanalysis and in particular in Lacan, which reverberates in Lefebvre's text, jouissance is contrasted to pleasure; Lacan himself was aware of the problems and suggested a combination of "enjoyment" and "lust," but most of his translators did not follow his advice and left the word untranslated; see Néstor A. Braunstein, "Desire and jouissance in the teachings of Lacan," in *The Cambridge Companion to Lacan*, ed. Jean-Michel Rabate (Cambridge: Cambridge University Press, 2003), 103; Jane Gallop, "Beyond the Jouissance Principle," *Representations* 7 (1984): 110–15.
160. Lefebvre, *Vers une architecture de la jouissance*, 172; chap. 8 in this volume.
161. Jacques Lacan, *The Ethics of Psychoanalysis, 1959–1960* (New York: Norton, 1992), 184; Dylan Evans, *An Introductory Dictionary of Lacanian Psychoanalysis* (London: Routledge, 1996), 93–94. For Lefebvre's reading of Lacan, see Steve Pile, *The Body and the City: Psychoanalysis, Space, and Subjectivity* (London: Routledge, 1996), 145–69; Derek Gregory, "Lacan and Geography: The Production of Space Revisited," in *Space and Social Theory: Interpreting Modernity and Postmodernity*, ed. Georges Benko and Ulf Strohmayer (Oxford: Blackwell, 1997), 203–31; Schmid, *Stadt, Raum und Gesellschaft*, 240–43.

162. See the following books by Lefebvre: *Métaphilosophie* (Paris: Éditions de minuit, 1965); *Le langage et la société* (Paris: Gallimard, 1966); *Position: Contre les technocrates* (Paris: Gonthier, 1967); *Manifeste différentialiste* (Paris: Gallimard, 1970); *Au-delà du structuralisme* (Paris: Anthropos, 1971); *La survie du capitalisme* (Abingdon, UK: Routledge, 2011).

163. Barthes, *Pleasure of the Text*, 14.

164. Lefebvre, *Vers une architecture de la jouissance*, 68–69; chap. 3 in this volume.

165. Lefebvre, *Vers une architecture de la jouissance*, 221; chap. 12 in this volume.

166. Lefebvre, *Vers une architecture de la jouissance*, 47; chap. 3 in this volume.

167. When interviewed about the manuscript, Nicole Beaurain recalled that "in the summer of 1973 Henri was writing a book about gardens, in particular about the Generalife" (interview with Nicole Beaurain, Paris, September 2011).

168. Henri Lefebvre, *Rabelais* (Paris: Éditeurs français réunis, 1955), 156–58, 204–5; Lefebvre, *Vers une architecture de la jouissance*, 68; chap. 3 in this volume.

169. Aaron Betsky, *Queer Space: Architecture and Same-Sex Desire* (New York: William Morrow, 1997).

170. Lefebvre, *Vers une architecture de la jouissance*, 202–3; chap. 11 in this volume.

171. Octavio Paz, *Conjunctions and Disjunctions*, trans. Helen R. Lane (New York: Arcade, 1990), 55. Lefebvre and Nicole Beaurain visited India in 1967; the route, including the visit to Agra, was suggested to them by the French scholar of religion and Indologist Charles Malamoud (e-mail exchange with Nicole Beaurain, March 2013).

172. Lefebvre, *Vers une architecture de la jouissance*, 205bis; chap. 11 in this volume.

173. Lefebvre, "Le philosophe et le poète," *La quinzaine littéraire* 139 (1972): 21; Paz, *Conjunctions and Disjunctions*, 131; for a reading of Paz, see Lefebvre, *Production of Space*, 184, 201–2, 259–60; for discussion, see Merrifield, *Henri Lefebvre*, 113.

174. Lefebvre, *Vers une architecture de la jouissance*, 210–11; chap. 11 in this volume; see Anthony Vidler, *Claude-Nicolas Ledoux: Architecture and Social Reform at the End of the Ancien Régime* (Cambridge, Mass.: MIT Press, 1990), 356; Charles Fourier, *Des modifications à introduire dans l'architecture des villes* (Paris: Librairie Phalanstérienne, 1849); Edouard Silberling, *Dictionnaire de sociologie phalanstérienne: Guide des oeuvres complètes de Charles Fourier* (Paris: Librairie des Sciences Politiques et Sociales, 1911).

175. "Un certain regard: Charles Fourier," Chanal 1, September 6, 1972, Inathèque de France, Paris.

176. Lefebvre, *Vers une architecture de la jouissance*, 104; chap. 5 in this volume; Roland Barthes, *The Fashion System*, trans. Matthew Ward and Richard Howard (Berkeley: University of California Press, 1990 [1967]); Jean Baudrillard, *The System of Objects* (London: Verso, 2005 [1968]). For discussion, see Stanek, *Henri Lefebvre on Space*, chap. 2.

177. See Norberg-Schulz, *Existence, Space, and Architecture*.
178. Gaviria, *Libro negro*.
179. "Présentation," in "Les équipements du pouvoir," 5.
180. Hess, "La place d'Henri Lefebvre," 209.
181. For bibliography and discussion, see Stanek, *Henri Lefebvre on Space*, chap. 1.
182. Manfredo Tafuri, "Towards a Critique of Architectural Ideology," in K. Michael Hays, *Architecture Theory since 1968* (Cambridge, Mass.: MIT Press, 1998 [1969]), 22.
183. "Trois milliards de pervers."
184. Nishat Awan, Tatjana Schneider, and Jeremy Till, *Spatial Agency: Other Ways of Doing Architecture* (Abingdon, UK: Routledge, 2011).
185. See "Espectros de Lefebvre," special issue, *Urban: Revista del Departamento de Urbanística y Ordenación del Territorio* 2 (2011); and "Right to the City," special issue, *Architectural Theory Review* 16, no. 3 (2011).
186. McLeod, "Henri Lefebvre's Critique of Everyday Life"; see also Upton, "Architecture in Everyday Life"; Crawford, "Introduction," 12; Wigglesworth and Till, "The Everyday and Architecture."
187. Lefebvre, "La dictature de l'oeil et du phallus," 52.
188. Ibid.
189. See Le Corbusier, *Toward an Architecture*, trans. John Goodman (Los Angeles: Getty Research Institute, 2007 [1923]).
190. Lefebvre, *Vers une architecture de la jouissance*, 89–90; chap. 5 in this volume. For a discussion on Marx's value theory and its relationship to Lefebvre's theory of production of space, see Stanek, *Henri Lefebvre on Space*, chap. 3.
191. Lefebvre, *Vers une architecture de la jouissance*, 89–90; chap. 5 in this volume.
192. Ernst Bloch, *The Spirit of Utopia*, trans. Anthony Nassar (Stanford: Stanford University Press, 2000), 15; Charles-Edouard Jeanneret, *Une maison—un palais: À la recherche d'une unité architecturale* (Turin: Bottega D'Erasmo, 1975 [1928]); Helena Mattsson and Sven-Olov Wallenstein, eds., *Swedish Modernism: Architecture, Consumption and the Welfare State* (London: Black Dog, 2010); Siegfried Giedion, "The Dangers and Advantages of Luxury," *Focus* 3 (1939): 38.
193. "Finding Freedoms: Conversations with Rem Koolhaas," *El Croquis* 53 (1994): 18.
194. Marco de Michelis and Georges Teyssot, *Les conditions historiques du projet social-démocrate sur l'espace de l'habitat* (Paris: Institut d'études et de recherches architecturales et urbaines, 1979); Ginette Baty-Tornikian and Marc Bédarida, *Plaisir et intelligence de l'urbain: Architecture et social-democratie* (Paris: Ministère de l'urbanisme, du logement et des transports, 1984); Ginette Baty-Tornikian, *Un projet urbain idéal typique: Un social-démocrate, Henri Sellier* (Paris: Institut d'études et de recherches architecturales et urbaines, 1978); Catherine Bruant,

ed., *Une métropole social-démocrate, Lille, 1896–1919–1939: Gestion urbaine et planification* (Paris: Institut d'études et de recherches architecturales et urbaines, 1979); see also Manfredo Tafuri, *Vienne la rouge: La politique immobilière de la Vienne socialiste, 1919–1933* (Brussels: P. Mardaga, 1981).

195. Łukasz Stanek, "Second World's Architecture and Planning in the Third World," *Journal of Architecture* 17, no. 3 (2012): 299–307; Łukasz Stanek, *Postmodernism Is Almost All Right: Polish Architecture after Socialist Globalization* (Warsaw: Fundacja Bęc-Zmiana, 2012).

196. Lefebvre, *Vers une architecture de la jouissance*, 199; chap. 10 in this volume.

197. Ananya Roy, "The 21st-Century Metropolis: New Geographies of Theory," *Regional Studies* 43, no. 6 (2009): 819–30.

198. *A cidade informal no século 21* (São Paulo: Museu da Casa Brasileira, 2011).

1. The Question

1. [I would like to thank Donald Nicholson-Smith for his translation of the first two pages of the manuscript, which exist only in Spanish. —Trans.]

2. [Presumably Lefebvre is referring to the daughter of Caecillius Metellus Creticus, a Roman consul (69 BC). Her tomb, now a famous tourist site, is located on the Appian Way. —Trans.]

3. Octavio Paz, *Conjunctions and Disjunctions*, trans. Helen R. Lane (New York: Arcade, 1990), 54–55.

4. Martin Heidegger, *Off the Beaten Track*, trans. Julian Young and Kenneth Haynes (Cambridge: Cambridge University Press, 2002), 20–21.

5. The bonzes, philosophers, and Buddhist theologians (Zen or otherwise) I tried to question did not respond to my queries. Either they failed to understand them or simply disdained to answer.

6. See Octavio Paz, "The Other Mexico", in *The Labyrinth of Solitude*, trans. Lysander Kemp, Yara Milos, and Rachel Phillips Belash (New York: Grove Press, 1985), 303–4.

7. See G. R. Hocke, *Labyrinthe de l'art fantastique: Le maniérisme dans l'art européen*, trans. from German by Cornélius Heim (Paris: Gonthier, 1967); and Claude Arthaud, *Enchanted Visions: Fantastic Houses and Their Treasures* (New York: Putnam, 1972).

8. [Lodovico Ariosto, *Orlando Furioso*, trans. William Stewart Rose (Indianapolis: Bobbs-Merrill, 1968 [1532]). —Ed.]

9. [*Oeuvres complètes de Stendhal*, ed. Henri Martineau (Paris: Le Divan, 1937), 10, no. 5, 63. —Ed.]

10. [Henry Wotton, *The Elements of Architecture* (Amsterdam: Theatrum Orbis Terrarum, 1970 [1624]). Wotton rephrased the Vitruvian triad: "All … [buildings], must be built with due reference to durability, convenience, and beauty." Vitruvius, *The Ten Books on Architecture*, trans. Morris Hicky Morgan (Cambridge, Mass.: Harvard University Press, 1914), 17. —Ed.]

2. The Scope of the Inquiry

1. Friedrich Nietzsche, *The Gay Science*, ed. Bernard Williams, trans. Josefine Nauckhoff, poems trans. Adrian del Caro (Cambridge: Cambridge University Press, 2001), aphorisms 291 and 374, 164–65, 239–40.
2. Ibid., aphorism 334, 186–87.
3. [Fyodor Dostoevsky, *The Brothers Karamazov*, trans. Constance Garnett (New York: Barnes & Noble, 1995 [1880]); Nietzsche, *The Gay Science*. —Ed.]

3. The Quest

1. [Stendhal, *De l'Amour* (Paris: Michel Lévy Frères, 1857), 34. —Ed.]
2. [Karl Marx, *Economic and Philosophic Manuscripts of 1844*, trans. Martin Mulligan (Moscow: Progress Publishers, 1959 [1932]); Friedrich Nietzsche, *The Gay Science*, ed. Bernard Williams, trans. Josefine Nauckhoff, poems trans. Adrian del Caro (Cambridge: Cambridge University Press, 2001 [1882]). —Ed.]
3. André Breton, *Mad Love*, trans. Mary Ann Caws (Lincoln: University of Nebraska Press, 1987), 39.
4. Ibid., 67.
5. Ibid., 70.
6. Ibid., 73.
7. Ibid., 75.
8. Ibid., 77.
9. Ibid., 80.
10. Ibid., 226.
11. Ibid., 88.
12. Ibid., 83.
13. Jean Anthelme Brillat-Savarin, *The Physiology of Taste, or, Meditations on Transcendental Gastronomy*, trans. M. F. K. Fisher (New York: Vintage, 2011), 38.
14. Ibid., 40.
15. Ibid.
16. Ibid., 41.
17. Ibid., 39.
18. [Presumably, Flemish painter Joachim Patinir's (1480–1524) painting of *Charon Crossing the River Styx* in the Prado Museum. —Trans.]
19. [Georges Bataille, *L'abbé C: A Novel*, trans. Philip A. Facey (London: M. Boyars, 1983 [1950]). —Ed.]
20. [Chrétien de Troyes, *Erec and Enide*, trans. Dorothy Gilbert (Berkeley: University of California Press, 1992). —Ed.]
21. [Thomas De Quincey, *Confessions of an English Opium-Eater* (Oxford: Oxford University Press, 2013 [1821]), 34–35. —Ed.]
22. Rabelais, *Gargantua and Pantagruel*, trans. Sir Thomas Urquhart of Cromarty and Peter Antony Motteux (Derby: Moray Press, 1894), book I, chap. 1, LIII.

4. Objections

1. Robert Jaulin, *Gens du soi, gens de l'autre* (Paris: Union générale d'éditions, 1973), 225.
2. Georg Wilhelm Friedrich Hegel, *Aesthetics: Lectures on Fine Art*, trans. T. M. Knox (Oxford: Clarendon Press, 1998), 2, pt. 3, section 1, chap. 2, 660.

5. Philosophy

1. [Aristotle, *The Nicomachean Ethics*, trans. David Ross (Oxford: Oxford University Press, 1980). —Ed.]
2. [Lefebvre refers to the selection of Friedrich Nietzsche's texts from 1872 to 1875, published in German and French as *Das Philosophenbuch, theoretische Studien / Le Livre du philosophe, études théorétiques* (Paris: Aubier-Flammarion, 1969); cf. *Nietzsche, Philosophy and Truth: Selections from Nietzsche's Notebooks of the Early 1870's*, ed. Daniel Breazeale (Atlantic Highlands, N.J.: Humanities Press, 1979). —Ed.]
3. ["Love is merely 'pleasure accompanied by the idea of an external cause'": Benedictus Spinoza, *Ethics: With the Treatise on the Emendation of the Intellect and Selected Letters*, trans. Samuel Shirley (Indianapolis: Hackett Publishing, 1992 [1677]), 112. —Ed.]
4. [Julien Offray de La Mettrie, *L'art de jouir* (Cythère, 1751). —Ed.]
5. [Karl Marx, *Economic and Philosophic Manuscripts of 1844*, trans. Martin Mulligan (Moscow: Progress Publishers, 1959 [1932]). —Ed.]
6. [Georg Wilhelm Friedrich Hegel, *Phenomenology of Spirit*, trans. A. V. Miller (Oxford: Clarendon Press, 1977 [1807]). —Ed.]
7. Friedrich Nietzsche, *Thus Spoke Zarathustra: A Book for None and All*, trans. and with a preface by Walter Kaufmann (New York: Penguin, 1966), 55.
8. Ibid.
9. Ibid., 34.
10. Ibid., 35.
11. Ibid., 45.
12. Ibid., 51.
13. Ibid., Second Part, "On the Famous Wise Men."
14. Ibid., First Part, "On Free Death."
15. Friedrich Nietzsche, *The Will to Power*, trans. Walter Kaufmann and R. J. Hollingdale (New York: Vintage, 1968), 373.
16. Ibid.
17. Ibid., 371.
18. Ibid., 373.
19. Martin Heidegger, "Poetically Man Dwells," in *Poetry, Language, Thought*, trans. Alfred Hofstadter (New York: Harper Collins, 2001), 214.
20. Ibid., 221.
21. Martin Heidegger, "Building, Dwelling, Thinking," in *Poetry, Language, Thought*, 157–58.

22. Friedrich Nietzsche, *The Gay Science*, ed. Bernard Williams, trans. Josefine Nauckhoff, poems trans. Adrian del Caro (Cambridge: Cambridge University Press, 2001), 7.

6. Anthropology

1. Robert Jaulin, *Gens du soi, gens de l'autre: Esquisse d'une théorie descriptive* (Paris: Union générale d'éditions, 1973), 102ff.
2. Ibid., 434.
3. Ibid., 32.
4. Ibid., 274–75.
5. Olivier Marc, *Psychology of the House*, trans. Jessie Wood (London: Thames and Hudson, 1977).

7. History

1. [The principle of *détournement*, popularized by the Situationists, involved taking an existing object—whether it be an ad, a work of literature, a painting or sculpture, a movie, a building, anything at all—and turning it toward an unrelated end, directed at new goals; subverting it, in other words. It is similar, but not identical, to the concept of appropriation and might be thought of as a form of repurposing. The Canadian organization Adbusters, for example, has used the concept of détournement to subvert the aims and goals of popular advertising ("culture jamming"). "The concept of détournement entails the notion of detour, the intent to circumvent an obstacle, and contains elements of game playing and warfare. Détournement makes the reader or public a warrior. It incorporates a strategy of blurring appearances, the rejection of comparative quotation demanded by the spectacle, which is currently so intrigued by the cliché of authenticity. Consequently it also involves a rejection of an entire order of discourse, a logic of allocation, of pigeonholing, of signatures and responsibility through which everyone is in some way put back in his place or finds himself back there." See Vincent Kaufmann, *Guy Debord: Revolution in the Service of Poetry*, trans. Robert Bononno (Minneapolis: University of Minnesota Press, 2006), 37. —Trans.]

8. Psychology and Psychoanalysis

1. Friedrich Nietzsche, *The Will to Power*, trans. Walter Kaufmann and R. J. Hollingdale (New York: Vintage, 1968), 106ff.
2. Jean Stoetzel, *La psychologie sociale* (Paris: Flammarion, 1963), 60–61.
3. See also Herbert Marcuse's discussion of instinctual dynamics in *Eros and Civilization* (London: Routledge, 1987), 107.
4. Maurice Blanchot, *The Space of Literature*, trans. Anne Smock (Lincoln: University of Nebraska Press, 1989), 164.
5. [Stéphane Mallarmé, "The Tomb of Edgar Poe" [1877], in *Selected Poetry and Prose*, ed. and with an introduction by Mary Ann Caws (New York: New Directions, 1982), 50. —Ed.]

6. Pierre Francastel, *Peinture et société: Naissance et destruction d'un espace plastique, de la Renaissance au cubisme* (Lyon: Audin, 1951), 217.
7. [Cf. Marcelle Wahl, *Le mouvement dans la peinture* (Paris: F. Alcan, 1936). —Ed.]
8. Stéphane Mallarmé, from "Hérodiade," in *Selected Poetry and Prose*, ed. Caws.
9. Marcel Proust, *Remembrance of Things Past*, trans. C. K. Scott Moncrief (New York: Random House, 1934), 118–19.

9. Semantics and Semiology

1. [Lefebvre refers here to his previous books, in particular *Le langage et la société* (Paris: Gallimard, 1966); see also his *Métaphilosophie* (Paris: Éditions de minuit, 1965); *Position: Contre les technocrates* (Paris: Gonthier, 1967); *Manifeste différentialiste* (Paris: Gallimard, 1970); *Au-delà du structuralisme* (Paris: Anthropos, 1971); *La survie du capitalisme: La reproduction des rapports de production* (Paris: Anthropos, 2002 [1973]). —Ed.]
2. I am referring, in particular, to research conducted by the group Tel Quel, which included Jacques Derrida, Julia Kristeva, Philippe Sollers, and Roland Barthes *(The Pleasure of the Text)*.
3. For an amusing reference, which goes straight to the issue, see Ludwig Harig, *Manuel de conversation à l'usage des membres du Marché commun dans le cadre de la coopération franco-allemande* (Paris: Belfond, 1973).
4. See Roland Barthes, *Writing Degree Zero*, trans. Annette Lavers and Colin Smith (New York: Hill and Wang, 1999).
5. Roland Barthes, *The Pleasure of the Text*, trans. Richard Miller (New York: Hill and Wang, 1975), 55. [It is worth noting that Miller, in his translation of Barthes, has translated French *jouissance* as "bliss" and, in this particular instance, as "the kind of bliss afforded literally by an ejaculation." This is a highly particularized interpretation of a lexeme with various senses, including those in law and economics, most of which are perfectly innocent and require no parental guidance. While French authors are, of course, free to take advantage of its ambiguity—as Barthes does—there is no comparable English word with a comparable semantic range. I have translated it as "enjoyment" throughout Lefebvre's text. To compound the problem, ever since its widespread use by Lacan, translation of the term has become unusually problematic for translators, many of whom opt not to translate it at all. —Trans.]
6. [Paul Claudel, *Knowing the East*, trans. James Lawler (Princeton, N.J.: Princeton University Press, 2004 [1900]); Saint-John Perse, *Exile, and Other Poems* (New York: Pantheon Books, 1949 [1942]); Gaston Bachelard, *The Poetics of Space*, trans. Maria Jolas (New York: Orion Press, 1964 [1957]). —Ed.]

10. Economics

1. [Lefebvre provides no source for his statement, but this is clearly a reference to the work of Donella and Dennis Meadows. In 1972, they coauthored,

together with Jørgen Randers and William Behrens III, *The Limits to Growth*, based on a two-year study conducted at MIT, which was funded by the Volkswagen Corporation and commissioned by the Club of Rome. The book provided a systems analysis and computer model of the consequences of unchecked economic and population growth in the face of finite global resources. Lefebvre's remark about Bertrand Russell likely refers to the fact that, on page 176, the authors of *The Limits to Growth* include a quote from Russell's *In Praise of Idleness and Other Essays* (London: Allen and Unwin, 1935), 15–17. —Trans.]

11. Architecture

1. [Octavio Paz, *Conjunctions and Disjunctions*, trans. Helen R. Lane (New York: Arcade, 1990), 55. —Ed.]

2. Hermann Goetz, *India: Five Thousand Years of Indian Art* (London: Methuen, 1959). [Lefebvre refers to the French translation, Paris: Albin Michel, 1960. —Ed.]

3. [Plato, *Timaeus and Critias*, trans. Robin Waterfield (Oxford: Oxford University Press, 2008); Plato, *The Republic*, trans. Desmond Lee (Harmondsworth: Penguin, 1974). —Ed.]

4. Claude-Nicolas Ledoux, *L'architecture considérée sous le rapport de l'art, des mœurs, de la législation* (Paris, 1804), a date that makes Ledoux a contemporary of Brillat-Savarin, Saint-Simon, Fourier, the ideologues, and others.

5. [Ibid., 114, 6, 172, 215, 200, 195, respectively. —Ed.]

6. Charles Fourier, from "The Phalanstery," in *Selections from the Works of Fourier*, with an introduction by Charles Gide, trans. Julia Franklin (London: Swan Sonnenschein, 1901), 143–44. [I have made some minor corrections to the Franklin translation. Additionally, Lefebvre's citation is inaccurate in parts and does not respect Fourier's original text. —Trans.]

7. See Hegel's *Aesthetics*, III, 58ff. [Cf. Georg Wilhelm Friedrich Hegel, *Aesthetics: Lectures on Fine Art*, trans. T. M. Knox (Oxford: Clarendon Press, 1998 [1835]), 2, pt. 3, section 1, "Architecture." —Ed.]

12. Conclusion (Injunctions)

1. Stéphane Mallarmé, *Collected Poems*, trans. and with a commentary by Henry Weinfield (Berkeley: University of California Press, 1996), 69.

INDEX

Page numbers in italics refer to illustrations and their captions.

Abbé C: A Novel, L' (Bataille), 44
Abbey of Thelema, 46–48, 141
absolute, the, 90, 111
absolute space, 8, 92, 119, 145. *See also* political space; religious space
abstract rationality, 90
abstract space, xxx–xxxi, xxxiv, 119
abstract utopias, xxxvi–xxxvii, xxxix, 93, 130, 141, 148
Actaeon, 15
Actuel (journal), xix–xxi, *xxii–xxv*, lx; Lefebvre's interviews in, xix–xxi, *xxiii*
Adbusters, 174n1
aestheticism, 41–42
aesthetics, 11, 36, 52–53, 78–79, 114, 115; monuments and, 17, 20
affects/affectivity, 75–76, 81, 83, 85, 86, 102–3, 123
Ajanta caves, India, lv, 8, *138–39*
Alberti, Leon Battista, 141
Alhambra, Grenada, lv, *22–23*
Ali Qapu palace, Isfahan, 42
ambiguity, 75–76, 108–11; and art, 109–10; and body, 109; and mirrors, 110–11
analogy, 5, 7, 13–14, 92, 98, 144–45; monuments and, 25, 77; of total body, 151–52

Anaximander, 63
Ant Farm, *xxiii*; inflatable structures, xxi
anthropology, liv, 51, 80–86; and sexuality, 82–86
appropriation, 5, 21, 58, 93–98, 140, 151, 152; Christianity and, 97–98; concrete utopia and, 141; and domination, 93–95, 98; and mastery, 90; of nature, 73, 78; of space, xxi, 100, 112, 124, 125–26. *See also* détournement
Archigram, *xxiii*; walking cities, xxi
architects, xxxiv–xxxv, xxxvi, lix, 4, 87, 126; and habitat, 5; law on (1973), xliv–xlv; and monuments, 17–18; and social practice, 151
architectural imagination, xxxvi, xxxix–xl
architectural rationality, 51–53
architectural revolution, 27–28
architectural utopias, 141, 148
architecture, 136–45; as communication, 53–54, 122; definition of, 3; and division of labor, 54–55; of enjoyment, 16–17; funerary, 6–7, 15, 24–25, 92; of habitation, xl–xlviii; and jouissance, liv–lv; military, 90–93; and mode of

177

production/changes in, xxxv; oneiric, 14–15; political, 13–16, 20; of power, 13–16, 20, 25; redefinition of, xiii–xv; religious, 7–8; and social hierarchies, xxxiii; as space, xxxiv–xxxv; tragic, 14; transdisciplinary understanding of, xiii; and urbanism, xxxvi; vernacular, 21; Vitruvius's definition of, 171n10; and will to power, 55–56; Wotton's definition of, 17
architecture d'aujourd'hui, L' (journal), xxix, xxxv
Architecture of Happiness (de Botton), xvi
Archizoom: "No-Stop City," xxxi
Ariosto, Lodovico: *Orlando Furioso*, 14
Aristippus, 63, 64, 65
Aristotle: happiness, 61; *Nicomachean Ethics*, 61; pleasure, 64–65
art: and ambiguity, 109–10; and death, 105; and freedom, 105; and immediacy, 115
art de jouir, L' (La Mettrie), 69
arte povera, 21
artistic mystification, 21–22
artworks, 52–53, 78
asceticism, 16–17, 42–43, 66; of Cartesianism/European Logos, 68; critique of, xviii–xix; intellectual, 68, 115; philosophical, 10
Atelier de Montrouge, xxxv
Aubert, Jean, xlviii
Aztec pyramids, 13–14

Bachelard, Gaston, 126–27
Balladur, Jean, xxxvi
Barthes, Roland, xv, liv, 120, 126, 175n2
basilicas, Roman, 97
Bataille, Georges, lii; *L'Abbé C: A Novel*, 44

Baths of Caracalla, 143–44
Baths of Diocletian, lv, lvii, 137–38, 143–44
Baudrillard, Jean, 160n33
Bauhaus, xxxiv, lx, 163n72
beaches, xxxi, 48–49
Beaurain, Nicole, xi, *xiv, xvii*, 169n167; visit to India, 169n170
beauty, 11, 15, 32, 88, 93, 140; and desire, 65; monumental, 6
Behrens, William, III, 175n1
Being (Heidegger), 9
Benidorm, xviii, xxviii–xxix, 160n40; tourist guide, *xx*
Benjamin, Walter, xviii, xxxii
Berlin Wall, xxxi
Beyond the Pleasure Principle (Freud), 104
Bidagor, Pedro, xxviii
bisexuality, 107
Bloch, Ernst, lx
body, li, lii, 38, 40, 43, 66, 100, 113, 123, 135; and ambiguity, 109; and jouissance, lii, liv–lv; Lefebvre's sense of, liv–lv, 34–36; and leisure spaces, xvii, xxxii, 100; Marxism and, xxi; as model of space, lii; Nietzsche on, 74; and nonbody, 7–8, 11, 77, 102, 127, 150–51; relationship with surroundings, 32–36, 137–38, 139; religion and, 7; and space, 10–11, 41; total, xxxii, lv, 41, 148–52
Bofill, Ricardo, xv, xlviii, *l*, 159n33; collaboration with Lefebvre, 160n33
Bologna, Italy, xlii
Borden, Iain, xiii
Brecht, Bertolt, 96
Breton, André: *Mad Love*, 36–38
Brillat-Savarin, Jean-Anthelme, xxxii; *Physiology of Taste*, 38–41

Index

buildings, 9, 20, 27, 152; functionality and, 19; and monuments, 17–18, 30
Burgos symposium, 159n33

Campanella, Tommaso, 141
Candilis-Josic-Woods, xxx, li
Cano Lasso, Julio, *xxvii*
capitalism, xvii, xxxiv, 4, 92, 134; anthropology and, 80; Marx on, 31, 128–30; mode of production, 121; neocapitalism, 121; and spaces of tourism in Spain, xvii
Caracalla, 143–44
Cartesianism, 25–26, 68
Castells, Manuel, xliv, 160n33
cathexis, 135
centrality, 91; concept of, lviii
Centre d'études, de recherches, et de formation institutionnelles (CERFI), xlviii–lii, lvii–lviii; CERFI-Sud (Marseille), li
Centre d'études sociologiques, xv
Charles III of Sicily, 15
Charter of Athens, xxvi–xxvii, liii
Château d'Anet, 21–22
Chaux: ideal city project, lv
Chemetov, Paul, xv, xxx, xlv
Choay, Françoise, xv
Christianity, 45, 121, 136; and appropriation, 97–98; and body, 7, 33; religious architecture, 7–8
cities, xxvii, xlii, 20, 140–42; "City in Space" project, 160n33; colonization and, 92; funnel cities, xxi; history of, 87–88, 99; ideal city project, lv; and meaning, 88–89; Parisian suburban, xliv; walking cities, xxi
"City in Space" project, 160n33
Claudel, Paul, 126–27
cloisters, 10–11, 24, 94
closure, 119–20, 122

Club de gauche, 164n100
Club of Rome, 132–33, 175n1
Colbert, Jean-Baptiste, xxxvii
colonization, 92
Common Program. See *Programme commun de gouvernement du Parti communiste français et du Parti socialiste*
communication, 30, 119, 124, 147, 151; architecture as, 53–54, 122
Concepción housing estate, Madrid, xxi, *xxv, xxvi*
concrete utopias, xvi, xxxvi–xxxvii, xxxix, 123, 141, 148, 153
consumer society/consumerism, xvii–xix. See also capitalism; tourism
consumption, xxxiv, lvii, 20–21, 83, 100; productive/unproductive, 130–31
contemplation, 10–12, 24, 72, 94, 95, 110
Corrales Gutiérrez, José Antonio, *xxvii*
Cosi fan Tutte (Mozart), 107
Côte d'Azur: holiday villages, xxix
Crawford, Margaret, xiii
Critias (Plato), 141
Critique of Everyday Life, The (Lefebvre): habitation, concept of, xv
Cyrenaic school, 63, 64

Daisen-in temple, Kyoto, lv; garden of dry ocean, 12
da Vinci, Leonardo, 141
death, 4, 105–7, 112, 132, 144–45; ambiguity and, 109; funerary architecture, 6–7, 15, 24–25, 92; tragic architecture, 14; Western orientation toward, 50–51
death drive (Thanatos), 104–5, 109
de Botton, Alain: *Architecture of Happiness*, xvi

De l'Etat (Lefebvre), xi
de l'Orme, Philibert, 22
De Quincey, Thomas, 39, 45–46
Deroche, Jean, xxxv
Derrida, Jacques, 120, 175n2
desire, xlix–li, liv, 38, 83, 104; and beauty, 65; and divine, 94; and needs, 72; in *Phenomenology of Spirit* (Hegel), 72; punishment of, 15; reflection and, 110–11; religion and, 7, 94, 112; self-destruction of, 72; and senses, 40–41
destruction, 99; of lived experience, 34; of meaning, 18, 19, 20; nature and, xxxi, 89; satisfaction and, 72; self-destruction, 51, 59, 70, 72; social costs of, 133–34
détournement, 95–99, 114, 152, 174n1; body and, 100
dialectical reduction, xxxix, 57
Diane de Poitiers, Duchesse de Valentinois, 22
Diderot, Denis, 68–69
Diocletian. *See* Baths of Diocletian
Diogenes the Cynic, 66
displeasure, 76
division of labor, xxx; architecture and, xxxiii, xxxv–xxxvi, 54–55. *See also* mode of production
domination, 13, 14, 70, 140, 141, 153; and appropriation, 93–95, 98; dominating-dominated space, 52, 89–93, 95, 98, 99–100. *See also* détournement
Dostoyevsky, Fyodor, 29
Drop City, *xxiii*; geodesic domes, xxi
Dubedout, Hubert, xli
Dumazedier, Joffre, xxix–xxx; civilization of leisure, xxix; new housing typologies, xxix–xxx
dwelling, 4, 53, 79. *See also* habitation

Eastern world: religious architecture, 7–8
Ecochard, Michel, xxxvi
"Ecologic study of urban concentrations created in Spain during the last years as centers for tourism" (Gaviria), xxx
ecology, xli, 90, 133
Economic and Philosophic Manuscripts of 1844 (Marx), 35, 70–71
economics, 128–35; growth, 132–33; productive/unproductive consumption, 130–31; use/exchange value, 128–30; and utopia, 131–32
economy: definitions of, 128
Eisenstein, Sergei, 96
Elden, Stuart, xiii
Eleatic school, 62
Elephanta caves, India, 8
Eluard, Paul, 103
Empedocles, 63
encoding, 119, 124, 144, 151–52; overencoding, liv, 124, 125–26, 152
enjoyment: architecture of, 16–17; Marx and theory of, 70–71; meaning of, 61–62; need-labor-enjoyment triad, 69–70; and pleasure, 111, 112, 115–16, 119, 123; utopias of, 68, 77, 132; and violence, 147. *See also* jouissance
environment, 5, 33, 93, 101, 149–50; of everyday life, xli, 27
Epicurus, 66
Erec and Enide (Chrétien de Troyes), 44–45, 112
Eros (life drive), 41, 104–5, 109
eroticism, 41, 44, 85, 104; baths and, lv, 137–38, 143–44; Gupta art, 8, 138–39, 143–44
Espace et sociétés (journal), xv
Esquizo (film), xlviii, l
ethnology, 51, 83–84

Index

everyday life, xiii–xv, xxix, xli, xliv, 27, 104; concept of, lviii; will to power in, 56
exchange value, 57, 94, 95, 100, 128–30
existentialism, 121
Existenzminimum housing, xlvi, lxi

Falkenstein Castle, Germany, 43–44
fecundity, 78, 85, 126, 144–45
festivals, xxx, xxxii, xlviii, 20, 67–68, 70, 101
"50 Years of Bauhaus" exhibition, 163n72
Filarete (Antonio di Pietro Averlino), 141
Foucault, Michel, xlviii–xlix
Fourier, Charles, lv–lvii; passions, lvii, 40, 71, 142–43; phalanstery, lv, *lvi*, 71, 142–43
France: civilization of leisure, xxix; housing estates, xxi
Frankfurt School, xviii–xix
freedom, 105, 121
French Communist Party (PCF): Common Program, xl–xli, xlv
Freud, Sigmund, 128; *Beyond the Pleasure Principle*, 104; Eros and Thanatos, 104–5
Fuencarral housing estate, Madrid, xxi, 159n31
Fuller, Buckminster: geodesic domes, xxi
functionalist urbanism, xxvii–xxviii, xxxiii
functionality, lx, 19, 98
funerary architecture, 6–7, 15, 24–25, 92

Gailhoustet, René, xliv, xlvi, *xlvii*
Gargantua and Pantagruel (Rabelais), 46–48

Gaviria, Mario, xi–xii, *xii*; and Benidorm, *xx*, xxviii–xxix, 160n40; Burgos symposium, 159n33; "Ecologic study of urban concentrations created in Spain during the last years as centers for tourism," xxx; and Lefebvre, xi; and Lefebvre, contribution of, xxvi–xxvii; March Foundation research report, lvii; on Pamplona, xxxii; on spaces of leisure, xvii–xviii; studies of Madrid housing estates, xxi, *xxv–xxvi*, xxviii
gay science, 26–27, 28–29, 69–70, 73, 74–75
Gay Science, The (Nietzsche), 35, 105–6
Generalife, Grenada, lv, 22
geodesic domes, xxi
Giedion, Siegfried, lx
Gothic art, 8
Gran San Blas housing estate, Madrid, xxi, *xxvii*, *xxviii*
Grapus collective, xlii, *xliii*, *xlvii*
Gropius, Walter, xxxiv–xxxv
Guattari, Félix, xlvi, xlviii–xlix, lviii
Gupta art, 8, 138–39, 143–44
Gutiérrez Soto, Luis, *xxvii*

habitat, 4, 16; architects and, 5
habitation, xvi, xxxvi, xxxix, 29, 141; architecture of, xl–xlviii; concept of, xiii–xv. *See also* dwelling
Habitation à Loyer Modéré (HLM; subsidized housing), xli
Habitat 67, xxi
Halles, Les, Paris, xxxvii, *xxxvii*, xlviii, 97
happiness, liv, 19, 25, 26, 50, 138; and beauty, 32, 88; philosophy and, 61, 62, 63–64; pleasure and, 65
Harvey, David, xiii

Haus-Rucker-Co, *xxii*; landscape interventions, xxi
Havel, Václav, xix
hedonism, xviii, lx–lxi, 64
Hegel, Georg Wilhelm Friedrich, xiii, 1, 29, 53, 60, 143; Breton and, 36; mastery, meaning of, 89–90; need-labor-enjoyment triad, 69–70; *Phenomenology of Spirit*, 72; satisfaction and destruction, 72
Heidegger, Martin, 9–10; Being, 9; dwelling, 79
Henri Lefebvre on Space (Stanek), xii, xvi
Henri II of France, 22
Heraclitus, 62
Hess, Rémi, xiii
history, 87–101
Hölderlin, Friedrich, 1
holiday villages: and housing typologies, xxix–xxx
Hollein, Hans: landscape interventions, xxi
homosexuality, 107
hospitals, xlix, li
housing: Existenzminimum, xlvi, lxi; HLM, xli; holiday villages, xxix–xxx; Madrid housing estates, xxi, *xxv–xxvi*, *xxvii*, *xxviii*; proletarian, 5; Quartier d'Italie, Paris, xxi, *xxiv–xxv*; typologies, xxix–xxx
Huet, Bernard, xv, xlii
hyperspace, 86

ideological reduction: and reductivism, 57
ideological utopias, 89
imaginary, the, xxxix–xl, 4–5, 10, 21, 27, 28, 32; in cloisters, 94
imagination, 42–49; architectural, rethinking, xxxix–xl

immediacy, 83, 86, 100, 109, 112, 113; absolute, 111; and art, 115; initial, 105, 106–7; and sensoriality, 114; ultimate, 105
India: Lefebvre's visit to, 169n170; religious architecture, lv, lvii, 7–8, 138–39, 143–44
indifference, 67, 81, 109, 110
inflatable structures, xxi
initial immediacy, 105, 106–7
In Search of Lost Time (Proust), 113
Institut de sociologie urbaine (ISU), xv, xxx, xxxix; research projects, xliv
Institut d'urbanisme de Paris, xv
Internationale situationniste, xix, xlviii
international symposium of urban sociology (1974), Barcelona, 160n33
International Union of Architects (UIA; Union internationale des architectes), xxix–xxx
Iribas, José Miguel, xviii
irreducible, the, 102, 119, 122, 146, 147
Ivry-sur-Seine, Paris: "Ivry! Centre ville" poster, *xlvii*; renovation project, xliv–xlv, xlvi, *xlvii*

Jaulin, Robert, 50–51, 81
Jencks, Charles, xv
Jonas, Walter, *xxii*; funnel cities, xxi
jouissance: and architecture, liv–lv; body and, lii; Lefebvre's concept of, liii–lv, lx; spaces of, xlviii–lvi; translation of, vii–x, liii–liv, lx, 168n159, 175n5. *See also* enjoyment
joy, 16, 25–27, 32, 51, 52, 75, 76–77, 84; art and, 78, 139; space of, 94–5; Spinoza's theory of, 60. *See also* enjoyment; happiness; jouissance; pleasure

Kant, Immanuel, 69
Khajuraho temples, India, lv, lvii, 8, 138–39
Klee, Paul, 127
knowledge, 25–26, 34, 90, 102–3, 119, 122, 147, 149; criticism of, 24; meaning and, 120; philosophy and, 64, 67, 68–69; and power, 58, 59; psychoanalytic, 106
Konarak Sun Temple, India, 8
Koolhaas, Rem, xxxi, lx–lxi
Kopp, Anatole, xv, xlii
Kristeva, Julia, 120, 175n2

labor: division of, xxx, xxxiii, xxxv–xxxvi, 54–55, 62; need-labor-enjoyment triad, 69–70; and needs, 60–61
"Laboratory of Urbanism," Barcelona, 160n33
Lacan, Jacques, liv, 168n159
Lachat, Marcel, xxi, *xxiii*
Lafargue, Paul: *The Right to be Lazy*, xix
La Mettrie, Julien Offray de: *L'art de jouir*, 69
Languedoc-Roussillon: leisure facilities/tourist towns, xxix
Lapassade, Georges, xlv–xlvi, lviii
Le Corbusier, xxxiv, xxxvii, lx; *Une maison—un palais*, lx; *Vers une architecture*, lx
Ledoux, Claude-Nicolas, 141–42; Oikéma, lv, 142
Lefebvre, Henri, *xii*, *xvii*, 176n1; anti-Stalinist publications (1957–58), 164n100; architecture, redefinition of, xiii–xv; architecture and social hierarchies, xxxiii; body as model of space, lii; centrality, concept of, lviii; collaboration with Bofill, 160n33; *The Critique of Everyday Life*, xv; *De l'Etat*, xi; everyday life, concept of, lviii; expulsion from PCF, xl; functionalist urbanism/1960 Mourenx study, xxvii–xxviii, xxix, xxxii–xxxiii; habitation, concept of, xiii–xv; interviews in *Actuel*, xix–xxi, *xxiii*; *jouissance*, concept of, liii–lv, lx; *The Limits to Growth*, xxxi; and Marxism, xxxiii; on May 1968, xlviii, lii–liii; on Nietzsche, xix–xxi; parenthesizing, xxxix–xl, lvii; on Paris Commune (1871), xlii; on Paz, xxi; *The Production of Space*, xi, xvi–xvii, xxxv, lix; rhythmanalysis, xxi, lii, 149; *The Right to the City*, xi, xxvii; right to the city, concept of, xlvi–xlviii, lviii, lix, lxi; on spaces of leisure, xxxi; in Spain, xxvi–xxvii, 159–60n33; theory of space, lix; *The Urban Revolution*, 163n72; *Vers une architecture de la jouissance*, xii–xiii, *xiv*; visit to India, 169n170; writing style, lviii
leisure: activities, 99–100; civilization of, xxix; landscapes of, xvi–xvii; spaces of, xvii–xviii, xxi, xxx–xxxii, xxxix, 99–101; and spaces of tourism, xxix; urbanism of, xxix
Lévi-Strauss, Claude, 80
life drive (Eros), 41, 104–5, 109
Limits to Growth, The (Meadows et al.), xxxi, 175–76n1. See also Meadows report
literature, 120, 123, 126
lived experience, lv, 5, 10, 109, 122, 123; body and, 33, 34; gay science and, 26–27
logical reduction, 56–57
logology, 117, 120, 121

Logos, 61, 69, 80; Cartesian, 25–26, 68; intellectual asceticism of, 68; Western, 29, 51, 149
Loiseau, Georges, xxxv
López de Lucio, Ramón, 160n33
Louis II of Bavaria, 14, 15
Lourau, René, xlv–xlvi, lviii

Mad Love (Breton), 36–38
Madrid housing estates, xxi, *xxv–xxvi, xxvii, xxviii*; Concepción, xxi, *xxv, xxvi*; Fuencarral, xxi, 159n31; Gran San Blas, xxi, *xxvii, xxviii*
magic, 6; symbolism and, 144–45
Mahabalipuram sanctuaries, India, 8
maison—un palais, Une (Le Corbusier), lx
Malamoud, Charles, 169n170
Manuscript Found in Saragossa, The (Potocki), xi
Marais quarter, Paris, 88, 97
Marc, Olivier, 85
March Bank, Mallorca, xxx, lvii
March Foundation, xxx, lvii
Marcuse, Herbert, 105; "On Hedonism," xviii
marriage, 21, 82–83
Marx, Karl, xiii, xlv, liii, 29, 38, 68, 69; analysis of capital, 128–30; and dialectical reduction, 57; *Economic and Philosophic Manuscripts of 1844*, 35, 70–71; and Hegelian dialectic, 96; mastery, meaning of, 89–90; and revolution, 73; superstructures, 31; and theory of enjoyment, 70–71; working class and revolutions, 70–71
Marxism, xv, xviii–xix; Lefebvre and, xxxiii
mastery: and appropriation, 90; meaning of, 89–90; of nature, 89; of space, 93. *See also* domination

May 1968, xlviii, lii–liii; graffiti, *xlix*, lii
McLeod, Mary, xiii, lix–lx
McLuhan, Marshall, 53
Meadows, Donella and Dennis, 175n1
Meadows report, 130, 132–33, 134. *See also Limits to Growth, The*
meaning: cities and, 88–89; destruction of, 18, 19, 20; of enjoyment, 61–62; loss of, 58; of mastery, 89–90; monuments and, 18–19. *See also* semantics
mental space, 117, 135
military architecture, 13, 90–93
mirrors: and reflection/ambiguity, 76, 110–11
Mitterand, François, xl
mode of production, xxxi, xxxix, 4, 54, 91, 121, 131; architecture and, xxxv–xxxvi. *See also* division of labor
modernism, xix, xxxiv; Swedish, lx
modernity, xvi–xxxiii, 99, 124
monasteries, 10–11, 24, 94
Montreal Expo 67, xlviii
monumentality, 20, 26, 28, 88, 124; philosophy and, 77; and power, 55, 58; State and, 19, 30
monuments, 6–7, 16, 17–19, 21, 26, 30, 88, 97, 124–25, 141, 142; architects and, 17–18; and buildings, 17–18, 30; funerary, 8, 92; and meaning, 18–19; military, 92–93; philosophy and, 77; and power, 20, 25, 26; State and, 19, 30
morality, xviii, 67, 119; and categorical imperative, 69; will to power and, 25
More, Thomas, 141
Mourenx, France, xi, xxix; Lefebvre's 1960 study, xxvii–xxviii, xxix, xxxii–xxxiii

Mozart, Wolfgang Amadeus: *Cosi fan Tutte*, 107
music, 94–95, 96, 110, 114

Nanterre, University of, xv
Narcissus, 110–11
nature, xxxi, 5, 33, 34, 44, 51, 77–78, 100, 138, appropriation of, 73, 78; destruction, costs of, 133–34; mastery of, 89; and use value, 129
Naville, Pierre, xix
needs: and desire, 72; and labor, 60–61; need-labor-enjoyment triad, 69–70; satisfaction of, 60–61
negation, xxxiii–xl, 131, 148
negative utopias, 18, 148
negativism, 131
Nicholson-Smith, Donald, liii–liv
Nicomachean Ethics (Aristotle), 61
Nietzsche, Friedrich, xiii, 68, 70, 72–73, 77, 88, 103; Breton and, 36; gay science, 26–27, 28–29; *The Gay Science*, 35, 105–6; Lefebvre on, xix–xxi; perspectivism, 73; *Das Philosophen-Buch*, 62; and satisfaction, 75; Superhuman, 28, 72, 74, 105–6; *Thus Spoke Zarathustra: A Book for None and All*, 74; will to power, 16, 25, 28, 30–31, 55–56, 70, 73–74, 76; Zarathustra, 28–29, 74
Nieuwenhuys, Constant, xv, xlviii, 95, 151
nihilism, 29, 73–74, 105–6
nonbody: and body, 7–8, 11, 77, 102, 127, 150–51
nonmeaning, 120, 122
nonwork, xxx, 132; and work, xix, xxxii
Norberg-Schulz, Christian, xv
"No-Stop City," xxxi
nouvelle critique, La (journal), xli–xlii

objections: architectural rationality, 51–53; communication, 53–54; philosophical, 50–51; political, 54–56
Oikéma, lv, 142
Oldenburg, Claes, *xxii*
oneiric architecture, 14–15. *See also* imagination
"On Hedonism" (Marcuse), xviii
open-plan offices, xxxi
Orlando Furioso (Ariosto), 14
Orsini, Prince, 15
overencoding, liv, 124, 125–26, 152

Padua, Italy, 140–41
pain: and pleasure, 50, 64, 74–77, 78, 102–3
palaces, 13, 15, 16, 20, 42–44; Alhambra, lv, 22–23; Ali Qapu, 42; Generalife, lv, 22; Palazzo Borromeo, 15
Palazzo Borromeo, Isola Bella, 15
Palladio, Andrea, 139–40
Pamplona, Spain, xxxii
Pantheon, Rome, 143–44
paradigmatic opposition, 126–27
paradise, 112
Parallèles (journal), li
Parametro (journal), xlii
parenthesizing, xxxix–xl, lvii
Paris Commune (1871), xlii
Paris Match (magazine), xxxvii, xxxvii, xxxviii
Parmenides, 62
passions, 14, 26, 68, 85, 88, 112, 138; combinatory passions, lvii, 40, 142–43; vocabulary of, 71
Patinir, Joachim, 42
Paz, Octavio, xxi, lv, 7–8, 138; Aztec pyramids, 13–14
PCF (French Communist Party): Common Program, xl–xli, xlv

People's Architecture, Berkeley, *xxiii*;
    appropriation of space, xxi
Perrottet, Jean, xxxv
perspectivism, 73
Petit Seminaire, Marseille, li
phalansteries, lv, *lvi*, 71, 142–43
phenomenological reduction, 57
Phenomenology of Spirit (Hegel):
    desire, 72
Philosophen-Buch, Das (Nietzsche), 62
philosophical asceticism, 10
philosophical utopias, 19
philosophy, 50–51, 123; Greek, 61,
    62–66; and monumentality, 77; of
    pleasure, 50, 51, 60–79; and
    politics, 77; post-Hegel, 67–76
Physiology of Taste (Brillat-Savarin),
    38–41
Pingusson, Georges-Henri, xv
Place des Vosges, Paris, 88
place names, 123–24
Plato, 64–65, 74–75; *Critias*, 141; *The
    Republic*, 141
pleasure, liv, 21, 42–44, 45, 49, 52,
    104, 105, 106, 109, 126; Aristotle
    and, 64–65; and enjoyment, 111,
    112, 115–16, 119, 123; and
    fecundity, 78; irreducible and, 119,
    122; Oikéma, 142; and pain, 50, 64,
    74–77, 78, 102–3; philosophy of,
    50, 51, 60–79; power and, 25, 56,
    111; space of, xviii
political architecture, 13–16, 20
political space, 89, 92. *See also*
    absolute space
politics, 54–55; architecture of
    habitation, xl–xlviii; philosophy
    and, 77
Porro, Ricardo, xv
positivity, 90
Potocki, Jan: *The Manuscript Found
    in Saragossa*, xi

"Pour un urbanisme..." (For an
    urbanism...) colloquium, xli–xlii,
    xliii
poverty, 13, 20–21
power, 25–26, 119; architecture of,
    13–16, 20, 25; and pleasure, 25, 56,
    111; utopias of, 68; and violence,
    91–92. *See also* will to power
Production of Space, The (Lefebvre),
    xi, xvi–xvii, xxxv, lix
*Programme commun de gouvernement
    du Parti communiste français et du
    Parti socialiste* (Common program
    of the government of the French
    Communist Party and the
    Socialist Party, 1972), xl–xli, xlv
proletarian housing, 5
proper names, 123–24, 125–26
Proust, Marcel: *In Search of Lost
    Time*, 113
PS (Socialist Party): Common
    Program, xl–xli, xlv
psychiatric hospitals, li
psychic analysis, 107–8
psychic identity, 108
psychoanalysis, liv, 102–16, 168n159
psychology, 102–16; gratifications, 50;
    social psychology, 103
public baths, 136–38, 143–44
punishment: of desire, 15
Pythagoras, 63

Quartier d'Italie, Paris, xxi, *xxiv–xxv*
queer space, lv
Querrien, Anne, li

Rabelais, François, lv, 141; *Gargantua
    and Pantagruel*, 46–48
Ramos, Vicente, *xx*
Randers, Jorgen, 175n1
rationality, 7; abstract, 90; architec-
    tural, 51–53

Raymond, Henri, xxxi, xlvi
reactive utopias, 98
reading space, 124–25
Recherches (journal), xlix, lviii
reduction: ideological, 57; logical/dialectical, xxxix, 56–57; phenomenological, 57; and reductivism, 57
reductivism, xxxix, 57–59, 119, 146; and reduction, 57
reflection, 110–11
regional train network (RER), xxxvii
Régulier, Catherine, 166n115
relationships, 80–82, 82–83; town and country, 87–88
relativism, 73–74
religion, 6, 7, 33, 36, 119; Aztec, 13, 14; Christianity, 7–8, 33, 45, 97–98, 121, 136; Greek, 9; and reductivism, 58; State, 9
religious architecture, 7–10; Eastern world, 7–8; Greek temples, 8–9; monasteries, 10–11, 24, 94; Western world, 7–8
religious space, 8, 89. *See also* absolute space
Renaudie, Jean, xv, xliv, xlv, xlvi, *xlvii*
Rendell, Jane, xiii
Republic, The (Plato), 141
RER (regional train network), xxxvii
resentment, 75
revolution, xix, 131–32, 134; architectural, 27–28; French, 18, 19; and subversion, 73; urban, xxxii, 87; "Vive la révolution" movement, xix; working class and, 70–71
rhythmanalysis, xxi, lii, 149
Riboulet, Pierre, xv, xxx, xxxv–xxxvi
Ricardo, David, 128
Right to be Lazy, The (Lafargue), xix
Right to the City, The (Lefebvre), xi, xxvii
Robles Jiménez, Francisco, *xxv*

Roch, Fernando, 160n33
Rodchenko, Aleksandr, xviii
Romero Hernández, Jacobo, *xxv*
Rome/Romans: basilicas, 97; public baths, 136–37, 143–44
Romero Requejo, Lorenzo, *xxv*
Rousseau, Jean-Jacques, 68
Royal Saltworks, Arc-et-Senans, 142
ruralization, 99
Russell, Bertrand, 130, 175n1

Sade, Marquis de, 14
sadism, 16, 25
Safdie, Moishe, *xxiii*
Saint-John Perse, 126–27
saltworks, Arc-et-Senans, 142
satisfaction, 17, 20, 51, 62, 69–70, 76, 104, 132; and destruction, 72; Hegel on, 60, 61, 72; Nietzsche and, 75
Schmarsow, August, xxxiii–xxxiv
Schmid, Christian, xiii
Schnaidt, Claude, xlii
Schöffer, Nicholas, xxxvii; center for sexual relaxation, xxi, *xxii*, liv, 48; "Super Eiffel Tower of Paris in the year 1990," xxxviii
Schopenhauer, Arthur, 75; pleasure and pain, 64; self-destruction of desire, 72
scientism, 10, 17
sculptures, 15, 25, 26, 52–53; Gupta temples, 138–39
seaports, 93
security, 104
Self: and Other, 80–81
self-destruction, 51, 59, 70, 72
semantics, 117–27. *See also* meaning
semiology, 117–27. *See also* signification
senses, 39–41; and desire, 40–41
sensoriality, 9, 95, 109–10, 113–15; asceticism and, 16; and immediacy, 114

sensuality, 9, 15, 22, 109–10, 112, 115; Gupta art, 138–39; public baths and, 137–38; will to power and, 25
sexuality: anthropology and, 82–86; types of, 107–8
sight, 41
signification, 18–19; architecture and, 25. See also semiology
signifieds, 12–13, 151; architecture and, 25, 124; and signifiers, 15, 34, 48, 58, 94, 126, 152
signifiers, 12–13; and signifieds, 15, 34, 48, 58, 94, 126, 152
Smith, Adam, 128
social costs: of destruction, 133–34
social hierarchies, xix; and architecture, xxxiii
socialism, xli; state, xix; utopian, 71–72
Socialist Party (PS), xl–xli, xlv
socialist realism, xix
social practice, xxxiii, 40, 51–52, 54, 113–14, 146; architects/architecture and, 4–5, 151
social psychology, 103
social space, xxxiii, lii, lxi, 4, 5, 33–34, 81, 83, 85, 86, 117, 148
Soja, Edward, xiii2
Solà-Morales, Manuel de, 159n33
Solans, Juan Antonio, 159n33
Sollers, Philippe, 120, 175n2
Sombart, Werner, xviii
space/spaces, 119; absolute space, 119; abstract space, xxx–xxxi, xxxix; appropriation of, xxi, 100, 112, 124, 125–26; architecture as, xxxiv–xxxv; body and, 10–11, 41; dominating/dominated, 90–93, 95; empty spaces, 99; history of, 89–90; of jouissance, xlviii–lvi; Lefebvre's theory of, lix; of leisure, xvii–xviii, xxi, xxx–xxxii, 99–101;
mental, 117, 135; reading, 124–25; social, xxxiii, lii, lxi, 4, 5, 33–34, 81, 83, 85, 86, 117, 148; tourism and, xvi–xvii, xxix; use value of, 131
Spain: Madrid housing estates, xxi, *xxv–xxvi, xxvii, xxviii*; spaces of tourism in, xvi–xvii
Spinoza, Benedictus, 35, 68; theory of joy, 60
State, 4, 18, 27, 29, 30–31; and monumentality, 19, 30; and religion, 9
state socialism: Central/Eastern Europe, xix
statues, 22, 126, 137–38
Stendhal (Henri Beyle), 15
Strasbourg, University of, xv
Stravinsky, Igor, 96
structuralism, liii, 80–81
subsidized housing (Habitation à Loyer Modéré; HLM), xli
subversion, 27, 77, 131–32, 134; revolution and, 73. See also détournement
suffering, 23, 111–12; jouissance as, liv. See also pain
"Super Eiffel Tower of Paris in the year 1990" (Schöffer), *xxxviii*
Superhuman, the, 28, 72, 74, 105–6
superstructures, 31
surrealism, 17, 36
symbolism, xxxi, xxxii, 7, 19, 22, 46, 82, 84–85, 110–11, 122; architecture and, 143–44, 151; Christianity and, 97–98; Gupta art, 138; and magic, 144–45; power and, 13; symbols and signs, 56–57, 94, 118

Tafuri, Manfredo, xv, xxxiv, xxxvi, lviii
taste, 39, 41

technological utopias, 18
Tel Quel group, 120, 175n2
tents, 83–85
Thanatos (death drive), 104–5, 109
theoretical reduction: and reductivism, 57
Thorez, Maurice, xli, 164n100
Thus Spoke Zarathustra: A Book for None and All (Nietzsche), 74
total body, xxxii, lv, 41, 148–52
tourism, xvi–xviii; debate about spaces of, xxix; Spain, xxx–xxxi; and traditional urban festivals, xxxii. *See also* Benidorm
tourist towns, xxvii, xxix
tourist urbanism, xxxii
tragic architecture, 14
transsexuality, 107
Tronçais forest, xxxvii
Tschumi, Bernard, xxxv
Turell Moragas, Federico, *xxv*
Tusquets, Óscar, 159n33

uncertainty, 102–3, 104, 107–8; of lived experience, 10, 63
Union internationale des architectes (UIA; International Union of Architects), xxix–xxx
urbanism, xl–xli; and architecture, xxxvi; functionalist, xxvii–xxviii; of leisure, xxix; in Spain, xxvi–xxvii; tourist, xxxii
"Urbanisme monopoliste, urbanisme démocratique" (Monopolist urbanism, democratic urbanism) colloquium, xli
urbanization, 99
urban revolution, xxxii, 87
Urban Revolution, The (Lefebvre), 163n72
urban utopias, 89, 141, 148
use, concept of, lx, lxi

use value, lxi, 94, 95, 100, 128–30; of space, 131
utilitarianism, 69
utopian socialism, 71–72
utopias, xxxii, xxxiii–xl, 87, 147–48; abstract, xxxvi–xxxvii, xxxix, 93, 130, 141, 148; architectural, 148; and architectural revolution, 27; concrete, xvi, xxxvi–xxxvii, xxxix, 123, 141, 148, 153; of contemplative life, 94; and economics, 131–32; of enjoyment, 68, 77, 132; ideological, 89; negative, 18, 148; of nonwork, 132; philosophical, 19; of power, 68; reactive, 98, technological, 18; urban, 89, 141, 148
Utopie Group, xxxvii, xlviii

Vago, Pierre, xxxv
Vázquez Molezún, Ramón, *xxvii*
Venice, Italy, 88, 93
Venturi, Robert, xv
vernacular architecture, 21
Vers une architecture (Le Corbusier), lx
Vers une architecture de la jouissance (Lefebvre), xii–xiii; discovery of manuscript, xii; Table of Contents, *xiv*
Vidal-Beneyto, José: Burgos symposium, 159n33
violence, lvii, 57, 72, 95, 122, 124; and enjoyment, 147; and power, 13, 59, 91–92; will to power and, 16
Vitruvius: architecture, definition of, 171n10
"Vive la révolution" movement, xix

Weber, Max, 58
will to power, 28, 30–31, 70, 73–74, 76; architecture and, 55–56; in

everyday life, 56; morality and, 25; and sadism, 16
Wogenscky, André, xxxvii
work: and nonwork, xix, xxxii
workerism, xxxiv, 134
working class, xvii–xviii, xliv, 29–30, 134; and revolutions, 18, 70–71

Wotton, Henry: architecture, definition of, 17
writing, 119, 124

yurts, 83–85, 86

Zarathustra, 28–29, 74